For Wendy Perkins

I know not why our editors should, with such implacable anger, persecute their predecessors . . . the dead it is true can make no resistance, they may be attacked with great security; but since they can neither feel nor mend, the safety of mauling them seems greater than the pleasure; nor perhaps would it much misbeseem us to remember, amidst our triumphs over the 'nonsensical' and the 'senseless', that we likewise are men; that *debemur morti*, and as Swift observed to Brunet, shall soon be among the dead ourselves.

Samuel Johnson, in his note on *Hamlet*, 3.2.121–2

Coláiste Oideachais Mhuire Gan Smál
Luimneach

The first developments in the editing of English literary texts in the eighteenth century were remarkable and important, and they have recently begun to attract considerable interest, particularly in relation to conditions and constructions of scholarship in the period. This study sets out to investigate, rather, the theoretical and especially the interpretative bases of eighteenth-century literary editing. Extended chapters on Shakespearean and Miltonic commentary and editing demonstrate that the work of pioneering editors and commentators, such as Patrick Hume, Lewis Theobald, Zachary Pearce, and Edward Capell, was based on developed, sophisticated, and often clearly articulated theories and methods of textual understanding and explanation. Marcus Walsh relates these interpretative assumptions and methods to seventeenth- and eighteenth-century Anglican biblical hermeneutics, and to a number of key debates in modern editorial theory.

CAMBRIDGE STUDIES IN EIGHTEENTH-CENTURY
ENGLISH LITERATURE AND THOUGHT 35

Shakespeare, Milton, and eighteenth-century literary editing

CAMBRIDGE STUDIES IN EIGHTEENTH-CENTURY ENGLISH LITERATURE AND THOUGHT

Some recent titles

Mania and Literary Style
The Rhetoric of Enthusiasm from the Ranters to Christopher Smart
by Clement Hawes

Landscape, Liberty and Authority
Poetry, Criticism and Politics from Thomson to Wordsworth
by Tim Fulford

Philosophical Dialogue in the British Enlightenment
Theology, Aesthetics, and the Novel
by Michael Prince

Defoe and the New Sciences
by Ilse Vickers

History and the Early English Novel: Matters of Fact from Bacon to Defoe
by Robert Mayer

Narratives of Enlightenment
Cosmopolitan History from Voltaire to Gibbon
by Karen O'Brien

A complete list of books in this series is given at the end of the volume

Shakespeare, Milton, and eighteenth-century literary editing

The beginnings of interpretative scholarship

MARCUS WALSH

University of Birmingham

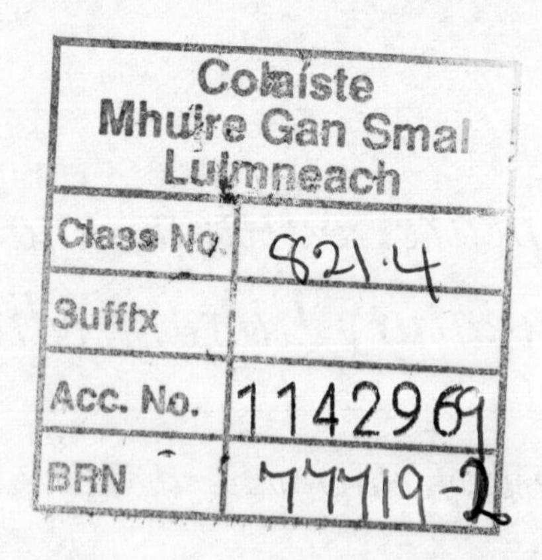

PUBLISHED BY THE PRESS SYNDICATE OF THE UNIVERSITY OF CAMBRIDGE
The Pitt Building, Trumpington Street, Cambridge CB2 1RP, United Kingdom

CAMBRIDGE UNIVERSITY PRESS
The Edinburgh Building, Cambridge CB2 2RU, United Kingdom
40 West 20th Street, New York, NY 10011–4211, USA
10 Stamford Road, Oakleigh, Melbourne 3166, Australia

First published 1997

Printed in the United Kingdom at the University Press, Cambridge

Typeset in Baskerville 10pt

A catalogue record for this book is available from the British Library

Library of Congress cataloguing in publication data

Walsh, Marcus.
Shakespeare, Milton and eighteenth-century literary editing: the beginnings of interpretative scholarship / Marcus Walsh.
p. cm. – (Cambridge studies in eighteenth-century English literature and thought : 35)
Includes bibliographical references (p.) and index.
ISBN 0 521 55443 8 (hardback)
1. English literature – Early modern, 1500–1700 – Criticism, Textual.
2. Criticism – Great Britain – History – 18th century.
3. Shakespeare, William, 1564–1616 – Editors.
4. Milton, John, 1608–1674 – Editors.
5. Editing – History – 18th century.
I. Title. II. Series.
PR418.T48W34 1997
801'.95'094109033 – dc20 96–43886 CIP

ISBN 0 521 55443 8 hardback

CE

Contents

Illustrations

Illustrations 1–9 are reproduced by permission of the Syndics of Cambridge University Library; illustrations 10–12 are reproduced by permission of Birmingham Public Libraries.

Acknowledgments

I have been fortunate to have many opportunities to discuss this book with colleagues and friends at the University of Birmingham, and I am grateful for advice, support, and information of many valuable kinds from Irena Cholij, Neville Birdsall, Stephen Bending, Tony Davies, Valerie Edden, Neville Davies, Bob Wilcher, Mark Storey, John Jowett, Kelsey Thornton, Stanley Wells, and Jonathan Laidlow. Perhaps more than anyone, Ian Small has shared, stimulated, and guided my enquiries into editing and its history. I have greatly appreciated the counsel and encouragement offered by Brean Hammond, Claude Rawson, and Karina McIntosh. My work has been very much assisted by Marcus Keidan's generous gift of a copy of the 1778 Johnson/Steevens Shakespeare. Denis Stratton provided wisdom and hospitality, as ever. Without the help of Alan Johnson and Mr Alastair Stirling, and their colleagues at ROH Woodlands, this book would not have been completed.

I thank the Faculty of Arts, University of Birmingham, for Study Leaves, Teaching Relief, and grants in support of the research for this book, and the British Academy for a Small Research Grant which enabled a period of study at Trinity College, Cambridge. I am grateful to the staffs of the British Library, the Wren Library at Trinity College, Birmingham Public Library, and Birmingham University Library. I am especially indebted to Ben Benedikz and Christine Penney of the Heslop Room at the University of Birmingham, and to Susan Brock, Librarian of the Shakespeare Institute. Preliminary versions of parts of these chapters have been presented as papers at the International Milton Symposium, and at research seminars in the School of English and Shakespeare Institute of the University of Birmingham. Professor Roy Flannagan and Professor Andrew Gurr have kindly given me permission to draw on my essays on Patrick Hume's annotations to *Paradise Lost*, published in *Milton Quarterly* in 1988, and on Swift's *Tale of a Tub*, published in *Modern Language Review* in 1990. An earlier (and very different) form of my work on Bentley appeared in *The Theory and Practice of Text-Editing*, a volume of essays edited by myself and Ian Small and published by Cambridge University Press in 1991.

Josie Dixon of Cambridge University Press has provided firm guidance and consistent and generous support.

This book is dedicated to Wendy Perkins, with love and gratitude.

Introduction

This book sets out to examine the theoretical bases, more especially the hermeneutic bases, of a remarkable and important cultural phenomenon, the eighteenth-century beginnings of the editing of English secular literature. The works of English poets and dramatists had in some sense been 'edited' before: the successive Shakespearean Folios, for instance, constitute a form of textual editing, and commentaries on English literary writings include E. K.'s Glosses on *The Shepheardes Calender*, and Sir Kenelm Digby's *Observations* (1644) on Spenser's Castle of Alma (*Faerie Queene*, 2. 9. 22). There is nothing however before the last years of the seventeenth century like the concerted project of 'intelligent' annotating and textual editing of Shakespeare and Milton (amongst other English writers) by such scholars as Patrick Hume, Alexander Pope, Lewis Theobald, Richard Bentley, Samuel Johnson, and Edward Capell.

The occasions for this development, and the reasons for its timing, lie partly no doubt in social, economic, and legal histories of the book and book readers, of the profession of letters, and of property and copyright. They lie too in the history of a more general process by which English culture required and developed a sense of its own identity and its own history, and began to seek literary classics of its own, comparable with, if not yet replacing, those of antiquity.

Many of the issues in this cultural process have already been discussed, in a number of distinguished studies. Accounts of the formation of an English literary history, of the ordering and canonizing of English literature, of the development of a new philological and historical scholarship concerned with vernacular writings, and the rise of a distinctively British literature have notably been provided by René Wellek, Lawrence Lipking, Joseph Levine, and Howard Weinbrot.

More particularly, in recent years there has been a gathering interest in, and to some extent a re-evaluation of, the work of the eighteenth-century literary editors, and more especially of editors of Shakespeare. Peter Seary has provided a scholarly reassessment of Lewis Theobald. Considerable attention has been paid to text-critical methods and policies, in Simon Jarvis's examination in his recent book of the work of Theobald and

Johnson, as well as by Steven Urkowitz, Grace Ioppolo, and other scholars. Perhaps above all recent work has been characterized by a focus on the scholarly assumptions and procedures of the eighteenth-century editors as responses to the social and cultural conditions of their own time. Margreta de Grazia argues that Edmond Malone's concern for 'authenticity' in his 1790 edition of Shakespeare is not neutral or essential but 'embedded in history', arising out of 'the determinate needs of a specific historical situation', that is, the Enlightenment. Simon Jarvis is concerned especially with conditions of literary production, and with constructions and representations of learning and scholarship, in the early and mid eighteenth century.

In all this there has been surprisingly little investigation of the theoretical foundations, and more especially the hermeneutic foundations, of eighteenth-century editing. Editing of course can never be wholly neutral, and can never be wholly divorced from its historical circumstances. Equally, however, editing is not merely a function determined by social or political or economic conditions, but a discipline possessed of its own principles, methods, procedures, and purposes, however variously defined and debated they have been, and remain. The first editors of English literature have been thought, and continue in some quarters to be thought, unmethodical, unprincipled, idiosyncratic. I attempt in this book to show that, on the contrary, the work of such figures as Lewis Theobald, Zachary Pearce, and Edward Capell was grounded in developed, sophisticated, and often clearly articulated theoretical understandings. I argue from the outset that editing is a necessarily interpretative activity, and I attempt to identify and illustrate the development and application of interpretative methods and assumptions in eighteenth-century editing. In particular I set out to demonstrate the extent to which editors in the period followed, in Peter Shillingsburg's phrase, an 'authorial orientation'. Many scholars and editors of the time sought to recover what their authors intended to write and what their authors intended to mean, and believed that such an enterprise was made possible by close examination of the text, and by knowledge of the author's writings and those of his contemporaries and, more generally, of the 'history and manners' of the author's time. I argue in my second chapter and elsewhere that what I take to be the essentially historicist and intentionalist methods and principles of much eighteenth-century secular literary editing may derive at least in part from those of Protestant, and more specifically Anglican, biblical hermeneutics of the previous century. With such issues in mind I concentrate less on the textual criticism as such of the eighteenth-century editors than on the interpretative grounds and rationales of their textual decisions, and, more broadly, on their attempt to understand and explain their texts. I shall be concerned, in fact, primarily with issues in the historiography of textual understanding.

I have focussed on the editing of Shakespeare and Milton, where the central issues are extensively debated, explored, and exemplified, aiming to provide, not a survey or a history of eighteenth-century editing, but an account of some of its important characteristics and tendencies, as revealed in the editorial practice, and theoretical and methodological statements, of some of its leading figures. The historical *termini* of my enquiry are Patrick Hume's *Annotations* on *Paradise Lost* (1695), the first full-length learned commentary on a major English literary work, and Edward Capell's editorial work on Shakespeare (1768–83), which seems to me in many ways a high point in the development and application of historicizing textual and interpretative scholarship.

It will be apparent that the work of the eighteenth-century editors raises issues that continue to be actively debated amongst modern editorial theorists, and I have attempted, at some length in my first chapter, and to some extent throughout this study, to assess the relation of eighteenth-century editing to the terms and categories of modern arguments about editing and interpretation. It is not my intention, however, to accommodate the eighteenth-century editors to our own positions. Indeed, one of my motives in writing this book has been the sense that, in some recent discussions, the eighteenth century has been judged, unsympathetically, by inappropriate and modern criteria. Notions in editorial theory – of the author, of authorial intention, and of commentary, most pertinently – need to be seen as historically specific. It is an essential part of my argument that the work of the first English literary scholars should be assessed in the light of their specific, and different, understandings of these and other key editorial and hermeneutic issues. Those understandings, and the use they made of them, may have some significant resonances for our own time.

I

Some theoretical perspectives for the study of eighteenth-century editing

Orientations of editing

To a modern eye, the work of the first editors of Shakespeare and Milton in the eighteenth century can seem most unfamiliar. While much has been written in appreciation of their work, some recent commentators have found many of them guilty of a tendency to the speculative and conjectural, of a preference for 'taste' over textual recension, and of a general ignorance of recent theory and practice in textual criticism. By contrast, I shall wish to argue that some at least of these editorial pioneers had a highly developed understanding, though not a modern understanding, of the problems and possibilities involved. The eighteenth-century editors were innovators facing particular, and new, sets of editorial and interpretative questions, within their own historical and intellectual setting. If we are to understand how they approached their task it is necessary for us to have a sense of how they conceived the questions which faced them, of what they took the functions of editing to be, and of what literary and intellectual resources were open to them, in their own time. If we are properly to envision their work, we need in fact to reconstruct (to borrow a Popperian terminology) their specific historical 'problem situation'.[1] In the course of this book I shall in particular attempt to argue that the emphases of many of the eighteenth-century literary editors were fundamentally interpretative, and to describe some of the grounds and characteristics of their interpretative methods. I shall begin by suggesting in this chapter how, and how far, their work might be related to some modern terms of the editorial debate.

The explosion of editorial and textual theorizing in this century has provided us not only with a range of conceptual and methodological tools for the reproduction and interpretation of past writings, but also with a number of positions from which we might view the editorial theories and practices of the past. For a number of reasons, however, we must choose

[1] See Karl R. Popper, *Objective Knowledge* (revised edn: Oxford: Oxford University Press, 1983), pp. 170–7. Popper applies the precept to the understanding of works of art, as well as to the understanding of scientific problem situations (see *Objective Knowledge*, p. 180).

the positions we adopt with some care. Many modern discussions address problems and subject matters which had scarcely begun to be recognized in the early eighteenth century, or start with assumptions more or less foreign to that period. To believe we have now achieved confident editorial enlightenment, and to describe the history of editing as a progress towards that enlightenment, would of course be merely another chapter in Whig history. And in fact, as most of their practitioners readily acknowledge, textual criticism and editing are now amongst the most contested and problematized areas of the humanities. If the specific character of eighteenth-century editing is to be understood, it will certainly be necessary to consider which modern conceptualizations of textual criticism and editing might possibly provide us with useful and appropriate optics for its examination, and which cannot.

I would like to begin that process of discrimination, for the purposes of this study, by an appeal to what seems to me the clearest and most useful modern taxonomy of textual editing, that presented by Peter Shillingsburg in his *Scholarly Editing in the Computer Age: Theory and Practice* (1986). I shall use Shillingsburg's taxonomy throughout this book as a heuristic tool in assessing the positions and directions of eighteenth-century editing, though it will be apparent that I understand and apply some of his categories in somewhat modified ways.

Shillingsburg argues that there are four possible formal orientations of textual editing, the historical (or documentary), the aesthetic, the authorial, and the sociological, depending on where the editor chooses to locate authority for the text. Though no edition is constructed purely and exclusively with regard to any one orientation, most may be characterized as predominantly pursuing one or another of these four defining possibilities. Shillingsburg thinks of his four formal orientations more particularly with reference to their effect on 'the readings preserved in an edition'. I shall however extend their application beyond the realm of pure textual criticism to the realm of interpretation, believing, for reasons which will I hope become clear later in this chapter, and throughout my discussion in this book, that the two realms have no clear boundary, and, indeed, cover some of the same terrain.[2] I shall be concerned, in fact, with the forms and the theory of exegesis, as well as of textual criticism. Eighteenth-century editors rarely drew an unbroken line between the two. It is a salient characteristic of the work of such scholar-editors as Lewis Theobald and

[2] Professor Shillingsburg has since considerably developed his position. In his later article, 'Text as matter, concept, and action' (*Studies in Bibliography*, 44 (1991), 31–82), he substantially redraws the map of relations between Work, Document, Language, Author, Reader, and Book, taking postmodern scepticism and relativism almost as givens. I believe his earlier statement of the orientations of textual editing in *Scholarly Editing in the Computer Age* (Athens, Georgia, and London: University of Georgia Press, 1986) nonetheless remains coherent.

Edward Capell that their textual choices are regularly made on explicitly formulated interpretative grounds.

Of the four orientations, the historical 'places a high value on the chronology of forms'.[3] Authority, for this orientation, resides primarily in the historical document. Historically orientated editors resist the eclectic mixing of discrete texts. In the pure or strong form of the historical orientation, as practised by professional historians rather than literary scholars, dealing especially with manuscript or typescript, a single document is treated as a particular piece of historical evidence, and reproduced more or less exactly, perhaps even by photographic or type facsimile or microfilm.[4]

At the beginning of the eighteenth century there was in some quarters a resistance to excessive faith in particular documents. The work of Richard Bentley did much to nurture a presumption that ancient manuscripts were corrupt, and required both correction against other available witnesses, and conjectural emendation. Alexander Pope attacked the pedantic antiquarianism which refused, out of a blind idolatry for ancient documents, to make necessary (and necessarily eclectic) editorial decisions. Thomas Hearne had boasted that it was 'a Principle with me not to alter MSS even where better and more proper Readings are very plain and obvious'. He would be immortalized as 'Wormius' in the *Dunciad*, and mocked in the poem's very first note: 'I can never enough praise my very good Friend, the exact Mr. *Tho. Hearne*; who if any word occur which to him and all mankind is evidently wrong, yet keeps it in the Text with due reverence, and only remarks in the Margin, *sic M.S.*'[5]

Eighteenth-century literary editing almost never follows a purely historical, or documentary, orientation. The question of the degree of status and authority properly to be accorded to particular surviving witnesses was nonetheless, as we shall see, at the centre of debates between, for example, Pope and Theobald, or Bentley and his answerers. And as the century progressed, such scholar-editors as Thomas Newton and Edward Capell took an increasingly exact approach to the original documents with which they dealt.

In the sociological orientation, authority is located 'in the institutional unit of author *and* publisher'. For sociological editors the contribution made by publishers, publishers' editors, and others is to be understood not as corruption or dilution of a pristine creative act, but as 'a social

[3] Shillingsburg, *Scholarly Editing*, p. 19.

[4] For important discussions of the rival claims of 'literary' and 'historical' editing see G. Thomas Tanselle, 'The editing of historical documents', *Studies in Bibliography*, 31 (1978), 1–56, and 'Historicism and critical editing', *Studies in Bibliography*, 39 (1986), 1–46 (pp. 3–4, 9).

[5] Hearne, *A Collection of Curious Discourses* (2nd edn enlarged, 2 vols., London, 1771), I. lxx (first published Oxford, 1720); *Dunciad Variorum* (1729), note on the title, and 3. 184.

phenomenon integral to the creative process'. A sociologically orientated edition is likely to be based not on an author's manuscript but on a published text precisely because it has 'passed through the normal social process of becoming a printed work'.[6] With the exception of the introduction of computerized technologies, there has been no more significant development in modern bibliography and editing than the pursuit of arguments for a sociological orientation.[7] Editors now may think of texts not as the communications of autonomous creative individuals but as indeterminate and changeable products of a variety of social forces operating over time. There is an obvious consonance with a number of modern movements away from the authorial and canonical, including New Historicism and reception theory.[8]

Eighteenth-century scholarly editors did not have an extensive modern knowledge of the conditions of production of earlier writing, and entertained as we shall see rather different ideas of the author and of the text. Eighteenth-century editing therefore offers very few anticipations of this distinctively modern revolution. Scholars were aware that Shakespeare's plays were altered in the playhouse, but they normally thought of that as corruption and degradation rather than cooperative creativity. In the century's main argument about the initial process of publication of *Paradise Lost*, Richard Bentley subjected the early texts to a process of amendment in order to remove what he thought or represented to be dishonest and inept changes introduced by Milton's first 'editor' and printer. His answerers defended the early text on the grounds that the process of publication of the first two editions adequately communicated the poem Milton intended, without such external intrusions. In this debate neither Bentley nor his opponents were inclined to describe contributions by anyone but the author John Milton as anything but contamination.

In the aesthetic orientation, according to Shillingsburg, authority is located 'in a concept of *artistic* forms – either the author's, the editor's, or those fashionable at some time'.[9] The aesthetic orientation may lie behind an editor's choice of the 'best' text of a work, or behind any particular choice of reading. Aesthetic editors choose between texts and readings on

[6] Shillingsburg, *Scholarly Editing*, pp. 24–6.

[7] See especially Jerome J. McGann, *A Critique of Modern Textual Criticism* (Chicago: University of Chicago Press, 1983); McGann, 'The monks and the giants: textual and bibliographical studies and the interpretation of literary works', in *Textual Criticism and Literary Interpretation*, ed. Jerome J. McGann (Chicago: University of Chicago Press, 1985), pp. 180–99; McGann, 'Interpretation, meaning, and textual criticism: a homily', *TEXT*, 3 (1987), 55–62; and Donald F. McKenzie's 1985 Panizzi Lectures, *Bibliography and the Sociology of Texts* (London: British Library, 1986).

[8] For a development of these points, see G. Thomas Tanselle, 'Textual criticism and literary sociology', *Studies in Bibliography*, 44 (1991), 83–143.

[9] Shillingsburg, *Scholarly Editing*, p. 22. It will be apparent that Shillingsburg's understanding of the aesthetic in relation to editing is a particular and restricted one.

the basis of their consistency with some artistic standard, of metre for example, or the linguistic proprieties of the author's or the editor's period, or consonance with the 'genre' of the piece of writing, or some ideal of poetic richness and suggestivity. If it is possible to distinguish, as E. D. Hirsch does,[10] between determinate 'meaning' inherent in the writing, and 'significance', which is the relationship of that meaning to anything else, then the aesthetic orientation is concerned chiefly with significance. An edition which adapts a text to the tastes and knowledges of either the editor or the reader is to that extent aesthetic. Modern scholarly literary editors appealing to this orientation 'usually restrict their selection of forms to those already existing in historical documents, though most will provide nonhistorical forms in the place of readings which they consider to be erroneous in all surviving texts' (Shillingsburg, *Scholarly Editing*, p. 22). In the strongest forms of the aesthetic orientation, editorial choices may be made on the basis of an essentially subjective taste.

The aesthetic orientation is rarely adopted, at least openly, by modern literary editors, but is not inherently criminal, even in its stronger forms. F. A. Wolf understood that the Alexandrian editors laboured more to present a consistent and elegant Homer than an accurate one, proceeding 'from poetic rather than from diplomatic standards of accuracy'.[11] In our own century, G. Thomas Tanselle has similarly argued that

> a person of taste and sensitivity, choosing among variant readings on the basis of his own preference and making additional emendations of his own, can be expected to produce a text that is aesthetically satisfying and effective . . . editing which does not have as its goal the recovery of the author's words is not necessarily illegitimate – it is creative, rather than scholarly, but not therefore unthinkable.[12]

The point may be made with a more general reference to literary interpretation. Michael Hancher amongst others has urged the necessity of providing for interpretations which, though unconcerned with the author's intended meaning, are nonetheless valuable; such interpretations 'will not be scientific in method', and 'will not issue in knowledge'.[13] E. D. Hirsch argues, more strongly, that no special privilege can be claimed for intrinsic principles, and that a 'judicial evaluation need fulfill only two criteria: (1) that it be a judgment about the work and not about a distorted version of

[10] *Validity in Interpretation* (New Haven: Yale University Press, 1967), p. 8.

[11] *Prolegomena to Homer* (1795), trans. and ed. Anthony Grafton, Glenn W. Most, and James E. G. Zetzel (Princeton: Princeton University Press, 1985), pp. 157–8.

[12] 'Textual study and literary judgment', in Tanselle's *Textual Criticism and Scholarly Editing* (Charlottesville and London: University Press of Virginia, 1990), pp. 325–37 (p. 329). Compare Tanselle, 'The editorial problem of final authorial intention', *Studies in Bibliography*, 29 (1976), 167–211 (p. 180 and n. 28).

[13] 'The science of interpretation, and the art of interpretation', *Modern Language Notes*, 85 (1970), 791–802 (p. 797). Compare Marcia Muelder Eaton, 'Good and correct interpretations of literature', *Journal of Aesthetics and Art Criticism*, 29 (1970–1), 227–33.

it, and (2) that the judgment be accurate with respect to the criteria applied . . . Judgments that are accurately made upon explicit criteria furnish the grounds of their own validation and therefore qualify as knowledge.'[14] So if we disagree with Thomas Rymer's attack on Shakespearean tragedy in his *Short View of Tragedy* (1693), where Rymer's neo-Aristotelian criteria are made sufficiently explicit, we must do so either on the grounds that Rymer distorts the plays he discusses, or that he applies those criteria to them inaccurately. We may consider Rymer's criteria wholly inappropriate, but (if we accept Hirsch's argument) that in itself would not disable Rymer's judgment as knowledge *in its own terms*.

Certainly the aesthetic orientation plays a major part in much eighteenth-century editing. Some eighteenth-century editors, notably Pope and Bentley and Warburton, have been accused of adopting a grossly subjective aesthetic approach, changing the texts of Shakespeare and Milton more or less freely in order to accommodate them to their own tastes. The appropriate question, however, is not whether they adopted an aesthetic approach, but whether they made their editorial decisions accurately and according to openly stated and coherent criteria. If Bentley and Warburton will emerge in my ensuing discussion as problematic at best from this point of view, it will also appear that some eighteenth-century editors, where they make editorial judgments on grounds at least partly aesthetic, do so 'accurately . . . upon explicit criteria'. Thomas Newton's *Milton* is perhaps the most obvious case. My main argument in relation to this issue however will be that, as the century progressed, eighteenth-century scholarly editing depended less on the aesthetic orientation, and more on the fourth of Shillingsburg's categories, the authorial.

In the authorial orientation, authority is located in the author. The editor seeks to include authorial forms, but, so far as is possible, to exclude errors and non-authorial forms, producing 'a purified authorial text' (Shillingsburg, *Scholarly Editing*, p. 28). Authorially orientated editors are likely to privilege holographs, and published versions which the author has proof-read. Shillingsburg's definition does not conceal the problematic nature of this orientation:

> Most editorial principles which discuss authorial intentions, whether 'original' or 'final', reveal an authorial orientation. Phrases such as 'the text the author wanted his readers to have', 'the author's final intentions', his 'artistic intentions', 'the product of the creative process', or even 'what the author did' reveal an authorial orientation.
>
> Authority for the authorial orientation resides with the author, though editors do not agree on what that means. (p. 24)

[14] *The Aims of Interpretation* (Chicago: University of Chicago Press, 1976), p. 108; Hirsch's essays here on 'Evaluation as knowledge' and 'Privileged criteria in evaluation' (pp. 95–109, 110–23) bear on this issue throughout.

The authorial orientation has been dominant in twentieth-century editing, from McKerrow and Greg through Bowers, and down to Bowers's heir, G. Thomas Tanselle. Greg declares that 'the aim of a critical edition should be to present the text, so far as the available evidence permits, in the form in which we may suppose that it would have stood in a fair copy, made by the author himself, of the work as he finally intended it'.[15] Fredson Bowers approved of Greg's 'Rationale of copy-text' as a method for producing 'the nearest approximation in every respect of the author's final intentions', and, in a late essay, insisted that 'the main scholarly demand is for an established critical text embodying the author's full intentions'.[16] Tanselle has explored a number of the theoretical implications of editing which seeks to reconstruct an author's developed intentions in an essay which is the fullest recent treatment of the issue, and has reaffirmed in many of his writings both the desirability and possibility of this orientation.[17]

The authorial orientation and ideas of the author

A central part of my thesis in this book is that, despite some early and persistent aesthetic tendencies, the authorial orientation was increasingly dominant in eighteenth-century scholarly editing of vernacular literary texts, and that the work of the eighteenth-century editors will not be well understood if the reasons for and the nature of their authorial orientation are not taken into account. Such editors as Theobald and Capell, and such commentators as Zachary Pearce, set out to establish and to explain, in the phrase they regularly used, 'what the author wrote'. In what remains of this chapter I shall explore some of the problems and implications of the authorial orientation in editing as they shed light on theory and practice in the eighteenth century.

Certainly the extent to which scholarship, commentary, and editing have focussed on the author has developed and varied historically with changes in the valuation of the status and agency of the author. A. J. Minnis has influentially argued that the author, both of Scripture and of non-scriptural texts, came into his own in the late middle ages. As the emphasis in biblical interpretation shifted from the allegorical to the literary sense, so it began to be possible to think that 'the intention of the human *auctor* was believed to be expressed by the literal sense'.[18] So texts,

[15] W. W. Greg, *The Editorial Problem in Shakespeare* (Oxford: Oxford University Press, 1942), p. x.

[16] 'Some principles for scholarly editions of nineteenth-century American authors', *Studies in Bibliography*, 17 (1964), 227; 'Remarks on eclectic texts', in Bowers's *Essays in Bibliography, Text, and Editing* (Charlottesville: University Press of Virginia, 1975), pp. 488–528 (p. 527).

[17] 'The editorial problem of final authorial intention'. Compare, for example, Tanselle's 'Historicism and critical editing', p. 21.

[18] A. J. Minnis, *Medieval Theory of Authorship* (2nd edn, Aldershot: Wildwood House, 1988), p. 5.

including the Bible, began to be theorised in more 'literary' ways; so the human author became possessed of 'a high status and respected didactic / stylistic strategies of his very own'; and so '*auctoritas* moved from the divine realm to the human'. The authority, and authenticity, of a piece of writing became associated with, and dependent on, its attribution to a named *auctor*. In the world of study, each discipline had its *auctores*: Aristotle, or Ptolemy, or Cicero, or Galen. The business of the student was not to compete with or query the status of the authoritative works associated with such authors, but to understand them.[19] The authorial text is there *to be interpreted*. Because its purpose is to be interpreted, to be understood, the authorial text becomes the object of glossary and commentary.

Despite the lapse of half a millennium, and despite all differences, the process which Minnis here describes offers some analogies with the beginnings of English literary editing. The project of editing secular scriptures was contemporaneous with the sense of a native literary history beginning to define itself in England in the early eighteenth century. In particular the two writers perceived as the pillars of an identifiably English tradition, namely Milton and Shakespeare, were invested with authority and their writings were implicitly identified as canonic, as scriptures, and hence as worthy of editorial attention, and explanatory commentary. Minnis tellingly denominates the process in medieval literature by which authority moved from the divine to the human, and from the past to the present, as a *translatio auctoritatis*, and finds in it 'one of the most significant movements in the history of vernacular literature' (p. viii). It seems to me that just such a *translatio auctoritatis* as Minnis describes, from the biblical and classical to recent vernacular scriptures, may be found in the period I am examining, and may have some importance there too. An author becomes ripe for commentary when he (or, more recently, and significantly, she) is perceived to have *auctoritas*. What Minnis says of medieval commentary might perhaps also be applied, *mutatis mutandis*, to editorial commentary in the eighteenth century: 'to provide vernacular texts with an apparatus . . . tacitly claimed a degree of prestige for them (because that apparatus was of the type which conventionally had accompanied the works of the revered auctores) . . . techniques of exposition traditionally used in interpreting "ancient" authorities are being used to indicate and announce the literary authority of a "modern" work' (pp. xi, xiii). This notion found clear expression in the eighteenth century in both positive and negative forms. The force and purpose of the elaborate *scholia* of the *Dunciad Variorum* is of course that, in mimicking aspects of the apparatuses employed in the editing of classical texts, they claim, inappropriately, a similar prestige for a parodic modern epic, and enact in Pope's view a

[19] Minnis, *Medieval Theory of Authorship*, pp. vii, 11, 13–14.

threatening and unwanted *translatio auctoritatis* parallel to the *translatio imperii* which the plot of the poem sets out. The force and purpose of the apparatuses which were developed by Theobald, Bentley, Johnson, or Capell for the poems of Milton and the dramas of Shakespeare is that they claim, appropriately and seriously, prestige for more genuinely canonical texts, and that they effect an analogous, and in their writers' view acceptable or desirable, translation, or at least extension or sharing, of authority. At many points the techniques of editorial annotation used by the editors of Milton and Shakespeare bear, as I shall attempt to show, a clear similarity to the methods of commentary which had been used for other scriptures, sacred and profane. Patrick Hume's *Annotations* on *Milton's Paradise Lost* (1695) are modelled on the formal Annotation and Paraphrase of seventeenth- and eighteenth-century Anglican biblical commentary, and many other editors, of Shakespeare as well as of Milton, draw on the methods and principles of that exegetical tradition. Theobald's edition of Shakespeare, and Newton's edition of *Paradise Lost*, amongst others, use some of the methods of learned commentary on the pagan classics, as well as those of biblical commentary.

If what I suggest here, and will attempt to argue in the following chapters, is true, it will appear that some at least of the eighteenth-century scholars granted to the authors that they edited a status, an autonomy, and an ultimate authority over meaning which many recent theorists, if not all recent editors, would consider unacceptably theological. Roland Barthes announced the death of the author, and argued for a movement from Work to Text. In the Work 'the *author* is a god (his place of origin is the signified); as for the critic, he is the priest whose task is to decipher the Writing of the God'; the Text, by contrast is a 'galaxy of signifiers', from which the author, as a delimiter of meaning, has been banished.[20] Barthes has not been alone in problematizing quasi-theological notions of authorship. Morse Peckham, questioning some of the assumptions that lie behind the Bowers school of author-centred textual criticism, argues that:

> In the theology and hagiography of literary humanism the term . . . 'author' is a sacred term . . . God inspired the authors of the Bible, and in the *Phaedrus* is a locus classicus for the notion that poets also are divinely inspired. To be sure, Plato was being ironic . . . But this irony has been traditionally ignored by literary humanists . . . Literary inspiration, then, descends upon the poet as grace descends upon the saint. 'Imagination' in literary theory is the equivalent of 'grace' in hagiology . . . In short, in literary humanism the term 'author' (the intensive is 'poet') ascribes to

[20] *S/Z*, trans. Richard Miller (London: Cape, 1975), pp. 5, 174. Seán Burke's discussion points out how Barthes's polemical construction of the author as 'tyrannical deity' goes beyond anything to be found in other critics, and is designed to 'create a king worthy of the killing' (*The Death and Return of the Author* (Edinburgh: Edinburgh University Press, 1992), p. 26).

a human organism conceived of primarily as producer of language the gift of God's grace, or charisma.[21]

No doubt the privileging of the author in textual editing and interpretation is an attribute of literary humanism, and more especially of the print culture which has allowed authors a measure of identity, property, and determinacy in their writings which they did not have in a manuscript culture, and will not have in a digital one. I shall in fact suggest at a number of points in this book that the work of the eighteenth-century editors privileges the values of print and the book, and in this respect is characteristically an expression of late humanism. Yet Peckham's words involve some overstatement. There is no necessary link between the ascription of authority to a given author and that author's writings, on the one hand, and a belief in the inspired state of that author on the other. The doctrine of inspiration, pagan or Christian, is not central or necessary to humanist conceptions of the author. It has indeed been dismissed by many humanist theorists (by Philip Sidney, for example)[22] as scornfully as it was by Plato, and a good deal more explicitly, and belongs rather, as Peckham indeed acknowledges, with certain Romantic doctrines of poetic imagination. Similarly, though constructions of literary canonicity derived at least in part from the Holy Book, and though the identifiably authored stood in relation to the canonical as the anonymous to the apocryphal, there is nonetheless also a distinction to be made between canonicity, and canonization. Shakespeare and Milton represented for the eighteenth century aspects of a characteristically English poetic talent, a genius which could be spoken of, metaphorically at least, as a divine gift. In the limit and exceptional case of *Paradise Lost*, authority depended partly upon the sacred truths that Milton's poem was seen to present.[23] These elements of the charismatic or quasi-charismatic were certainly a vital part of what made these authors appropriate and necessary objects of editorial attention. Nonetheless, it is only in the figures of poetic representation that Milton and Shakespeare achieved anything like a Barthesian apotheosized status. And certainly the scholarly editors were not in the business of eliciting the traces of divine grace. In the process of editing, the object of attention was not some notion of the author's statement of divinely communicated truth, but literal, authorially intended, meaning. Milton and Shakespeare had gained the right as authors to be interpreted, to be understood.

21 'Reflections on the foundations of modern textual editing', *Proof*, 1 (1971), 122–55 (pp. 136–7).

22 See *An Apology for Poetry*, ed. Geoffrey Shepherd (London: Nelson, 1965), p. 130.

23 See below pp. 55–7.

The authorial orientation in editing and interpretation

Though all editing inescapably involves interpretation, the authorial orientation is by its nature more essentially interpretative than others, for it seeks to reconstruct a posited authorial text which is most unlikely to be perfectly represented in any single surviving document. The editor who locates authority in the author will choose a text closest to the author, where possible a manuscript, or a printed text known to have been authorially proof-read. Rather than accepting the authority of that single witness, however, the authorial editor will seek to identify and correct apparent errors, purge the text of non-authorial elements, and draw on other authoritative source texts where they exist, in the attempt to approximate the author's 'original intentions', or 'final intentions'.[24]

This process is, at every stage, necessarily dependent on interpretative judgment (some use the phrase 'critical judgment'). Errors may be more or less obvious or obscure. The identification of even the most 'obvious' error, however, is an act of interpretation, which needs to be based on knowledge of the particular author. Shakespeare's standards of metre, orthography, syntax, lexis, and semantics, and the consistency of his conformity to those standards, were different from ours. His text is to be judged (authorial editors would agree) by his standards in these matters, not by ours. Those standards are to be known through scholarship, not subjective taste. The identification of frank error is not sufficient. A reading may be possible, and yet be unlikely to represent the intention of the author in question.[25]

Editors vary in the energy and freedom with which they seek error. In the extreme case, the authorial orientation may be used as a cloak by which the rather different business of aesthetic editing might be carried on, as has been thought to be the case in Bentley's edition of *Paradise Lost.* Most scholarly editors however take the view that knowledge of the particularities of the writing and its context will often allow us to explain what might have otherwise seemed alien and incomprehensible. The more such knowledge we have, the more we shall be able to avoid unnecessary and inappropriate emendation. Housman offers a classic statement of this view in the Preface to his edition of Manilius:

Latin poets compose Latin poetry, which is very unlike English or German poetry;

[24] For fuller discussion of these points, see, for example, Bowers, 'Eclectic texts', pp. 488, 527; Shillingsburg, *Scholarly Editing*, pp. 26–8; Tanselle, 'Textual criticism and literary sociology', p. 142.

[25] For a particularly cogent formulation of this point, see Alice Walker, 'Principles of annotation: some suggestions for editors of Shakespeare', *Studies in Bibliography*, 9 (1957), 95–105 (p. 96). For examples of other recent discussions, see Martin L. West, *Textual Criticism and Editorial Technique Applicable to Greek and Latin Texts* (Stuttgart: B. G. Teubner, 1973), especially p. 48; Tanselle, 'The editorial problem of final authorial intention', especially pp. 173, 186.

and each writer has his own peculiarities and the peculiarities of his generation and his school, which must be learnt by observation and cannot be divined by taste . . . A properly informed and properly attentive reader will find that many verses hastily altered by some editors and absurdly defended by others can be made to yield a just sense without either changing the text or inventing a new Latinity.[26]

Better information will not free us however from the responsibility of interpretative judgment. Housman himself also argued, perhaps more famously, that 'the art of explaining corrupt passages instead of correcting them' was as likely to do harm as the excesses of unbridled correction.[27]

Similarly, interpretative judgment is necessary in deciding on the validity of alternative readings where they exist, and in choosing between them. The editor cannot trust that the reading of a chosen base text at any given point is more likely to be that of the author than that of an alternative witness. In the case of any substantive variant reading in surviving witnesses, the authorially orientated editor is, according to Housman or Greg, both free and obliged to exercise choice, drawing on 'critical' judgment, as well as on purely textual or bibliographical data.[28] In some cases – where there is an error in a sole surviving authoritative witness, or where none of several surviving witnesses supplies a satisfactory reading – the editor must at least diagnose the fault, and may wish to take the further interpretative step of making a conjectural emendation. Conjectures *ex ingenio* are more likely to be required where the authorial text is lost, as in the case of the classics, or the Bible, or Shakespeare, and less likely to be required where texts close to the authorial original survive, as in the case of Milton.

Such exercises of conjectural emendation are a further step in the interpretative process by which authorially orientated editing proceeds, and are not essentially different in nature from acts of interpretative choice between witnessed readings. Richard Bentley notoriously argued, in his edition of Horace, that conjectures should be treated on their merits, and that conjectures made *ex ingenio* were (at least) no more hazardous than conjectures *ex codicibus*.[29] The point is not merely Bentleian eccentricity. Housman similarly insists that the appearance of a reading in a codex merely confirms a case made on prior interpretative grounds.[30] 'Conjecture', or interpretative choice, is an essential part of eclectic, authorially orientated, editing. Conjecture begins at the point where an editor makes any change to the base text, whether that change is based on documentary evidence or not. An editorial conjecture, as Tanselle puts it in the most

26 Manilius, *Astronomicon*, ed. A. E. Housman, I (London, Grant Richards, 1903), xl.

27 *Astronomicon*, I. xxxii, xli.

28 See Greg, 'The rationale of copy-text', in *Bibliography and Textual Criticism*, ed. O. M. Brack and Warner Barnes (Chicago and London: University of Chicago Press, 1969), pp. 41–58 (p. 51).

29 See below, p. 64.

30 See especially *Astronomicon*, I. lx.

persuasive and extended recent discussion of this issue, 'may be more certainly what the author wrote than any of the alternative readings at a point of variation'.[31]

Eighteenth-century editing, especially early eighteenth-century editing, can appear to modern eyes to be characterized by a freedom, even a dangerous freedom, in finding error, in resorting to alternative readings, and particularly in proposing frankly conjectural emendation. Yet a distinction has to be made between the (aesthetically orientated, in Shillingsburg's understanding of the term) attempt to improve a work by an editor's own standards, and an editor's employment of appropriate interpretative criteria in an attempt to reconstruct an author's intended reading.[32] Conjectural criticism as practised in Bentley's edition of *Paradise Lost*, or William Warburton's *Shakespeare*, might well be thought frequently to fall into the first category. Conjecture as practised in Theobald's *Shakespeare*, supported (I shall argue) on the whole by a conscious exercise of rational interpretative principles, belongs to the second category.

The practice of conjecture *ex ingenio* in literary editing declined even during the eighteenth century. In the early twentieth century, with the growth of analytical bibliography, the prestige, and even the respectability, of conjecture dwindled further in the face of the new emphasis on mechanical explanations, and scientific or quasi-scientific standards of proof. Most commentators have thought this on the whole a positive development, which has set powerful controls and limits upon editorial sophistication. There have however been a number of persuasive advocates for conjectural emendation where essential, in the fields of classical, New Testament, medieval,[33] and Shakespearean editing. In the last of these, Gary Taylor in particular, while commending the salutary effects of modern textual conservatism, has argued that, nonetheless, analytical bibliography has 'generally inhibited editorial creativity and undermined editorial confidence in the validity of critical judgements', and urged a new freedom in proposing characteristically Shakespearean emendations.[34] Certainly, few would now urge a return to the kind of conjectural freedom

[31] 'Classical, Biblical, and medieval textual criticism and modern editing', *Studies in Bibliography*, 36 (1983), 21–68 (p. 55; see also pp. 26, 62–3). For further significant discussions, see Bowers, 'Eclectic texts', p. 527; E. J. Kenney, *The Classical Text* (Los Angeles and London: University of California Press, 1974), pp. 72–3, 74.

[32] My formulation here echoes one by Tanselle in his 'Historicism and critical editing', p. 45.

[33] Broadly reasoned cases are presented by George Kane, 'Conjectural emendation', in *Medieval Literature and Civilisation*, ed. D. A. Pearsall and R. A. Waldron (London: Athlone, 1969), pp. 155–69; and John Strugnell, in 'A plea for conjectural emendation in the New Testament, with a coda on 1 Cor 4:6', *Catholic Biblical Quarterly*, 36 (1974), 543–58. Günther Zuntz argues for the correction of authorial 'slips of the pen', and insists that 1 Cor. 6:5 requires emendation, in '"The critic correcting the author"', *Philologus*, 99 (1955), 295–303.

[34] Gary Taylor, 'Inventing Shakespeare', *Deutsche Shakespeare-Gesellschaft West Jahrbuch 1986*, pp. 26–44 (pp. 30, 33); Stanley Wells and Gary Taylor, with John Jowett and William

to be found in Bentley or Warburton. Modern editorial theory however need have no difficulty in understanding as part of the interpretative process of authorially orientated editing the more rational methods of such eighteenth-century editors as Theobald or Capell or Newton.

Nonetheless, eighteenth-century editors of Shakespeare and Milton will inevitably prove inconsistent and wanting when tested against the demanding standards of twentieth-century editorial science. The New Bibliography has tended to concentrate on physical textual evidence rather than interpretation, on the methods of *recensio* rather than *emendatio*. W. W. Greg for example stressed the factual or historical as against the interpretative in his important lecture on 'Principles of emendation in Shakespeare'. While acknowledging from the start that a conjectural emendation must provide 'exactly the sense required by the context', he stresses throughout that the justifiability of any act of conjecture ultimately rests on the facts of the history of textual transmission. For Greg emendation is in itself 'devoid of principle', a statement which begs the question of whether emendation might possibly be validated by an interpretative logic.[35]

Almost all modern textual theorists nonetheless reject the notion of a wholly mechanistic system of editing. Greg himself disapproved not only 'unprincipled eclecticism' but also the 'attempt to substitute objective or mechanical rules in place of personal judgement'.[36] In his most famous philippic, Housman insisted that textual criticism cannot be based merely on mechanical sciences, complaining that 'one sees books calling themselves introductions to textual criticism which contain nothing about textual criticism from beginning to end; which are all about palaeography and manuscripts and collation'; which confine textual criticism, that is, essentially to matters of *recensio*. Rather, Housman insists, quoting Haupt, 'the prime requisite of a good emendation is that it should start from the thought'.[37] Similarly E. D. Hirsch, the leading modern theorist of textual interpretation in relation to authorial intention, briefly but emphatically endorses this received view amongst editors of an authorial orientation: 'Textual choices frequently depend upon interpretations, just as interpretations depend upon texts. The aim of the textual editor is to determine what the author wrote or intended to write, and no purely mechanical system which ignores interpretation could ever reliably reach such a determina-

Montgomery, *William Shakespeare: a Textual Companion* (Oxford: Oxford University Press, 1987), pp. 18, 58–60.

35 'Principles of emendation in Shakespeare', *Proceedings of the British Academy*, 14 (1928), 147–216 (pp. 147, 149, 151, 172–3).

36 *The Works of Thomas Nashe*, ed. R. B. McKerrow, rev. F. P. Wilson, v (1958), Supplement, 33. Compare Walker, 'Principles of annotation', p. 96; Kane, 'Conjectural emendation', p. 160.

37 'The application of thought to textual criticism', *Proceedings of the Classical Association*, 18 (1921), 67–84 (pp. 67, 77).

tion.'[38] As Hirsch's words imply, at issue here is the nature of the relation of two aspects of authorial intention, the intention to set down a sequence of words, and the intention to mean something by those words. Tanselle, amongst a number of other recent commentators, has argued the inextricability of these two levels of intention, and the consequent inevitable involvement of the editor in questions of intention to mean:

The editor may at first feel . . . that he is concerned with establishing intended *wording*, not with explicating intended *meaning* . . . But he soon realizes that his discovery of textual errors or his choice among textual variants involves his understanding of the intended meaning of the text . . . The scholarly editor is in the same position as the critic who is concerned with the author's intended meaning . . . the scholarly editor makes corrections or emendations on the basis of the one he judges most likely to have been the author's intended meaning.[39]

Those who fall within the range of Tanselle's remark would certainly include twentieth-century editors whose decisions are based primarily on 'factual' textual evidence. Some eighteenth-century editors, on the other hand, have been thought guilty of the opposite sin of interpretative speculation with little reference to the constraints imposed by the nature of the surviving textual evidence. George Steevens, as often both profound and strikingly 'modern' in his remarks, complained in 1765 that William Warburton, amongst other failings in his edition of Shakespeare, 'has taken more pains to understand Shakespeare's meaning than his words, two studies which have so mutual a relation that they ought to be inseparable'.[40]

One of the constant concerns of this book will be to examine to what extent the inseparability of these two studies was understood amongst Miltonic, and more particularly amongst Shakespearean, editors, in the four decades before Steevens wrote these words. Certainly most of the editors I shall discuss seem to a modern eye biassed to meanings rather than words, to judgments made on 'critical' grounds rather than to careful consideration of physical evidence and the facts of textual transmission. Most of their more consequential theoretical statements, and by far the greater number of their practical textual decisions, involved issues of interpretative judgment rather than of textual description, collation, or

38 *Validity in Interpretation*, pp. 171–2 n.

39 'The editorial problem of final authorial intention', pp. 179, 181. Compare Hirsch's definition of verbal meaning as 'whatever someone has willed to convey by a particular sequence of linguistic signs and which can be conveyed (shared) by means of those linguistic signs' (*Validity in Interpretation*, p. 31). Tanselle's view is not universal; for significant differing views, see Shillingsburg, *Scholarly Editing*, pp. 36–8; and James McLaverty, 'The concept of authorial intention in textual criticism', *Library*, sixth series, 6 (1984), 121–38 (especially p. 127).

40 Review of Benjamin Heath's *Revisal of Shakespeare's Text*, *Critical Review*, 19 (1765); ascribed to Steevens by Brian Vickers, and reprinted in his *Shakespeare. The Critical Heritage* (6 vols., London: Routledge and Kegan Paul, 1974–81), IV. 565–73 (p. 573).

genealogy. The emphasis of the present study will for much the greater part therefore be firmly on their treatment of matters of *emendatio*. To concentrate on their work in *recensio* (as some recent historiography has done) is likely to reveal areas of weakness rather than of strength, or rather to show them in the early stages of what might credibly be thought an evolutionary science. Preceding Lachmann and his co-workers they knew very little about formal stemmatics. They had not of course developed anything resembling complex and modern theorizings of copy text, authorial revision, or the ontology and treatment of multiple authorial versions. This is not to say that the period did not witness important explorations, and applications to secular literary editing, of themes and techniques of *recensio*. Some editors, notably Theobald, knew enough of paleography to apply the principle of the *ductus litterarum* with some credibility; there was a developing sense of the unique authority of the first text, the Shakespearean first Folio for instance, in a line of succession; the collection and collation of surviving documents was practised with increasing energy by a number of scholars, and with real thoroughness by Newton, Capell, and Charles Jennens; and Capell practised sophisticated and detailed methods of bibliographical description. Nonetheless, a very high proportion of the annotations written by these and other scholar-editors, and a very high proportion of the examples cited in this book, are arguments *in which they choose between readings by an interpretative process*; rejecting existing readings, or defending them, on interpretative grounds; proposing new readings, and defending them, on interpretative grounds; addressing themselves in fact to what they evidently understood as two interrelated interpretative questions: what words an author intended to set down, and what he intended to mean by the words he set down.

Valid interpretation: principles and criteria

So far I have outlined the argument that authorially orientated editing is necessarily interpretative, concerned with meaning as well as with words, and that the authorially orientated editor stands in the same relation to the text as the critical interpreter. It will already have become clear that this position begs a fundamental question: can interpretation be a knowledge-based activity, capable of reaching valid conclusions by rational argument and evidence? Or, to apply the question more specifically to textual editing and its history, can editors hope ever to escape their own personal and cultural position, and move beyond the accommodation and appropriation of past texts to their own tastes and circumstances, to a genuine and objective knowledge of the original (what the authorial orientation aspires or claims to achieve)? The question is central to our assessment of eighteenth-century editing, as it attempted to leave the value judgments of

Pope, Bentley, and Warburton behind in the quest for acceptably stable, and adequately explained, texts of an English literary inheritance.

Though this question has of course been much contested, a number of modern hermeneutic theorists have argued that interpretation is a process by which valid provisional knowledge may be reached, as in any discipline, by a process of hypothesis formation and testing. Karl Popper has insisted that the fundamental method of conjecture and refutation is applicable to the humanities as well as to the sciences, 'in reconstructing a damaged text as well as in constructing a theory of radioactivity':

the interpretation (*hermeneutics*) of texts . . . is indeed almost as risky as the interpretation of nature. It is a matter in which we must work with conjectures *and* refutations: that is, we must try to refute our conjectures until they fit fully into the context of the problem situation, lose arbitrary features, and achieve something like a maximum of explanatory power of what the author wanted to say.[41]

E. D. Hirsch has similarly argued that the interpretation of a literary work is an exercise in hypothesis formation, itself grounded in 'numerous subhypotheses (i.e. constructions of individual words and phrases)'. Validation of an interpretation of a text 'is achieved only with respect to known hypotheses and known facts: as soon as new relevant facts and/or guesses appear, the old conclusions may have to be abandoned in favor of new ones'.[42] Such a view is pertinent to editing's detailed engagement with the words and the meanings of the words of a text, and with the process by which interpretations may be disputed and modified in successive editions, and has been accepted implicitly or explicitly by many textual theorists, and many writers of editorial commentary.[43] If this position is accepted, the interpretative element in editing need be considered no less 'scientific' than the bibliographical or the paleographical. It may be objected, however, that in interpretation, unlike the predictive sciences, it is not always possible to generate data allowing us to choose between one or more rival hypotheses by demonstrating one of them to be false. In a celebrated essay in an aspect of interpretative scepticism, Stanley Fish has argued that the parading of editorial disagreement in the Milton *Variorum* demonstrates that cruxes 'are not *meant* to be solved', and that consequently 'any procedure that attempts to determine which of a number of readings is correct will necessarily fail', that is, that hypotheses (or some hypotheses) in interpretation are not capable of falsification.[44] It is possible to concede this point without abandoning the possibility of knowledge in interpreta-

[41] *Objective Knowledge*, pp. 185, 190n. [42] *Validity in Interpretation*, p. 170.

[43] See, for example, Kenney, *The Classical Text*, p. 147; Kane, 'Conjectural emendation', pp. 165–6; G. Thomas Tanselle, 'Recent editorial discussion and the central questions of editing', *Studies in Bibliography*, 34 (1981), 23–65 (pp. 26, 62).

[44] 'Interpreting the Variorum', in his *Is there a Text in this Class? The Authority of Interpretive Communities* (Cambridge, Mass., and London: Harvard University Press, 1980), pp. 147–73 (pp. 148–9).

tion. Choices may nonetheless be made between conflicting hypotheses, Hirsch has argued, by probability judgments on the basis of available evidence, according to 'objectively defined and generally accepted principles'.[45] If this is the case, supporters of the hypothesis view of interpretative procedure can still assert, in answer to Fish, that the debates in modern, or in eighteenth-century, variorum commentaries may be seen, not as a demonstration of the impossibility of solving interpretative problems, but as a contest of hypotheses which is in principle capable of resulting in valid knowledge as in other disciplines. What is at issue is not the fact of disagreement, but whether or not individual competing hypotheses are susceptible to discrimination by the adequacy of the criteria on which they are based and the evidence to which they resort. That more than one hypothesis exists for the meaning of the 'two-handed engine' of *Lycidas*, and indeed had already appeared in eighteenth-century commentaries, does not rule out the possibility of ultimate choice between these hypotheses on rational grounds. Nor does it rule out the possibility of new knowledge resolving the issue.

If the hypothesis-making activity which is authorial editing and interpretation is not to be thought merely individual and subjective, if in fact it can aspire to be a science, it has then to be shown that adequate criteria are available by which evidence for deciding authorial readings and authorial meanings may be selected and assessed. The criteria of interpretation employed by editors and discussed by editorial theorists are in principle of the same kind as those discussed more generally by hermeneutic theorists. Discussion of such criteria has of course a very long history. In editorial theory we may trace it at least as far back as Robortello's advice, in his textbook of textual criticism *De arte critica sive ratione corrigendi antiquorum libros disputatio* (1557), that the critic's conjectural ideas should be governed by considerations of paleography, style, and understanding of the subject.[46] Some criteria of course relate to mechanical evidence: matters of bibliography, stemmatics, paleography, typography, and scribal and printing-house practice. Editorial theorists and editors have also argued for, and applied, interpretative criteria having to do with evidence ranging from particular words and their immediate connections to very much more widely derived cultural, intellectual, and historical contextual data. A choice between readings or conjectural emendation must provide exactly the sense required by the local verbal context.[47] It should be coherent with the thought of the passage and, more broadly, with the author's intended meaning in the whole of the

[45] Hirsch, *Validity in Interpretation*, pp. 180–1, 183.
[46] L. D. Reynolds and N. G. Wilson, *Scribes and Scholars* (3rd edn, Oxford: Oxford University Press, 1991), p. 167.
[47] Housman, *Selected Prose*, ed. J. Carter (Cambridge: Cambridge University Press, 1961), p. 51;

text.[48] It should be consistent with, or not impossible by, the *langue* of the author's time, in its syntax, lexis, semantics, and other linguistic characteristics.[49] More narrowly, it should be compatible with the author's *usus scribendi* (or 'idiom', or 'style'), so far as that may be established from knowledge of the whole of the author's work.[50] And it will be controlled by what is known of the author, of the author's habits and taste as a writer, of the genre within which the author wrote, and of the period, including literary and historical information of a wide variety of kinds.[51]

These are familiar editorial statements of criteria which acquire sharper focus and greater cogency in the writings of a number of hermeneutic theorists. They map well, for example, on to the four essential criteria of interpretation as stated by E. D. Hirsch: of 'legitimacy' ('the reading must be permissible within the public norms of the *langue* in which the text was composed'), of 'correspondence' ('the reading must account for each linguistic component in the text'), of 'generic appropriateness' ('if the text follows the conventions of a scientific essay, for example, it is inappropriate to construe the kind of allusive meaning found in casual conversation'), and the decisive criterion of 'coherence' (or 'plausibility', 'a sense of the whole meaning, constituted of explicit partial meanings plus a horizon of expectations and probabilities').[52] Validity in interpretation depends upon the precision with which criteria are defined, and the accuracy with which they are applied. Most of the criteria of interpretation identified by editorial theorists have to do with matters of 'context'. Understanding of an author's intended meaning is possible to the extent that we share, or can reconstruct by a process of research, and as editors can offer in commentary, the context within which the author's utterance was made. In common usage we mean by 'context', as Hirsch points out, 'a very complex and undifferentiated set of relevant factors, starting with the words that surround the crux and expanding to the entire physical, psychological, social, and historical milieu in which the utterance occurs'.[53] Interpretation, however, cannot work validly with a criterion so undefined, or with data from so wide a possible field. Modern interpretative theorists have posited, and most modern editors would wish to work with, rather rigorous

Greg, 'Principles of emendation in Shakespeare', p. 149; West, *Textual Criticism and Editorial Technique*, p. 48.

48 Housman, *Astronomicon*, I. xxxix; 'The application of thought to textual criticism', pp. 77 ff.; Tanselle, 'The editorial problem of final authorial intention', pp. 182–3.

49 Shillingsburg, *Scholarly Editing*, pp. 36–7; Strugnell, 'A plea for conjectural emendation in the New Testament', p. 553.

50 Kane, 'Conjectural emendation', pp. 164–5; West, *Textual Criticism and Editorial Technique*, p. 48; Tanselle, 'The editorial problem of final authorial intention', p. 173.

51 Tanselle, 'Literary editing', in *Literary and Historical Editing*, ed. George L. Vogt and John Bush Jones (Lawrence, Kansas: University of Kansas Libraries, 1981), pp. 49–50; Housman, *Astronomicon*, I. xvii; Kenney, *The Classical Text*, p. 146.

52 *Validity in Interpretation*, pp. 236–7.

53 *Validity in Interpretation*, pp. 86–7.

standards of evidential relevance, working not from the general background or milieu of the work they seek to explain, but establishing from the work itself which particular ideas or conventions are drawn on by the author, and testing the provenance and availability of particular ideas and the process of transmission.[54]

One of my concerns in this book will be to explore the extent to which eighteenth-century scholarly editors began to identify pertinent contextual knowledges, and the ways in which they exploited those knowledges in interpreting Shakespeare and Milton. Their turn from an aesthetic to an authorial orientation involved a movement away from absorption in the editor's personal taste and contemporary culture, towards a belief that earlier literature must be interpreted, as well as evaluated, within the horizons of its own moment of production. Their development of historicizing scholarship is highly significant in relation to this turn. Equally significant, from the point of view of the validity of their interpretations, is the exactness with which evidence was applied. Such editors and commentators as Theobald, Pearce, Upton, Newton, and Capell use their scholarship not as mere background, or as a source of analogues, but frequently to allow that identification of precise sources and allusions which makes interpretation possible. Theobald's extensive and vital knowledge of Elizabethan and Jacobean drama, the copious and various materials of Capell's *School of Shakespeare*, and Newton's detailed professional knowledge of Holy Writ, are not inert pedantry or antiquarianism, but the necessary resources on which they drew as interpreters, and which make their interpretations at least potentially cogent.

Editing and commentary

Modern scholarly editors of literary texts normally make a clear formal distinction between explanatory commentary and textual notes. Most eighteenth-century editors did not (Edward Capell is the most obvious, and significant, exception). Partly this was because they did not have a modern conception of the necessity of detailed textual apparatus providing the factual record, and had not therefore evolved a modern methodology of textual apparatus (though in Capell we clearly see the beginnings of such a methodology). A second reason, however, was that their textual decisions

[54] These are ideas of common currency, but see, notably, R. S. Crane, 'The Yahoos, the Houhynhnms, and the history of ideas', in his *The Idea of the Humanities and other Essays Critical and Historical* (2 vols., London and Chicago: University of Chicago Press, 1967), II. 261–82 (especially pp. 267–9); P. D. Juhl, *Interpretation: an Essay in the Philosophy of Literary Criticism* (Princeton: Princeton University Press, 1980), especially ch. 5; Herman J. Real and Heinz J. Vienken, ' "Interpretations the author never meant": problems of annotation in *A Tale of a Tub*', *Notes and Queries*, 230 (1985), 201–3; and Hirsch, *Validity in Interpretation*, *passim*.

constantly emerged out of, and were the subject of, interpretative discussion. To a greater degree than in most modern editing, their editorial work was constituted of commentary.

It is possible to identify two historically opposed conceptions of commentary. In the first of these, the commentary usurps the place of the text, and itself claims or becomes or rewrites the text's (authorially intended or literal) meaning. This conception has a long history and many representatives and versions, including ancient allegorizings of Homeric myth and moralizings of Ovid's tales, and reinterpretations of the Old Testament both by Cabbalists and by Christian exegetes. A later example is the assertion of Roman Catholic hermeneutic theorists in the seventeenth century that sense inheres, not in Scripture, but in the commentary, the tradition, of the Church (against this, as we shall see, English scholarly interpreters working in a broadly Protestant and humanist tradition to some extent defined themselves). Some kinds of modern theory describe all forms of commentary as primarily political and social, rather than neutrally or objectively interpretative, functions. Annotation is inevitably 'appropriation', more or less aggressive and more or less open, 'an apparatus' (as Laurent Mayali puts it, in an essay appearing in a recent collection on the subject) 'for reproducing knowledge in a form that legitimates the annotator, the annotation, and the social structures within which they exist'. According to Mayali, 'the relationship of annotation to the text is less a relation of meaning than it is a relation of power'.[55] For Ralph Hanna, writing in the same collection, commentary cannot be a 'benign mediation' of the work to the reader, but must inevitably create the community it purports to serve: 'In this way, the forms of annotation speak what is not: they exist deliberately to obscure the aggressive act of controlling audience consumption of the text.'[56] All of the many possible versions of this subjective conception of annotation start with some form of the assumption that meaning is not stably and determinately *in* the text, and problematize notions of annotation as explanation or mediation. Famously Stanley Fish has argued, with particular reference to forms of commentary employed in the Milton *Variorum*, that meanings are not 'embedded or encoded in the text' but are the product of prevailing interpretative assumptions.[57] Under this first pole, commentary is regularly imaged as repetition and deferral, part of an inevitably limitless semiosis, which neither can nor should achieve 'closure'. Honesty requires that annotators acknowledge their participation in this infinite process, rather than 'aggressively' lay claim to real knowledge or real meanings.

[55] 'For a political economy of annotation', in *Annotation and its Texts*, ed. Stephen A. Barney (New York: Oxford University Press, 1991), pp. 185–6.

[56] 'Annotation as social practice', in Barney, ed., *Annotation and its Texts*, p. 181.

[57] 'Interpreting the Variorum', *Is there a Text in this Class?*, p. 158.

The second pole of annotation depends on the assumption that the text contains a literal sense, or determinate meaning, and that it is the annotator's business to understand this sense (*ars intelligendi*) and to explain it to the reader (*ars explicandi*). Under this conception annotation may claim to be a rational and evidential activity. It professes not to replace or stand for the text, but to cast light on the text's meaning. This alternative understanding of annotation, which has strong and necessary associations with print culture, humanism, and Protestantism, has underwritten most scholarly editorial commentary on secular literary texts. Eighteenth-century editors (I shall argue) increasingly adopted this assumption. They distinguished between the scholastic commentary, which they generally perceived and portrayed as self-obsessed, self-serving, parasitic, not seeking to explain the text but to replace it, on the one hand, and the explanatory commentary, designed to explicate and mediate, on the other.[58] The conception of commentary as explication and mediation remains broadly characteristic of modern scholarly editing, despite the theoretical attacks upon it of the last decades.

There has been considerable debate about the kinds of information it is necessary or desirable for the annotating editor to provide, and about the nature of the annotating editor's mediating role. The two issues are not unconnected. Ian Jack, discussing the policies of the Clarendon edition of the Brontë novels, defines the principal duty of an annotator as being 'to attempt to enable his contemporaries to read a book as its original audience read it. This calls for the explanation of words which are unfamiliar or which have changed their meaning, the provision of information about social customs and historical events, and the identification of quotations and allusions.'[59] Commentary, by this familiar conception of its function, sets out to recover and make available the information which is necessary to understanding. Some at least of that information was part of the shared horizon which enabled communication between the author and the original readership, but has become lost with the passage of time. Several theorists have been prepared to argue for both the recoverability of such information by scholarly effort, and its value in interpretation. Alice Walker for instance, in a well-known essay on the annotation of Shakespeare, grounding her argument on the assumption that the editor is concerned with 'Shakespeare's words' and 'the sense . . . Shakespeare intended', insists on the necessity of knowledge of Shakespeare's idiom and

[58] See below, pp. 48–9.

[59] 'Novels and those "necessary evils": annotating the Brontës', *Essays in Criticism*, 32 (1982), 321–37 (p. 323). Martin Battestin is one of a number of practising annotating editors who have offered formulations to a broadly similar effect: see 'A rationale of literary annotation: the example of Fielding's novels', in *Literary and Historical Editing*, ed. George L. Vogt and John Bush Jones (Lawrence, Kansas: University of Kansas Libraries, 1981), pp. 57–79 (pp. 60, 76).

the language of his time, and finds that, for modern editors, the *Oxford English Dictionary* makes available the linguistic knowledge which was lost and which we need.[60] Speaking more generally, in a brilliantly suggestive essay which has everything to do with the theoretical issues involved in explicatory commentary, George Steiner writes of interpretation as a process that begins with 'looking up', and argues that, for the majority of problems posed by historically distanced texts, there is no necessary theoretical bar to understanding: 'conceivably, the distance between a culture and certain texts can grow so drastic that *everything has to be looked up* . . . In practice this may make the given text inaccessible; it slips over the horizon of pragmatic perception . . . But the point *is* pragmatic, not ideal or theoretical. Granted time and explicative means, even *everything* can be looked up.'[61] Allowing that, as most practising literary annotators would accept, such 'contingent' difficulties (as Steiner calls them) are for the most part, for most texts, recoverable, there nonetheless remain questions of relevance and annotator's function. A first criterion of relevance for the information adduced in commentary, essential to any claim it may make to interpretative validity, is the precision of its relation to the text. As E. D. Hirsch argues, the interpreter is concerned not with the author's general milieu, but with specific meanings actualized from the milieu.[62] Evidence supplied in a commentary is of greater evidential value as it is closer in time and currency to the author, and of greatest evidential value when it relates most exactly to the author's specific meaning and intention.[63] A second criterion of relevance in annotation is the judgment of what information the audience for an edited literary text requires. Like modern editors, scholarly editors in the eighteenth century attempted, by the recovery of knowledge necessary to understanding, to make the writings of authors from a past and distant culture available to contemporary readers, many of whom were likely to find Shakespeare in particular considerably more alien, linguistically and culturally, than they thought Homer or Virgil. Such judgments, then as now, depend on the editor's understanding of the culture of his audience, as well as assessments of historical difference between the text's historical moment and the present

[60] 'Principles of annotation', pp. 96–8. Not all modern editors would share Walker's view that the *Oxford English Dictionary* is so lexicographically complete as to obviate the need for resort to parallels.

[61] 'On difficulty', in his *On Difficulty and Other Essays* (Oxford: Oxford University Press, 1980), pp. 18–47 (p. 27). I have addressed this issue, with some illustrations from my editorial annotations in the Oxford University Press edition of Christopher Smart, in 'Editing poetry: theory and practice', in *Talking about Text*, ed. Malcolm Coulthard (Birmingham: English Language Research, 1986), pp. 75–87.

[62] *Validity in Interpretation*, p. 87.

[63] See Battestin's expansion of Arthur Friedman's axioms, 'Rationale of literary annotation', pp. 71–4.

time.[64] They may well involve, in the eighteenth century as now, aspects of the aesthetic as well as the interpretative, of significance as well as of meaning.

There has been much anxiety in recent years amongst professional annotators lest they become vulnerable to the charge of attempting coercive and aggressive control of the meanings of the text. Martin Battestin has insisted that, though the annotator is 'responsible for supplying essential information', he 'should strive to avoid imposing on the reader his own interpretation of a passage. His aim is to make the act of criticism possible, not to perform it.' Nonetheless, however, and regrettably, 'by making available the elements out of which the reader may construct his own interpretation of the text, the editor to some extent will unavoidably control his reader's understanding of the text . . . the editor cannot help governing, to some degree, the reader's response to the text'.[65] In one of the most important methodological and theoretical discussions in recent years, the Introduction to the *Notes* of the Florida edition of *Tristram Shandy*, Melvyn New has also addressed this anxiety, urging that editors must resist the temptation to incorporate a text 'into their own coherent (self-satisfying) systems of order and belief', and insisting that 'a strong measure of self-awareness and a consistent concern with the problem can allow the editor to untangle at least some of the linkages and to establish patterns of annotative commentary that work to keep elucidation and interpretation apart'.[66] Commentary sets out to provide information that makes possible the reader's act of interpretation. The commentator must not give, *ex cathedra*, an overall, closing, reading of the work, nor attempt to persuade the reader to accept definitive interpretations of particular passages.

New's distinction between 'elucidation' and 'interpretation' describes a practice which New himself has used in his Florida *Notes* to *Tristram Shandy*, and which most modern scholarly annotating editors would recognize and aim to follow. I would wish to insist, however, that the choice of what information is necessary to 'elucidate' the text is itself an interpretative judgment. Knowledge of allusion, reference, context, are conditions that make understanding possible. An interpretation is made (at the least, begun) at the moment the editor judges that one piece of information, one allusion or reference, is more relevant than another. To offer information

[64] This issue is cogently discussed in Ian Small, 'Annotating "hard" nineteenth-century novels', *Essays in Criticism*, 36 (1986), 281–93.

[65] Battestin, 'Rationale of literary annotation', pp. 69–70.

[66] 'Introduction', in Laurence Sterne, *Tristram Shandy*, volume III: *The Notes*, ed. Melvyn New, with Richard A. Davies and W. G. Day (Gainesville: University Presses of Florida, 1984), pp. 1–31 (p. 5). Compare New's '"At the backside of the door of purgatory": a note on annotating *Tristram Shandy*', in *Laurence Sterne*, ed. Valerie Grosvenor Myer (London: Vision and Totowa, N.J.: Barnes and Noble, 1984), pp. 15–23 (p. 21).

as interpretatively relevant is to interpret. 'Interpretation' however seems now a word to be avoided in modern editorial discussion (as we have seen, it is regularly, and symptomatically, replaced by the word 'criticism'). The fear of imposing interpretation upon the reader is expressed by Martin Battestin in figures – 'controlling', 'governing' – that remind us of the tendentious rhetoric of Ralph Hanna ('the aggressive act of controlling audience consumption of the text'), or of Jonathan Lamb, who finds that an 'unhappy' result of the labours of the Florida editors has been 'to re-position Sterne in a grid of borrowings, quotations and allusions that considerably restricts the freedom to read beyond the annotated pale'.[67] It would be naïve to imagine of course that such editions as the Florida *Sterne*, or the Oxford *Shakespeare*, are not in their different ways part of an institutional economy, and carry a certain perceived authority which is partly institutionally derived. It is also however naïve to imagine that students and scholars and teachers are helpless innocents who, if an editor interprets, are bound to believe.[68] 'Interpretations' in editions, as anywhere else, are not papal edicts, but hypotheses, which may be deemed to be valid or not on rational and evidential grounds; eighteenth-century editors of secular literary texts, as well as Anglican commentators on Holy Scripture, had a sense of this distinction, and frequently articulated it.[69] The personal interests, beliefs, and competencies of the individual editor inescapably, as both New and Battestin rightly insist, play a part in the process of editorial annotation, but it does not therefore follow that, because perfect objectivity and final knowledge are not available, all knowledge is merely personal, or, to put it another way, that no distinction can be made between the interpretative methods of a Richard Bentley and an Edward Capell. To make this further concession would be simply to beg once more the question, so often begged in this debate: can interpretation not be a rational and knowledge-based activity?

Of course, editing has a political and a cultural history. English eighteenth-century editions of Shakespeare and Milton are products of their time and place, and reflect the understandings, attitudes, and purposes of the scholars who produced them, as well as of the readers for whom they were intended. Like any edition produced at any time they involve processes of accommodation and appropriation, not merely innocent transmission and neutral elucidation. Like any edition, in fact, they are at some level irreducibly 'aesthetic'. Much recent discussion has concentrated on the 'ongoing process of literary and cultural appropriation in which

[67] *Sterne's Fiction and the Double Principle* (Cambridge: Cambridge University Press, 1989), p. 2.

[68] As Battestin himself acknowledges ('Rationale of literary annotation', p. 70).

[69] On the distinction as it operated amongst, and was expressed by, Anglican biblical exegetes, see my 'Profession and authority: the interpretation of the Bible in the seventeenth and eighteenth centuries', *Literature and Theology*, 9 (1995), 383–97.

each new generation attempts to redefine Shakespeare's genius in contemporary terms', and some important recent studies have entirely convincingly demonstrated how far editorial scholarship in the eighteenth century, far from being (as scholarship never entirely can be) an essentially autonomous activity, must be seen in the light of contested practices, constructions, and representations of learning, scholarship, and reading in the period.[70] But that does not tell the whole story. Editing, particularly within a humanist tradition, has been able to claim also a function of interpretation, and it has been possible to describe and value it in those terms. Eighteenth-century scholarly editors, late humanists in many of their attitudes though working on secular rather than classical or sacred letters, continued to think this project of understanding and explanation natural, central, and possible, and it may not be appropriate to read back into their work modern scepticisms and anxieties about the functions of textual editing and commentary. This book sets out to demonstrate the extent to which the eighteenth-century scholarly editors of English literary texts were and thought of themselves as interpreters, who set out to construe and communicate their author's sense, and who developed, often consciously, a theory and a practice of interpretation, coherent in its own terms, and rooted in earlier interpretative theories and practices.

[70] Jean I. Marsden, ed., *The Appropriation of Shakespeare* (London: Harvester Wheatsheaf, 1991), p. 1. I refer particularly to Gary Taylor, *Re-inventing Shakespeare* (New York: Vintage, 1991); Joseph M. Levine, *The Battle of the Books* (Ithaca and London: Cornell University Press, 1991); Margreta de Grazia, *Shakespeare Verbatim* (Oxford: Oxford University Press, 1991); Simon Jarvis, *Scholars and Gentlemen* (Oxford: Oxford University Press, 1995).

2

Making sense of Scripture: biblical hermeneutics in seventeenth- and eighteenth-century England

The first editors and commentators of Shakespeare and Milton in the eighteenth century were pioneers, working in a virtually new field of understanding and enquiry. Those who involved themselves in the task of editing national secular scriptures had to adopt methods and approaches from established areas of scholarship and critical discourse, or develop their own. I have already argued that the editing of literary texts is inevitably a process in which concern with the text is inextricably bound up with questions of interpretation. Where might such innovators as Lewis Theobald, Zachary Pearce, or Edward Capell have found models for their textual and interpretative theories and practices?

One important source was the long-established study and editing of classical literary texts. At the beginning of the eighteenth century English letters could boast arguably the most famous and accomplished classical scholar of his time, Richard Bentley. Bentley, who had first established his reputation in this field with his *Epistula ad Millium* (1691), published editions of Horace (1711), Terence (1726), and Manilius (1739). Late in his life he turned his attention to a modern native literary classic, publishing his edition of *Paradise Lost* in 1732. In his edition of Milton's great poem Bentley employed some of the methods of his classical editing, notably in identifying presumed errors in surviving textual witnesses, and proposing and supporting conjectural emendations. The methods of classical editing, more especially Bentley's own distinctive methods, had a significant effect on the early editors of Milton and Shakespeare. Lewis Theobald's *Shakespeare Restored* (1726), and his edition of Shakespeare's plays, are heavily influenced in their critical procedure by Bentley's classical scholarship, as Theobald, happy to endow his own work with some of the prestige of the greatest practitioner of an established learning, acknowledged. After Theobald, Bentley and classical scholarship remained, for many of the eighteenth-century scholars and editors of English literature, a significant shaping force.

The connections of this tradition with the beginnings of the editing of modern English secular texts are well known, and I shall return to them particularly in discussing Bentley's *Paradise Lost* and Theobald's Shakespearean scholarship. In the present chapter, however, I wish to suggest that some of the methods and assumptions which dominated most editorial work in the eighteenth century, and indeed have operated powerfully since, may well have derived from Protestant biblical hermeneutics, and more especially from the biblical hermeneutics of the English Church.[1] This of course need be no surprise: the extensive and various literature of biblical scholarship and criticism remained the main forum for statement and discussion of issues of interpretative theory in the seventeenth century, and for much of the eighteenth. It might very well be argued that a credible history of literary criticism, interpretation, and scholarship, at least to the eighteenth century, and arguably later, must be predominantly a history of the reading and interpretation of the Bible.

I shall offer here, not a detailed account of Anglican hermeneutics in the seventeenth and eighteenth centuries, but an attempt to illustrate some of its essential themes. It is clear that amongst the many writers who dealt with issues of biblical exegesis there were a variety of views on, for example, the proper status and spheres of reason, faith, and authority. Nonetheless, in matters pertaining to scriptural interpretation, it is possible to identify some broad agreements regarding both principle and method.

The reformed Church was of necessity founded on the Scriptures: 'The Bible onlie is the Religion of Protestants', as Chillingworth famously put it.[2] In order to defend the Scripture as the Rule of Faith, writers of the English Church had to argue that it was capable of interpretation, and that a method and standard of interpretation could be formulated. They had to find and assert what William Chillingworth called 'a middle way betwixt a *publique externall*, and a *private internall* voyce',[3] between, that is, the Romanist insistence that scriptural interpretation can rest securely only on the authority of the Church of Rome, and the Puritan reference of interpretation to private reason or the individual spirit. These Romanist and Puritan positions might be thought of as varieties of textual scepticism and subjectivism, claiming that the text cannot be reliably interpreted without reference to extrinsic principles of validation. Against these opponents Anglican theorists and controvertists argued that Scripture contained a true sense, interpretable by rational and mostly, though not exclusively, intrinsic criteria. Reason, Chillingworth insists, is 'a Publique and certain

[1] I should note that here and elsewhere I use the word hermeneutics to refer (not to 'modern' or philosophical hermeneutics but) to 'classical' hermeneutics, concerned with the theory and practice of interpretation. 'The term hermeneutics is derived from *hermeneia*, which . . . has long signified . . . the work of the interpreter. As such it is not essentially different from *exegesis*, and the two words may be used as synonyms' (Philip August Boeckh, *Encyclopedia and Methodology of the Philological Sciences*, in *The Hermeneutics Reader*, ed. Kurt Mueller-Vollmer (Oxford: Blackwell, 1986), p. 134).

[2] *The Religion of Protestants* (Oxford, 1638), p. 376.

[3] See *Religion of Protestants*, pp. 94–5.

thing and exposed to all mens tryall and examination'. The Puritan who appeals to the Holy Spirit 'saying, *the Spirit of God tels me that this is the meaning of such a Text*' makes a claim that cannot possibly be validated, 'it being a secret thing'; the Roman argument that 'the sense of Scripture was not that which seem'd to mens reason and understanding to be so, but that which the Church of Rome should declare to be so, seem'd it never so unreasonable and incongruous' is merely furthering the 'ambitious pretence' of Rome to exploit her power over scriptural interpretation. The Anglican interpreter however may credibly account for his procedures by saying, '*these & these Reasons I have to shew, that this or that is the meaning of such a Scripture*'.[4] Later in the seventeenth century John Wilson, in his *The Scriptures Genuine Interpreter Asserted* (1678), a particularly sophisticated example of a significant genre of guides to scriptural interpretation, could similarly insist on 'the true Sense of Scripture', ascertainable by the application of 'objective Evidence', according to a 'Rule of Interpretation'.[5]

In writings of seventeenth-century and early eighteenth-century Anglican scholars and controvertists may be found a hermeneutics which could in principle be applied not only to Scripture but to all kinds of texts. The belief that there is no 'different rule to be follow'd in the Interpretation of *Scripture* from what is common to all other Books' was regularly stated, not only by confessed rationalists such as Spinoza or, as here, John Toland,[6] but, as we shall see, by many Anglican apologists. The formulation of a general hermeneutics is thought of, no doubt not unreasonably, as a development of the last two centuries. Anglican writers, however, in discussing scriptural hermeneutics, frequently addressed, and were aware of addressing, more general questions of textual hermeneutics, and some of their formulations anticipate the hermeneutical canons of, for example, Schleiermacher.[7] The Bible was of course a special book, written by uniquely divine inspiration, and some Anglican apologists specifically stated the need for the assistance of the Spirit in its interpretation. Nonetheless, Anglican hermeneutics were founded on the belief that it is amenable to broadly rational interpretative assumptions and procedures. Hence their rules of interpretation held in principle not only for the understanding of the Bible, but for the understanding of all books.

[4] *Religion of Protestants*, pp. 52, 95.

[5] *The Scriptures Genuine Interpreter Asserted*, p. 6. Compare John Owen, *The Causes, Ways, and Means of Understanding the Mind of God as Revealed in his Word* (1678); William Lowth, *Directions for the Profitable Reading of the Holy Scriptures* (London, 1708). Wilson's book, which received its imprimatur on 9 December 1676, was intended as an answer to L. Meijer's *Philosophia S. Scripturae interpres* and L. Wolzogen's *De Scripturarum interprete*. Wilson was Vicar of Kimpton in Hertfordshire from 1657 to his ejection in 1662.

[6] *Christianity Not Mysterious* (London, 1696), p. 46.

[7] Compare Schleiermacher as extracted by Mueller-Vollmer, *The Hermeneutics Reader*, pp. 73–96, especially pp. 78, 84, 86, 90.

In their controversy with Rome, Anglican writers had to mount a defence of writing and of the printed book. Roman Catholics argued that the meaning of Scripture was inherently equivocal and indeterminate; that interpretation was a fundamentally subjective activity, different for every man according to his preconceptions; and that where Scripture was left to be construed by the individual the sense was inevitably wrested and forced. The great historian of the text of Scripture, the Oratorian Richard Simon, insists that 'the Hebrew Text of the Bible may be interpreted several ways by reason of the Equivocation of the Hebrew words', and John Gother, the most effective Romanist writer in England in the 1680s, points out that no single text in the New Testament has escaped interpretative dispute.[8] Extreme Roman textual sceptics in the mid seventeenth century could argue that any writing consists merely of 'bare and dead words', 'dead Letters' which bear no sense of their own but are 'yet to be senc't', and that only 'Tradition gives us *Christ's Sence*'.[9] Roman Catholic controvertists insisted also on the uncertainties of textual transmission. That the text of Scripture was subject to error and variation was regularly asserted in the seventeenth century, and 'the great alterations which have happened . . . to the Copies of the Bible since the first Originals have been lost', and perhaps especially 'in these latter Ages', is demonstrated in devastating scholarly detail by Richard Simon.[10]

Against the uncertainties of textual meaning, understanding, and transmission, Roman Catholic apologists emphasized what they thought to be the stability and continuity of tradition, primarily though not exclusively oral, as preserved in the Church, and the necessity of tradition to any safe understanding of Holy Scripture. Bossuet, in his *Exposition de la Doctrine de l'Eglise Catholique*, regarded by many as an official account of belief, insists that the Church is founded on an original unwritten word: 'JESUS-CHRIST ayant fondé son Eglise sur la prédication [spoken preaching], la parole non écrite a esté la premiere regle du Christianisme; & lors que les Ecritures du Nouveau Testament y ont esté jointes, cette parole n'a pas perdu pour cela son autorité.'[11] So the oral discourse takes precedence over the written text. The word of truth has been passed down in unbroken series from Christ to his Apostles, and thence through the agency of the Church to the modern believer. The true Bible exists not in the printed book, but in the

[8] Simon, *A Critical History of the Old Testament* (London, 1682), III. 7; Gother, *Reason and Authority* (London, 1687), pp. 35–6.

[9] William Rushworth, *The Dialogues of William Richworth or the Iudgment of Common Sense in the Choise of Religions* (Paris, 1640), pp. 277, 290; John Sergeant, *Sure-Footing in Christianity* (London, 1665), pp. 13, 127, 149, 194. On Rushworth and Sergeant, see Philip Harth, *Contexts of Dryden's Thought* (Chicago: University of Chicago Press, 1968), pp. 248–57.

[10] *Critical History of the Old Testament*, sig. a3^{v}–4^{r}, III. 160.

[11] *Exposition* (Paris, 1671), pp. 158–9. For an English statement of this view, compare John Gother, *The Catholic Representer* (2nd part, London, 1687), p. 45.

institution of the Roman Church. 'The Church . . . alone is possess'd of the Scripture', argues Richard Simon, 'because she possesses the true sence thereof'. Even if 'there were no Copies of the Bible in the World, Religion would be preserv'd, because the Church would always subsist'.[12] By contrast with the institutionalized certainty of the chain of oral tradition, Scripture was characterized by Roman polemicists as inadequate, on its own, as a rule of faith; uncertain in its transmission, dubious in its translation, and dangerously ambiguous in its sense. Without the sure guidance of oral tradition the text itself can never be enough.

Anglican writers resisted the privileging of the spoken word, and defended the determinate meaning, the comprehensibility, and the reliability of transmission of Scripture. Writing is neither an accident nor a substitute, but original, apostolic, fully equal to speech. If speech may be plain and comprehensible, so equally, argues Chillingworth, may writing: 'They that heard our Saviour and the Apostles preach, could they have sufficient assurance, that they understood at any time, what they would have them doe? . . . If they could, why may we not be as well assured, that we understand sufficiently what we conceive plaine in their writings?'[13] John Tillotson thought the Romans like the Pharisees, who 'equalled their own unwritten word and traditions with the Word of God'.[14] In his response to William Rushworth's claim in his *Dialogues* (1640) that only the living presence of a speaking subject can guarantee the accurate transmission of the word of truth, Tillotson questions with a deft irony the foundations of the claims of a primarily oral tradition: 'I hope that Oral and Practical Tradition . . . hath deliver'd down Christ's Doctrine with all the right *Traditionary Accents*, *Nods* and *Gestures*, necessary for the understanding of it; otherwise the omission of these may have so altered the sense of it, that it may be now quite different from what it was at first.'[15] Tillotson insisted that the Scriptures, not the oral tradition preserved in Peter's Church, 'are the means whereby the Christian Doctrine hath been brought down to us'. Like many of his Anglican contemporaries Tillotson understood that the defence of the Scriptures as a rule of faith inevitably depended on a defence of all writing and of all printed text as a determinate and reliable vehicle for the communication of meaning, and the safe conveyance of knowledge through the centuries: 'any kind of Doctrine may be sufficiently conveyed, by Books, to the knowledge of After-ages'. What may be spoken, may be written, and retains its intelligibility in full when written: 'whatever can be spoken in plain and intelligible

[12] *Critical History of the Old Testament*, III. 160.
[13] *Religion of Protestants*, p. 111.
[14] Sermon 30, 'The necessity of the knowledge of the Holy Scriptures', in *The Works of the Most Reverend Dr John Tillotson* (3rd edn, London, 1701), p. 349.
[15] *Rule of Faith* (1666), in *Works*, p. 696.

words, and such as have a certain sense, may be written in the same words ... words are as intelligible when they are written as when they are spoken'.[16] John Wilson offers a particularly resonant endorsement of the principle that there is a determinate sense, inherent in Scripture itself, intended by its original author, stable and unchanging over time. He begins by stating two principles 'which to a sober and considerate reader need no proof':

First, that the Scriptures are not a heap of insignificant Words, or unsens'd Characters, as some late Romanists, who cry up Oral Tradition for the only Rule of Faith ... have ridiculously and profanely affirm'd: but that they have a true Sense *Originally* and *Essentially* in themselves, given them by their Author when they were first indited ... Secondly, That the Sense of Scripture is fixt and immutable, not varying with the times, or altering according to the differing practice of the Church ... the Sense of Scripture is no other than what it always had, and ever will have to the World's end. (*Scriptures Genuine Interpreter*, p. 5)

Wilson's formulation is in many respects close to the arguments of E. D. Hirsch that determinacy is a necessary feature of any sharable meaning, and that verbal meaning is determinate and immutable over time, 'what it is and not something else, and ... always the same'.[17] Implicit in Wilson's formulation too is Hirsch's distinction between determinate meaning, and significance, which may indeed vary with the times or the differing practice of the Church.

Simon's researches into the history of the text of the Scriptures had led to conclusions about their diverse authorship and fractured transmission which no apologist for the English Church was in a position to controvert, and which most, indeed, were in no position to understand.[18] One possible and familiar response was Dryden's: Scripture is 'uncorrupt ... In *all* things which our needful *Faith* require'.[19] An argument of more general import, though not necessarily a less problematic one, is that in its textual variations the Bible resembles other books, and is like other books none-theless capable of communicating meaning. 'The Books of Scripture are conveyed down to us', insists Tillotson in his *Rule of Faith*, 'without any material corruption or alteration'. To deny this would be to adopt an absolute scepticism, forcing us to 'reject the authority of all Books, because we cannot be certain whether they be the same now as they were at first'.[20] Perhaps the best-known Anglican affirmation of the textual adequacy of

16 *Rule of Faith*, in *Works*, pp. 658, 659, 674.

17 *Validity in Interpretation* (New Haven: Yale University Press, 1967), pp. 1–23, 9, 46.

18 For a persuasive account of Simon and his reception by English thinkers, see Gerard Reedy, *The Bible and Reason* (Philadelphia: University of Pennsylvania Press, 1985), pp. 104–18.

19 *Religio Laici*, lines 299–300. This was a commonplace: compare, for example, Arthur Bury, *The Naked Gospel* (London, 1690), p. 43.

20 *Works*, pp. 660–1.

Scripture is to be found in Richard Bentley's *Remarks upon a Late Discourse of Free-thinking* (1713), a reply to Anthony Collins's assertion that the existence of some 30,000 textual variants in modern texts of the Greek New Testament showed that 'nothing certain can be expected from Books, where there are various Readings in every Verse'.[21] Bentley is quite untroubled by this revelation: such a degree of textual variation, he acknowledges, 'must necessarily have happened from *the Nature of Things*', and is 'common and in equal proportion in all Classics whatever'. The presence of numerous though mostly minor textual variations in Scripture as in the writings of classical antiquity, however, does not necessarily obscure 'the Writer's Design' or 'darken the whole Context'.[22] Bentley's argument like Tillotson's is ultimately concerned to assert, not only that the text of Scripture as transmitted is 'competently exact', but the very possibility of the communication of knowledge in writing in general. Such a resistance to textual scepticism is fundamental, of course, not only to the Protestant defence of the Scripture, but to the whole enterprise of textual humanism, including the possibility of editing.

Anglican writers agreed in founding their hermeneutics on the understanding that the true meaning of Holy Scripture (as of any other text) was that intended by its author. That Scripture is a special case, written by divine inspiration, posed no serious theoretical problems for them. Scripture's meaning is that of its author, whether that author is God himself, or human penmen more or less consistently guided by him.[23] Most Roman Catholic controvertists shared this position;[24] their difference with Protestants came at a later stage of the hermeneutic process, with the question of how, or rather whether, intention might validly be determined. Amongst Protestant writers the notion that the object of interpretation is the intended meaning of the holy penmen was a given. Spinoza's important chapter, 'Of the interpretation of Scripture', in the *Tractatus Theologico-Politicus*, is clear that it is the business of 'the true method of interpreting Scripture' to infer 'the intention of its authors'.[25] The idea was fundamental for English Protestant writers. Tillotson asserts that the Scriptures

[21] *A Discourse of Free-Thinking* (London, 1713), p. 89. Collins's words paraphrase the 'late Learned *Critique* of Dr WHITBY'.

[22] *Remarks upon a Late Discourse of Free-Thinking* (London, 1713), pp. 64, 76. Bentley realized that, by resort to the oldest existing codices, the number of variations could be reduced from 30,000 to, as he estimated, 200: letter to Archbishop Wake, 15 April 1716, in *The Works of Richard Bentley*, ed. Alexander Dyce (3 vols., London: Macpherson, 1836–8), III. 477; *Proposals for Printing a New Edition of the Greek Testament* (London, 1721), p. [4].

[23] On this theoretical issue, see Hirsch, *Validity in Interpretation*, p. 126n.

[24] See, for example, John Sergeant, *Sure-Footing in Christianity*, p. 26; John Gother, *A Papist Misrepresented and Represented* (London, 1685), p. 28.

[25] *A Theologico-Political Treatise*, trans. R. H. M. Elwes (New York: Dover, 1951), p. 99. Cf. pp. 106, 107, 111.

'sufficiently express the sense and meaning of Christ's Doctrine'.[26] John Wilson insists that the words of Scripture can have no other sense than 'what the Author intends, seeing . . . they are signs or notes of the Conceptions of his Mind'.[27] This idea has a humanist as well as a rationalist history, corresponding for example to Philip Sidney's assertion that 'uttering sweetly and properly the conceits of the mind . . . is the end of speech'.[28] John Locke was to provide just after the turn of the century a similarly decisive and explicit endorsement of the central importance of authorial intention to scriptural interpretation in the 'Essay for the understanding of St Paul's Epistles by consulting St Paul himself', prefixed to his *Paraphrase and Notes on the Epistles of St Paul* (1707). Intention is the ally of interpretative objectivity and good faith, against an irresponsible subjectivism: 'sober inquisitive Readers had a mind to see nothing in St *Paul*'s Epistles but just what he meant; whereas those others of a quicker and gayer sight saw just what they pleased'. The author's intention, 'St Paul's end in Speaking', is assumed as the criterion of valid interpretation. Words and phrases are to be explained 'according to the Apostle's Meaning'.[29] A year later William Lowth, father of that Robert Lowth who was to be the eighteenth century's greatest English hebraic scholar and biblical critic, insists in decisive terms that the Holy Scriptures communicate as effectively as other books an authorially intended meaning: 'The Design of all Writing is to convey our Thoughts intelligibly to others: and it would be a great Reflection upon God's Wisdom, if a Book written by his Direction, and for the Instruction of Mankind, should fall short of that end which Human Composures do generally attain to.'[30] Historically, nothing has been more damaging to the prestige of intentionalist theories of interpretation than the accusation that they concern themselves with the mental state, rather than with the verbal meaning, of the author. Opponents of the use of intention in interpretation have regularly created the straw man of a naïve psychologistic intentionalism, which imagines that the meaning of a text might be interpreted by reference to the general life, or consciousness, or personality, of the artist. W. K. Wimsatt accused intentionalist critics of 'wishing to throb in unison with the mind of the artist'.[31] Such critics, presumably, would wish to know, as Swift's hack in *A Tale of a Tub* argues,

[26] *Rule of Faith*, in *Works*, p. 673. For two of the many similar statements, see Edward Fowler, *The Texts which Papists Cite out of the Bible, for the Proof of their Doctrine, Concerning the Obscurity of the Holy Scriptures, Examined* (London, 1688), pp. 23, 47.

[27] *The Scriptures Genuine Interpreter Asserted*, p. 209.

[28] *An Apology for Poetry*, ed. Geoffrey Shepherd (London: Nelson, 1965), p. 140.

[29] *A Paraphrase and Notes on the Epistles of St Paul* (London, 1707), pp. x, xiii, xvii.

[30] *Directions for the Profitable Reading of the Holy Scriptures*, pp. 29–30.

[31] 'Genesis: a fallacy revisited', in David Newton-de Molina, ed., *On Literary Intention* (Edinburgh: Edinburgh University Press, 1976), p. 117.

all the dreary and irrelevant *impedimenta* of an author's circumstances and state of mind:

Whatever Reader desires to have a thorow Comprehension of an Author's Thoughts, cannot take a better Method, than by putting himself into the Circumstances and Postures of Life, that the Writer was in, upon every important Passage as it flow'd from his Pen; For this will introduce a Parity and strict Correspondence of Idea's between the Reader and the Author. Now, to assist the diligent Reader . . . I have recollected, that the shrewdest Pieces of this Treatise were conceived in Bed, in a Garret: At other times . . . I thought fit to sharpen my Invention with Hunger; and . . . the whole Work was begun, continued, and ended, under a long Course of Physick, and a great want of Money.[32]

Most authors, however, and certainly those of Scripture, are dead, and can provide no answers. Their writings, as an English Romanist apologist wrote in 1640, are 'full of equivocal ambiguitie, their sense and meaning lying in the brest and minde of him who is not to be found, but deceased manie ages agone'.[33] Certainly, throbbing in unison with the sacred penman, or with Swift's hack, is a pointless and hopeless enterprise, which Anglican theorists did not advocate; such a psychologistic intentionalism is for the most part a Romantic, and post-Romantic, idea. A rather more sophisticated intentionalism concerns itself not with the irrelevant, and unknowable, psychological accompaniments of expression, but with *verbal* intention; in Hirsch's words, 'that aspect of a speaker's "intention" which, under linguistic conventions, may be shared by others'.[34] It is quite clear that Anglican writers of this period understood that they were addressing the question of verbal intention. When John Eachard was accused of having had, in his *Grounds and Occasions of the Contempt of the Clergy* (1670), 'a designe to bring the whole Office of Preaching into Contempt', he replied by distinguishing his verbal or active intention – that is, his (knowable) intention to mean, as expressed in the words he used – from any possible programmatic intention – the intention (unknowable in this case) of an author to effect a particular result by a piece of writing:[35] 'Who can tell, Sir, what my design was, but my self, any further than it may be judged by

[32] *A Tale of a Tub*, ed. A. C. Guthkelch and D. Nichol Smith (2nd edn corrected, Oxford: Oxford University Press, 1973), p. 44. Swift's satiric parody of a crude psychologizing intentionalism is quite mistakenly compared by Thomas Docherty with E. D. Hirsch's argument that valid interpretation must be founded on the author's verbal intention (Thomas Docherty, *On Modern Authority* (Brighton: Harvester, 1987), p. 247).

[33] Rushworth, *Dialogues*, p. 321. Cf. Joseph Johnston, *A Reply to the Defence of the Exposition of the Doctrin of the Church of England* (London, 1687), p. 133.

[34] *Validity in Interpretation*, p. 218.

[35] I borrow the terms 'active intention' and 'programmatic intention' from Michael Hancher's cogent modern re-statement of this rather older distinction, in his 'Three kinds of intention', *Modern Language Notes*, 87 (1972), 827–51.

my words?'[36] There is a similar insistence on the specifically verbal aspect of intention in Wilson's *dictum* that 'Real interpretation' is concerned with 'the Exposition of the Author's Mind *Signified by those Words as they are so and so placed*'.[37] Locke is equally explicit: 'till we from [St Paul's] Words paint his very Ideas and Thought in our Minds we do not understand him'.[38]

In post-structuralist theory the author's intending, independent voice is an illusion; rather, authors are spoken by a discourse from which they can never escape. Their writing is enmeshed in a system of intertextuality, conditioned by a complex of cultural and linguistic circumstance they cannot transcend. Under such views, cultural or linguistic factors on the one hand, and authorial intention on the other, are to a greater or lesser extent mutually exclusive hermeneutic criteria. Objectivist hermeneutics have, by contrast, assumed or defended the author's freedom to mean, and have typically seen context and intention as necessarily interdependent criteria. In the theory of E. D. Hirsch, meaning is not *determined* by the larger cultural or linguistic context. Rather it is willed by the author. The context however suggests 'a probable type of meaning', provides limits for the possible implications of the word sequence produced by the author.[39] Wendell Harris insists that 'an author's intended meaning *can* be understood with reasonable probability and accuracy, but only through knowledge of as much of the context assumed by the author as possible'.[40]

The argument that knowledge of cultural and linguistic context is a necessary factor in the valid construction of an author's willed meaning is a common and fundamental assumption of seventeenth-century Protestant hermeneutics. Spinoza, for example, writes, in the *Tractatus Theologico-Politicus* (1670): 'If we read a book . . . written in a very obscure style, and if we know nothing of its author, nor of the time or occasion of its being written, we shall vainly endeavour to gain any certain knowledge of its true meaning. For being in ignorance on these points we cannot possibly know the aim or intended aim of the author'.[41] English writers regularly argued that the intention of the scriptural authors is to be understood in terms of the specific meaning intentions available to them in their own historical time and place. Locke begins his *Reasonableness of Christianity* (1695) by insisting that the Bible is 'in general and necessary points to be understood in the plain direct meaning of the words and phrases such as they may be supposed to have had in the mouths of speakers, who used them according

36 [Eachard] *Some Observations upon the Answer to an Enquiry into the Grounds and Occasions of the Contempt of the Clergy* (1671), p. 54.
37 *The Scriptures Genuine Interpreter Asserted*, p. 159; my italics.
38 *A Paraphrase and Notes on the Epistles of St Paul*, p. xxiii.
39 See *Validity in Interpretation*, pp. 47–8, 66, 86–7, 219–22.
40 Wendell V. Harris, *Interpretive Acts* (Oxford: Oxford University Press, 1988), p. 168.
41 *Theologico-Political Treatise*, trans. R. H. M. Elwes, p. 111.

to the language of that time and country wherin they lived'. The cultural and historical knowledges requisite to valid interpretation include, according to John Wilson, 'some insight into the Peculiar Laws, Customs and Proverbial Speeches of those times and places that the Scripture relates to', as well as knowledge of 'the known Customs of the Gentiles, as in their Divinations, Idolatrous Worships, Publick Games' (*Scriptures Genuine Interpreter*, p. 10). William Lowth, arguing for the necessity of appropriate knowledge in the interpretation of Scripture, again makes the point that, in this respect as in others, the hermeneutics appropriate to Scripture are appropriate to all texts: 'no book can be so plain, but that 'tis requisite for the perfect understanding of it, that Men should be acquainted with the Idioms and Proprieties of the Original Language, and the Customs and Notions which were generally receiv'd at the time when it was writ . . . This is a Difficulty common to Scripture, with all other Books of Antiquity.'[42] English biblical commentators of the seventeenth century lacked no doubt the archaeological and anthropological sophistication achieved by the German *höhere kritik* a century later, but Henry Hammond was one of the many who were conscious that 'the change and diversity of customes in divers countries is very ordinary', and aware, too, that this has consequences for the implications of scriptural meanings and scriptural metaphors: so in his *Paraphrase and Annotations upon All the Books of the New Testament* (1653) he explains Christ's account of the good shepherd, whose sheep know his voice and follow him (John 10:3–5), by referring to the pastoral customs of the Hebrews. For Anglican writers the interpretative authority of the Church Fathers is seen as not simply prescriptive, but founded on their privileged knowledge of the original context. William Sherlock argues that the chief cause of possible ambiguity in the Epistles is that, written as they were to those who knew the 'daily practice', the 'Rules of Order and Discipline' of the early Church, they naturally did not include a 'punctual, and particular . . . account of these matters'. Hence the best possible guide towards determinate meaning in such texts is 'to know what the practice of the Apostles was in these Cases', and this may most readily be learnt from those who were closest in place and time to the original writers: 'the best way to understand the practice of the Apostles, is from the Practice of the Catholick Church in succeeding Ages, especially when the memory of the Apostles was fresh'.[43] By the same principle William Lowth suggests interpretation should refer to 'such Ancient Authors as were most likely to be acquainted with the Notions which were then generally received'.[44]

[42] William Lowth, *Directions for the Profitable Reading of the Holy Scriptures*, p. 35.

[43] [William Sherlock] *The Protestant Resolution of Faith* (London, 1683), pp. 15–16.

[44] *A Vindication of the Divine Authority and Inspiration of the Writings of the Old and New Testament* (Oxford, 1692), p. 36. Cf. William Wake, *A Defence of the Exposition of the Doctrine of the Church of England, against the Exceptions of Monsieur de Meaux, late Bishop of Condom* (London, 1686), p. 76.

In appealing to contextual warrants of meaning, the Anglican writers were not working with a generalized sense of background, but with an acute apprehension of the necessity of reference to the particular proprieties, cultural and linguistic, of Scripture writing. John Wilson insists that the linguistic context within which we interpret Scripture must not be a generalized, or modern, *usus loquendi*, the 'common use of Speech', but the special historical *usus loquendi scripturarius*, 'the *Scripture use* of Speaking' (*Scriptures Genuine Interpreter*, pp. 160, 163). (This looks like an argument for the uniqueness of Scripture; in logic it implies no more than that any text, of which Holy Scripture is one, belongs to its own class.) John Locke similarly argues, in the prefatory essay to his *Paraphrase and Notes on the Epistles of St Paul*, that, as Paul's subject was 'wholly new', so 'most of the important Terms in it have quite another Signification from what they have in other Discourses' (p. v). The idiom of the Bible is specific: the New Testament is written in a Greek which 'has a Peculiarity in it, that . . . obscures and perplexes the Meaning' (p. iv). The special status and extraordinary currency of the Bible creates an interpretative problem: readers commonly accommodate the meaning of the biblical text to their own linguistic understanding, as well as to their particular prejudices or belief. Paul's Epistles are 'now by long and constant Use become a part of the English language . . . This everyone uses familiarly, and thinks he understands, but . . . always according to the Sense of his own System, and the Articles or Interpretations of the Society he is engaged in.' This however cannot be true interpretation. The Apostle 'writ not by that Man's System, and so his Meaning cannot be known by it' (p. xi). Scripture has to be saved from unguarded accommodation to inappropriate, and subjectively selected, frameworks. Just as Spinoza had argued against 'explaining the words of Scripture according to our preconceived opinions' (p. 117), so Locke insists that 'he that would understand St *Paul* aright, must understand his Terms in the Sense he uses them, and not as they are appropriated by each Man's particular Philosophy, to Conceptions that never entered the Mind of the Apostle' (pp. xxii–xxiii). What entered the mind of the Apostle can only come from the horizon of his historical place and moment. It is therefore folly to interpret Scripture according to the lights of a system not available to its author. Samuel Clarke similarly argues, in his *Scripture-Doctrine of the Trinity* (1712), against taking 'Humane and perhaps Modern Forms of speaking' as 'the Rule of . . . Faith', or interpreting the ideas of Scripture 'according to the Notions which may happen at any particular Time to prevail', and insists on understanding any Scripture word 'as it really signifies in the original Texts of Scripture'.[45]

[45] *The Scripture-Doctrine of the Trinity* (London, 1712), pp. xix, xxiii. Compare William Lowth's argument that true interpretation of the Scriptures depends upon 'respect to the Sentiments and Exigencies of the Age wherein they were written', the 'Genius of the Language which the

The theoretical argument for the interpretative value of knowledge of the cultural and linguistic context of Scripture was underwritten by some substantial achievements in biblical scholarship. Brian Walton's *Biblia Sacra Polyglotta*, published in six volumes from 1655 to 1657, looks back to the concern of the Renaissance humanists with the original languages of Holy Writ, and to the great Continental polyglots, and offered the reader in its prefatory treatises a *chronologia sacra*, treatises on weights, coins, and measures, a wonderfully illustrated account of the temples of Jerusalem, and Prolegomena on the language, letters, editions, and versions of the Bible. Edward Leigh's *Critica Sacra*, in its enlarged third edition (1650), is a Hebrew dictionary of the Old Testament and Greek dictionary of the New Testament. John Pearson's *Critici Sacri: sive Doctissimorum Virorum in SS. Biblia Annotationes, & Tractus* (9 vols., 1660), later revised by Matthew Poole, collected the Latin learned scholarship of the Reformation and later, including writing by Erasmus, Valla, Scaliger, Casaubon, and Grotius. Matthew Poole's *Annotations upon the Holy Bible* (2 vols., 1683, 1685) was the most significant of the many late seventeenth-century commentaries, and would be succeeded by Matthew Henry's *Exposition of All the Books of the Old and New Testaments* (1708–14), and the *Critical Commentary and Paraphrase of the Old and New Testaments* (1727–60) put together from the work of Simon Patrick, William Lowth, Daniel Whitby, and other divines.[46] Irène Simon has remarked upon the Church of England's 'resistance to historical and philological scholarship' in the post-Restoration period.[47] Certainly English scholars were unable to engage with the historico-textual work of Richard Simon on his own terms, and certainly the achievements of the German higher criticism, or of such later eighteenth-century British scholars as Robert Lowth, Benjamin Kennicott, and Alexander Geddes, lay in the future. The English reader of the Bible in this period, nonetheless, was provided with materials which allowed at least the beginnings of contextualization.

Some of the most powerful and prevalent principles of Anglican biblical interpretation derive from a Protestant understanding and application of the Analogy of Faith, a doctrinal idea which goes back to Augustine. Scripture is at some points, to use a phrase of St Peter's that reverberates through late seventeenth-century controversies, 'hard to be understood' (2 Peter 3:16).[48] Nonetheless, argued Augustine, what is unclear in any given

Holy Writers used', and 'the State of the Church in their Time' (*A Vindication of the Divine Authority*, p. 36).

46 For a convenient account, see Thomas R. Preston, 'Biblical criticism, literature, and the eighteenth-century reader', in *Books and their Readers in Eighteenth-Century England*, ed. Isabel Rivers (Leicester: Leicester University Press, 1982), pp. 97–126.

47 *Three Restoration Divines: Barrow, South, and Tillotson* (2 vols. in 3, Paris: Société d'Edition 'Les Belles Lettres', 1967), I. 100.

48 This and all my biblical quotations are from the Authorized Version.

place may be explained by reference to the essential tenets of Christian belief. For Protestant exegetes, who believed that those tenets are to be found in Scripture, this meant that obscurities could be clarified by invoking 'the constant and perpetual Sentence of Scripture in those places that are undoubtedly plain and obvious to our understandings'.[49] That 'there is nothing spoken under dark Mysteries in one place [in Scripture], but the self same thing in other places is spoken more familiarly and plainly' was made explicit for example in the Homily 'Exhortation to the reading and knowledge of the Holy Scripture', and was a commonplace in the writings of Anglican apologists.[50]

Of the many interpretative consequences of this principle, two are especially significant. Firstly, the comparison of parallel places in the interpretation of difficult passages acquired and maintained a key role in the armoury of most Protestant, and virtually all Anglican, biblical scholars and exegetes. The essential form of annotation of the Authorized Version of 1611, which survives into modern editions, was prescribed in the seventh of the Rules for the translators: 'such Quotations of Places to be marginally set down, as shall serve for the fit reference of one Scripture to another'.[51] This principle of the conference of places is asserted time after time in the work of Anglican theorists of interpretation, most carefully perhaps in Locke who, after warning against unsystematically heaping together 'a Multitude of Texts', concludes that, if genuinely analogous places are compared, 'one part of the Sacred Text could not fail to give light unto another'.[52] The resort to parallel places was pervasive and fundamental in English biblical commentary.

Secondly, the way in which many Anglican theorists understood and applied the principle of the Analogy of Faith amounted to a rather well-articulated coherence theory of interpretation. In the formulation provided by E. D. Hirsch in his early essay, 'Objectivity in interpretation', coherence is an over-riding criterion by which the sense of a particular passage may be tested against the norms of meaning established by its context: 'one meaning coheres with another because it is typical or probable with reference to the whole'. The 'whole' which Hirsch here stipulates is not only the text within which the crux is situated, but, more broadly, 'the author's horizon, his disposition toward a particular type of meaning'.[53]

49 Whitaker, quoted by John Wilson, *The Scriptures Genuine Interpreter Asserted*, p. 169.

50 In late seventeenth-century writings on the topic, compare, for example, Simon Patrick, *Search the Scriptures* (1685), pp. 111–15; Edward Fowler, *The Texts which Papists Cite*, p. 21.

51 See Gilbert Burnet, *The History of the Reformation of the Church of England* (3 parts, 1679, 1681, 1715), II. 368.

52 *A Paraphrase and Notes on the Epistles of St Paul*, pp. xx–xxi. Compare, for example, John Wilson, *The Scriptures Genuine Interpreter Asserted*, pp. 12, 165.

53 Hirsch, *Validity in Interpretation*, p. 237. This is an appeal, of course, to the verbal meaning intentions of the author, not to the author as a particular historical subject: see *Validity in*

Similar appeals from particular passages to the text as a whole and the 'scope' or meaning of its author formed a frequent part of Anglican defences of the possibility of interpretation of the Bible. John Wilson offers one of the clearest and most theoretically self-conscious statements. One of the 'immediate Means' of interpretation of scriptural passages is 'the consideration of the coherents with antecedents and consequences, together with the scope and design of the Speaker'. The sense intended by God is determinable from both the local and the larger textual context: 'the Words and Sentences of Scripture taken in such a coherence among themselves, and connexion with the whole, . . . do exhibit to the Reader no other Sense than what is indeed the Authors Meaning'.[54] John Locke, concentrating in his *Paraphrase and Notes on the Epistles of St Paul* on particular books which he understood to have been written by the same author, could found his interpretative procedure on a sense of the textual whole, and on an assumption that the object of interpretation was the author's coherent 'System' (p. xxi). The interpretation of particular passages is quite explicitly validated by reference to the intention of the whole. Generally, and distinctively, the stress in Protestant applications of the principle is on the Scriptures themselves, on Scripture as 'its own interpreter'. Individual texts, Samuel Clarke insists, must be accommodated to the 'whole Scope and general Tenour of Scripture'.[55] By contrast, Roman Catholic apologists were more likely to base their application of the Analogy of Faith on grounds at least partly outside the text, and foreign to the intending author, in the opinion of the Fathers, and the Tradition of the Church.

The principle of coherence, and the practice of interpreting scriptural statements by reference to their immediate and broader textual contexts, was for many English writers in this period a fundamental element in the defence of the possibility of 'true' interpretation against the subjectivisms and scepticisms of a number of their opponents. One of the characteristics of Jack, the Calvinist brother in Swift's *Tale of a Tub*, is that, by a decontextualized and subjective reading of individual scriptural verses, he is able to turn Holy Writ to all the purposes and occasions of his own life. Against such methods Thomas Hobbes had grounded his argument, in chapter 43 of the *Leviathan*, on scriptural texts which are 'agreeable to the harmony and scope of the whole Bible', for:

> it is not the bare Words, but the Scope of the writer that giveth the true light, by which any writing is to bee interpreted; and they that insist upon single Texts, without considering the main Designe, can derive no thing from them cleerly; but rather by casting atomes of Scripture, as dust before mens eyes, make every thing

Interpretation, pp. 242–3.

[54] *The Scriptures Genuine Interpreter Asserted*, pp. 11, 207.

[55] *Scripture-Doctrine of the Trinity*, pp. xix–xx. Compare Simon Patrick, *Search the Scriptures*, pp. 118–19.

more obscure than it is; an ordinary artifice of those that seek not the truth, but their own advantage.[56]

John Locke, in the prefatory essay to his paraphrase of the Pauline Epistles, insisted that to cite isolated verses of Scripture, instead of understanding them as part of 'a continued coherent Discourse', is to deprive them of the 'Tenour of the Context' which limits and defines the sense. Since the factitious division of the Epistles into chapters and verses, we have become 'accustom'd to hear them quoted as distinct Sentences, without any limitation or explication of their precise Meaning from the Place they stand in, and the Relation to what goes before, or Follows'. This breakdown of discursive coherence makes valid interpretation impossible, and, worse, allows the subjective 'wresting' of the meaning as odd words are snatched out 'to serve a Purpose'. To interpret fragments out of context would 'disturb the Sense, and hinder the Understanding of any Book whatsoever'. To set any verse in its verbal context, however, provides a narrowing of the possible sense and makes reliable and unprejudiced interpretation possible. Words, whether in St Paul's Epistles or in any other text, receive 'a determin'd Sense from their Companions and Adjacents'.[57] For most eighteenth-century writers the notion remained a truism. Ephraim Chambers, in the *Cyclopaedia* which is perhaps as reliable a guide as any to received knowledge in the period, could state quite unproblematically that 'to take the full sense of the text, the *context* should be regarded'.[58]

A cornerstone of theories of determinate meaning and valid interpretation is that a meaning is not confined to a unique form of words, but may be reproduced in other words. 'Synonymity', argues Hirsch, 'is in fact possible, and . . . on this possibility depends the determinacy of meaning, the emancipation of thought from the prison house of a particular linguistic form, and the possibility of knowledge generally.' This has two important consequences for the debate between Anglicans and Romans: first, if we deny that 'a difference in linguistic form compels a difference in meaning', it becomes possible to believe that a translation may adequately reproduce the meaning of an original text.[59] Secondly it becomes possible, as Hirsch explains, to think of commentary on a text not as inevitably foreign and parasitic, but as genuinely explicatory:

> if we isolate . . . the interpretive function of commentaries . . . from their critical function, we will observe that the art of explaining nearly always involves the task of discussing meaning in terms that are not native to the original text . . . A translation or paraphrase tries to render the meaning in new terms; an explanation tries to point to the meaning in new terms. (*Validity in Interpretation*, p. 136)

56 *Leviathan*, ed. Richard Tuck (revised edn, Cambridge: Cambridge University Press, 1996), p. 415.

57 *A Paraphrase and Notes on the Epistles of St Paul*, pp. vii–x.

58 *Cyclopaedia* (5th edition, 2 vols., 1741, 1743), under 'context'.

59 E. D. Hirsch, *The Aims of Interpretation* (Chicago: University of Chicago Press, 1976), pp. 10, 50.

This justification of the interpretative validity of translation or paraphrase is of fundamental consequence for the defence of the Scriptures as a Rule of Faith. It is also crucial for the possibility of explication of secular, as well as of sacred, scriptures.

The Reformation project of making the Bible available to the people was founded on the assumption that God's word remained in essentials the same when translated into vernacular languages. This assumption the Roman Church questioned from the beginning. Sarpi reports André de Vega, at the Council of Trent, insisting that it is 'impossible de traduire d'une langue dans une autre sans restraindre ou sans etendre le sens du Texte'.[60] De Vega is speaking of the Vulgate, but his view held for translation in principle. The most powerful late seventeenth-century attack on Protestant assumptions about translation came from Père Richard Simon, who documented in telling detail the faults of all the chief biblical translations in all languages, and flatly concluded 'that it is almost impossible to translate the Holy Scripture'.[61] William Rushworth states two of the key Roman Catholic theoretical objections to both translation and paraphrase. Firstly, it is impossible to translate from one language into another: 'since no two languages jumpe equaly in their expressions, it is impossible that everie word of the one should have a full expression of everie word of the other'. Secondly, any two translations from a given passage of Scripture into the same language will employ different forms of words, and therefore will bear a different meaning, because ''tis impossible to put fully and beyond all quarrel the same sense in divers words'.[62]

Anglicans do not seem to have formulated a clear theoretical response to such charges, partly no doubt because of their concern to refute the contrary Roman argument that oral tradition is effective precisely because it enables the communication of truth to men in a variety of different verbal forms.[63] In practice however paraphrase was a dominant mode of Anglican scriptural hermeneutics, providing the foundation of the great majority of works which set out to explain the text of Scripture. It was the means by which commentators understood themselves to be unfolding the genuine sense of Scripture to their readers.[64] By paraphrase they expanded what was elliptical, drew out the implications of metaphor, explained allusions, and pointed to evident typological elements, often of course with purposes, especially evangelical and moral purposes, of their own, but normally with a careful literalism. In John 10:16 Christ speaks in a parable to the Pharisees: 'And other sheep I have, which are not of this fold: them

[60] *Histoire du Concile de Trente* (2 vols., London, 1736), I. 248; cf. I. 243–4.
[61] *Critical History of the Old Testament*, sig. b1^r. [62] *Dialogues*, pp. 266–7.
[63] See, for example, Tillotson, *Rule of Faith*, in *Works*, pp. 682–3.
[64] For a typically explicit statement of this understanding, see Edward Wells, *An Help for the More Easy and Clear Understanding of the Holy Scriptures* (6 vols., Oxford, 1709–28), I. i.

also I must bring, and they shall hear my voice; and there shall be one fold, and one shepherd'; in Henry Hammond's widely used *Paraphrase and Annotations upon all the Books of the New Testament* (1653) the verse is paraphrased: 'But for you Jewes let me tell you, my flock is not all within this pale of Judaea, I have others that will believe and obey me . . . beside and beyond the Jewish nation, and the care and rule of those I must undertake, . . . and all believers . . . shall unite very sociably together, and become one fold, under me, the one shepheard of them all'.

English biblical commentaries very commonly and characteristically adopted a twofold method of paraphrase and annotation. Hammond's *Paraphrase and Annotations* again provides a representative example. Here each verse of the sacred text is printed with a marginal paraphrase which explicates, and somewhat expands (particularly by the citation of biblical parallels), the sense. Each chapter of Scripture is followed by Annotations, whose business is a more learned analysis of the text, with discussion of the sense of the original Greek, and reference to the Church Fathers and other commentators (including the cabala and Talmud), to classical and natural historians, and to much else. So Matthew 9:23, 'And when Jesus came into the ruler's house, and saw the minstrels and the people making a noise', is paraphrased thus: 'And found them very busily preparing for the interment of the rulers daughter, with Musick and other solemnities for the funerall'; and Hammond's Annotation spends half a page exploring 'this custome of having *musicall instruments* in *funeralls*', with reference to the Mishna, Josephus of Archelaus, Schickard, Apuleius, Aristotle, Lucian, Artemidorus, Homer, Flavius Josephus, and a number of scriptural texts.

Of course the nature of both paraphrase and annotation varied according to the beliefs, purposes, and audience of the commentator. In Richard Baxter's *Paraphrase on the New Testament, with Notes, Doctrinal and Practical* (1685), for example, which was intended for daily use by 'Religious Families' and 'the Younger and Poorer Sort of Scholars and Ministers', the paraphrase is brief and rather literal, and the notes offer doctrinal, moral, or practical applications to the reader. Whatever the differences, however, Baxter is adopting essentially the same structure of commentary as Hammond: a paraphrase giving a more or less straightforward explication of literal meaning, and annotations exploring more freely the contexts and significances of Holy Writ. Variations of this format were and remained normal in the genre of English biblical commentary.[65]

[65] A representative sample might include, beside Hammond, Baxter, and Locke's *Paraphrase and Notes on the Epistles of St Paul*: [Abraham Woodhead, Obadiah Walker, and Richard Allestree] *A Paraphrase and Annotations upon the Epistles of St Paul* (Oxford, 1675); Daniel Whitby, *A Paraphrase and Commentary on the New Testament* (2 vols., London, 1703); George Stanhope, *A Paraphrase and Comment upon the Epistles and Gospels* (4 vols., London, 1705–8); Edward Wells, *An Help for the More Easy and Clear Understanding of the Holy Scriptures. viz. 1. The Common English Translation render'd more*

Almost all varieties of editing have included some form of commentary or annotation on the text. As I suggested in chapter 1 there has been a tendency, in a number of versions of recent theory, to see every kind of commentary as 'appropriation', a matter of power rather than of explication, a means by which the annotator, and the institutions within which the annotator operates, are legitimated and can exercise control. This political, rather than functional, view may well be persuasive in its own terms, but it gives very little credence to the annotator's usual open or implicit claim of clarifying the sense of a difficult text for the reader. The claim that commentary might and should offer explication of the literal sense, rather than appropriate the text and replace its meaning, goes back to the Reformation and indeed to the late middle ages, to the work notably of Nicholas of Lyra (1270–1349) and of Erasmus.[66] Anglican writers of the seventeenth and eighteenth centuries similarly felt able to differentiate between commentary which they perceived as subjective and usurping, and therefore illegitimate, and commentary which set out to provide objective explication of the true sense. They clearly and repeatedly asserted the primary authority of the text itself, as the 'measure and standard' of the original author's meaning,[67] as against the authority of any commentary that might be written about it. They warned, time and again, of the danger that the meaning of a commentary might supplant the true meaning inherent in the original. Samuel Clarke for instance wrote that 'a Comment may in effect come into the place of the Text . . . till in process of Time, men . . . depart entirely from the Meaning of the Text, and Human Authority swallows up that which is Divine'.[68] And they anathematized in particular what they saw as 'the *wanton Wits* . . . of the Schools',[69] the subjective excesses of scholiastic commentary, aiming to impose on Scripture Rome's preferred meaning. Nonetheless, though commentary may be abused, it has a genuine function. In Samuel Clarke's view it has 'Authority' when, though only when, ''tis evidently agreeable to the Text itself', a statement which implies of course that commentary may be a true exposition of a true meaning. John Wilson distinguishes between

Agreeable to the Original. II. A Paraphrase III. Annotations (6 vols., Oxford, 1709–28); Thomas Pyle, *A Paraphrase with Short and Useful Notes on the Books of the Old Testament* (4 vols., London, 1717–25); James Peirce, *A Paraphrase and Notes on the Epistles to the Colossians, Philippians, and Hebrews* (London, 1727); George Benson, *A Paraphrase and Notes on the Epistles of St Paul* (London, 1734).

[66] For a discussion of the history and the issues, see Jerry H. Bentley, *Humanists and Holy Writ* (Princeton: Princeton University Press, 1983), chapters 1 and 4.

[67] Tillotson, *Rule of Faith*, in *Works*, p. 668. I have discussed this issue more fully in 'Text, "text", and Swift's *Tale of a Tub*', *Modern Language Review*, 85 (1990), 290–303 (see especially p. 296).

[68] Samuel Clarke, *Scripture-Doctrine of the Trinity*, p. xxii. Compare Spinoza's complaint in the *Tractatus Theologico-Politicus* against those who 'hawk about their own commentaries as the word of God' (*Theologico-Political Treatise*, p. 98); Locke, *A Paraphrase and Notes on the Epistles of St Paul*, pp. xi–xiii.

[69] Edward Fowler, *The Texts which Papists Cite*, p. 47.

commentaries which disqualify themselves by making Scripture 'more intricate and perplex'd', and commentaries which fulfil their purpose by clarifying and explaining Scripture.[70] For many Anglican writers it is the function of the cleric to act as a rational explicator and teacher of the true meaning,[71] and this purpose certainly lies behind a great many of the plethora of Anglican commentaries on Scripture.

Historians and critics are nowadays very much aware of the great eighteenth-century literary parodies and re-workings of the pedantic excesses of self-indulgent textual commentary, especially in *A Tale of a Tub*, and in the *Dunciad Variorum* (and all its various progeny). It is also true, and in no way a contradiction, that it was the ordinary eighteenth-century conviction that the primary and proper purpose of commentary was to clarify and explain a text, not to impose the commentator's meaning or to burden it with irrelevance. In his *Cyclopaedia* Ephraim Chambers notes the unfortunate possibilities of the subjective and obfuscatory abuse of commentary, citing St Evremond to the effect that 'commentators commonly spend a great part of their time in finding out beauties the author never dreamt of, and in enriching him with their own thoughts', and the proverbial French notion of the '*glose d'Orleans, plus obscure que la texte*'. Chambers's definitions of the headwords 'annotation', 'commentary, or comment', and 'gloss', however, begin by emphatically asserting that it is their normal function 'to clear up some passage', 'to render . . . more intelligible . . . some ancient, obscure, or difficult author', 'to explain [an author's] sense more fully, and at large'.

In the course of their defence of the Bible as a Rule of Faith, Anglican apologists and scholars adopted and developed a various but broadly unified hermeneutics which was capable of application to secular as well as sacred literature. In many of their arguments they were concerned to offer, and were conscious of offering, a general defence of the coherence, transmissibility, and comprehensibility of written and printed books. Their principles were enormously persuasive, if not prescriptive, during the course of the eighteenth century, and very often operated as unstated, though certainly not untheorized, assumptions in critical and editorial writing of the period. Strikingly explicit evidence of the prevalence of such principles in all kinds of interpretation is to be found in Isaac Watts's *The Improvement of the Mind*, first published in 1741 as a supplement to his *Art of Logick*. This is a textbook, delineating 'a Variety of . . . Rules for the Attainment and Communication of Useful Knowledge, in Religion, in the

[70] *The Scriptures Genuine Interpreter Asserted*, pp. 212–13.

[71] See, for example, William Sherlock, *A Discourse Concerning a Judge of Controversies in Matters of Religion* (London, 1686), p. 47. I have discussed this issue more fully in 'Profession and authority: the interpretation of the Bible in the seventeenth and eighteenth centuries', *Literature and Theology*, 9 (1995), 383–97.

Sciences, and in common Life', designed to be 'useful to Persons in Younger Years', and offering what Watts might reasonably have thought received and uncontroversial guidance.[72] Chapter 8, specifically, sets out to provide its young readers with a set of the basic procedures for 'Enquiring into the Sense and Meaning of any Writer or Speaker, and especially the Sense of the Sacred Writings'. Watts begins with an entirely familiar statement of position. The object of interpretation is the author's intention; written language is capable of ambiguity; it is therefore necessary to follow criteria or methods which will help us to ascertain the author's intended meaning:

It is a great Unhappiness that there is such an Ambiguity in Words and Forms of Speech, that the same Sentence may be drawn into different Significations; whereby it comes to pass, that it is difficult sometimes for the Reader exactly to hit upon the Ideas which the Writer or Speaker had in his Mind. Some of the best *Rules* to direct us herein are such as these. (p. 118)

The rules that Watts goes on to offer cover a good deal of theoretical ground, including the language and general cultural and historical context of the text, the uses of comparison of places, ways of determining intention, and the overriding requirement to read the text not according to our own tastes and opinions, but with respect for the author. It is necessary to be acquainted specifically with 'the . . . *Language* wherein the Author's Mind is exprest' (p. 118), not merely with general or modern senses and constructions: 'Consider the Signification of these Words and Phrases, more especially in the *same Nation*, or near the same *Age* in which that Writer lived, and in what Sense they are used by Authors of the same *Nation, Opinion, Sect, Party*, &c.' (p. 119). The student is advised, in what is in every sense a textbook definition of the principle of conference of places, to clarify the meaning of some obscure place in an author's writing by putting it beside another genuinely analogous passage, comparing 'the Words and Phrases in *one Place of an Author*, with the same or kindred Words and Phrases used in *other Places* of the same Author which are generally called *parallel Places*'; for 'a Writer best interprets himself' (p. 120). Hence it is that concordances are 'of excellent Use for Interpretation'. Interpretation of 'particular Sentences' will be aided by setting them in the light of the author's '*Scope and Design*' (pp. 120–1). A sense of the particular and varying historical contexts of the different penmen is vital to the clarification of their intended meaning: 'In order to interpret Scripture well, there needs a good Acquaintance with the *Jewish* Customs, some Knowledge of the

[72] Title, and Preface, p. xi. For an account of rival interpretative theories in the century from the perspective of a more recent reading theory, see David Bartine, *Early English Reading Theory* (Columbia: University of South Carolina Press, 1989). Bartine gives an account of Watts's position which seems to me to overstate the degree of freedom he allowed 'to the reader as interpreter, even when reading sacred texts': see especially pp. 49–50.

ancient *Roman* and *Greek* Times and Manners, which sometimes strike a strange and surprizing Light upon Passages which were before very obscure' (p. 122). Finally the student is warned against '*warping* the Sense of the Writer to *your own Opinion*'. We must come to the work of any author with 'an honest Design to find out his true Meaning', for it is only passion, prejudice, and prepossession which 'has given such a Variety of Senses both to the sacred Writers and others' (p. 123).

Watts's brief chapter seems to me striking and significant in several ways. It is clearly based on principles of biblical interpretation of late seventeenth- and early eighteenth-century English Protestantism, with particularly marked affinities with Locke's Preface to his *Paraphrase and Notes on the Epistles of St Paul.* Those principles are referred perhaps even more explicitly than in his predecessors to the interpretation of secular as well as of sacred texts. In a chapter whose scope extends to interpretation in general, the Scriptures remain a focus. Even as late as 1741, the methods of scriptural exegesis remain a standard, no doubt the most important standard, for any possible textual hermeneutics.

In the remaining two chapters of this book I shall set out to illustrate how the editing of secular literary texts in the eighteenth century began to be thought a critical, that is an interpretative, procedure, capable of being carried out by rational criteria. Increasingly editors came to think that their object was a determinate meaning intended by the original author. They believed, or at least claimed to believe, that it was both possible and desirable to establish 'what the author wrote', even where they thought the textual tradition radically faulty. A number of editors made a serious attempt to make sense of Shakespeare and of Milton in the light of those authors' own linguistic, cultural, and intellectual contexts, enabled by a growing and more and more particularized knowledge of the language, history, and literature of their times. As the century went on, the explanatory usefulness of commentary was more confidently assumed and exploited. Amongst explanatory techniques, paraphrase, the comparison of parallel places, and reference both to local verbal contexts and to the larger tendencies of meaning within the work were extensively used. Some of this derives, often demonstrably, from Renaissance and post-Renaissance classical editing and scholarship. These methods and principles of the eighteenth-century editors may well be founded at a yet deeper level, however, on the theory and practice of biblical commentary and exegesis, as expressed in the writings of Watts, Locke, and their English predecessors.

In the following chapters I shall try, too, to illustrate the importance, for many of the first editors of an English national scripture, of a tenet which had been basic in the Anglican approach to Scripture, though it is less familiar to us now. At the end of Watts's chapter the student is solemnly enjoined to treat not only the Holy Scriptures but all writings according to the golden rule of Christian charity, and to regard their authors with a respect which amounts to reverence:

LASTLY, remember that you *treat every Author, Writer or Speaker, just as you yourselves would be willing to be treated by others*, who are searching out the Meaning of what you write or speak: And maintain upon your Spirit an awful Sense of the Presence of God who is the Judge of Hearts, and will punish those who by a base and dishonest turn of Mind wilfully pervert the Meaning of the sacred Writers, or even of common Authors. (pp. 123–4)

Such a view of the central status of authorial intention is of course theological. True interpretation is a sacred duty, carried out under God's eye and judgment. To use Roland Barthes's terminology, Watts thinks of such writings as the Bible, or *Hamlet*, or *Paradise Lost*, as Works, not Texts, bearing their author's message, which it is the priest-like duty of the interpreter, or editor, to decipher, though Watts stops well short of a frankly Barthesian apotheosis of secular authors. Eighteenth-century editors could think of the greatest of the national scriptures of the past, the writings of Shakespeare and Milton, as sacred in this way, and similarly worthy of interpretative respect. Not all of the eighteenth-century editors, of course, were consistently theological, or pious, or charitable. It remains nonetheless true that Shakespeare and Milton were edited as authors, whose meanings were to be elicited with the honesty and care which Watts demands of interpreters of the Bible and of all other books; and that the methods and principles of interpretation employed by some of the pioneers of English literary editing derive in significant respects from scholars and thinkers who had been concerned with another kind of scripture.

3

Making sense of Milton: the editing of *Paradise Lost*

Beginning to edit a national scripture

For the eighteenth century no poet seemed closer to the divine than Milton, and no poem seemed closer to the sacred Scripture than *Paradise Lost*. Though some critics had doubts about its verse, its language, its originality, and even its theology, no literary work was in general more admired, more canonical, more scriptural. This had, as we shall see, powerful and immediate effects on how it was edited and interpreted, and, indeed, on how models of editorial interpretation in general were put together and developed in the course of the century.

Within few years of its appearance, and well before the end of Milton's own century, *Paradise Lost* had become established as the great central work of the nascent English literary canon. The poem was reasonably successful on its first publication in 1667: Samuel Johnson remarks that 'the sale of thirteen hundred copies in two years', in view of the small size of the reading public, a new verse form, and the public odium of the poet, 'was an uncommon example of the prevalence of genius'.[1] The status and reputation of *Paradise Lost* became firmly established with the publication in 1688 of the fourth edition of the poem, Jacob Tonson's great subscription-published folio, adorned with twelve 'Sculptures', and bearing in its frontispiece Dryden's famous epigram:[2]

> Three *Poets*, in three distant *Ages* born,
> *Greece*, *Italy*, and *England* did adorn.
> The *First* in loftiness of thought Surpass'd;
> The *Next* in Majesty; in both the *Last*.
> The force of *Nature* cou'd no farther goe:
> To make a *Third* she joynd the former two.

[1] 'Life of Milton', in his *Lives of the English Poets*, ed. G. Birkbeck Hill (3 vols., Oxford: Oxford University Press, 1905), I. 144. The authoritative account of the bibliographical and textual history of *Paradise Lost* is R. G. Moyles, *The Text of Paradise Lost* (Toronto: University of Toronto Press, 1985).

[2] There is some evidence that the text of the 1688 *Paradise Lost* bears some signs of editorial attention, possibly by Tonson himself: see Moyles, *The Text of Paradise Lost*, pp. 32–7; and Stuart Bennett, 'Jacob Tonson an early editor of *Paradise Lost*?' *Library*, 6th ser., 10 (1988), 247–52.

Already English Milton is claimed to be the ultimate epic poet, possessed of all the gifts of natural genius, who can not only match but exceed both Homer and Virgil.

Despite persistent hostility to Milton the man – the advocate of divorce, the republican, and the anti-prelate – and despite relative neglect both of the prose writings and even of most of his other poems, the status, reputation, and influence of Milton the poet of *Paradise Lost* continued to develop.[3] Successive editions by Jacob Tonson and his heirs, and (especially after the effective lapse of copyright in 1731) by other publishers, supplied the poem's extensive readership.[4] The first full-scale critical examination and evaluation of *Paradise Lost*, and indeed the first of any English poem, were the influential series of eighteen *Spectator* essays in which Joseph Addison analysed *Paradise Lost* according to essentially classical categories and standards, but also celebrated it as 'the greatest Production, or at least the noblest Work of Genius, in our Language'.[5] Addison's essays were read on their first appearance by some 60,000 subscribers, and repeatedly reprinted in editions of the poem. They were followed by a voluminous scholarly and critical debate about the poem throughout the century.[6]

But *Paradise Lost* was frequently figured almost from the beginning not merely as a canonical but also as a sacred text, and its poet not merely as a national property, 'our Milton' or 'our mighty Bard',[7] but as a writer touched by the divine, in whom Isaac Watts's distinction between 'sacred Writers' and 'common Authors' almost disappears. At least in poetic hyperbole Milton was becoming, as Shakespeare also would become, godlike. Andrew Marvell, in the poem on *Paradise Lost* that was printed in the second edition of 1674, suggested that heaven had requited Milton's blindness with 'prophesie'. Addison in 1694 attributed to Milton 'hallow'd rage', a Christianized version of the *furor poeticus*. Later writers referred to 'our Godlike Milton', a 'Divine Author' who had written a 'Divine Poem'.

[3] For a recent account, see Howard D. Weinbrot, *Britannia's Issue* (Cambridge: Cambridge University Press, 1993), especially pp. 115, 118–21. A classic study of the early formation and description of an English literary canon is René Wellek, *The Rise of English Literary History* (New York: University of North Carolina Press, 1941).

[4] Moyles provides a useful list, *The Text of Paradise Lost*, pp. 171–7.

[5] *Spectator*, 321. Joseph Addison, Richard Steele, *et al.*, *Spectator*, ed. Donald F. Bond (5 vols., Oxford: Oxford University Press, 1965), III. 169. All references are to Bond's edition. Addison's essays appeared in Saturday issues between 5 January (no. 267) and 3 May 1712 (no. 369).

[6] Eighteenth-century responses to Milton are valuably and selectively anthologized in two volumes edited by John T. Shawcross: *Milton: the Critical Heritage* (London: Routledge and Kegan Paul, 1970), covering the period 1628 to 1731; *Milton, 1732–1801: the Critical Heritage* (London: Routledge and Kegan Paul, 1972). These are hereafter referred to as Shawcross I and Shawcross II respectively.

[7] Q. Horatii Flacci, *Epistola ad Augustum . . . To which is added, A Discourse Concerning Poetical Imitation*, ed. Richard Hurd (1751), 180–1, quoted by Shawcross II. 199; Samuel Johnson, 'A New Prologue Spoken at the Representation of Comus' (1750), line 15.

Such mid-century poets as Thomas Gray, conscious of their belatedness, aware that the bowers of heaven-touched genius were overthrown, could lament that:

> not to one in this benighted age
> Is that diviner inspiration given,
> That burns in Shakespeare's or in Milton's page,
> The pomp and prodigality of heaven.[8]

As an object of idolatry, however, *Paradise Lost* had the advantage over Shakespeare's works that it was itself based on sacred narrative, and especially on the originary myth of the Creation, Paradise, and Fall. The poem was regularly equated, in terms of quality or authority, with Holy Writ. Where Dryden had asserted the poem's primacy in comparison with classical epic, Thomas Newton, amongst others, makes the obvious evaluative parallel with the Bible: 'whoever has any true taste and genius . . . will esteem this poem the best of modern productions, and the Scriptures the best of all ancient ones'.[9] The incidents and images of *Paradise Lost* were regularly justified by their scriptural provenance. The 'many surprising Incidents' with which Milton's narrative is filled may please even the most delicate reader, argues Joseph Addison, because they 'bear so close analogy with what is delivered in Holy Writ'. So, for example, Milton's image of the holy scales which decide the battle at the end of Book 4 is 'the more justified . . . as we find the same Allegory in Holy Writ', and in Book 10 Milton 'has . . . kept religiously to the form of Words, in which the three several Sentences were passed upon *Adam*, *Eve*, and the Serpent'.[10] The sublimity which for Addison, as for other writers, was the characteristic excellence of *Paradise Lost* is vitally connected with its divine subject. Milton can exceed the writers of ancient epic because his poem is based on the truth of Christian belief, and the 'Unquestioned Magnificence in every Part of *Paradise Lost*' is 'much greater than could have been formed upon any Pagan System'.[11]

[8] W. Worts, 'To my friend on his character of the English poets', in Samuel Cobb's *Poetae Britannici* (London, 1700), sig. B2^r (quoted by Weinbrot, *Britannia's Issue*, p. 120); Joseph Addison, 'An Account of the Greatest English Poets' (1694; quoted by Shawcross I. 105) and *Spectator* 267 (1712; Addison, *Spectator*, II. 538); Jonathan Richardson, father and son, *Explanatory Notes and Remarks on Milton's Paradise Lost* (London, 1734), Preface, p. cxxxvi; Thomas Newton, ed., *Paradise Lost* (2 vols., London, 1749), II. 431; William Collins, *Ode on the Poetical Character* (1746), line 75 (*The Poems of Thomas Gray, William Collins, Oliver Goldsmith*, ed. Roger Lonsdale (London: Longmans, 1969), p. 435); Thomas Gray, 'Stanzas to Mr Bentley' (written 1751–3; first printed in *Poems of Mr Gray*, 1775), lines 17–20 (*Poems*, ed. Lonsdale, pp. 154–5).

[9] Newton, ed., *Paradise Lost*, II. 432.

[10] *Spectator*, 267; *Spectator*, 321 (referring to *Paradise Lost* 4. 1010–15 and Daniel 5:27); *Spectator*, 357 (referring to *Paradise Lost* 10. 102ff., and Genesis 3:8 ff.). Addison, *Spectator*, II. 543, III. 174, 330.

[11] *Spectator*, 267. Addison, *Spectator*, II. 542. This argument for *Paradise Lost* as the sublime poem of revealed religion became a commonplace; compare Jonathan Richardson's assertion that the sublimity of Milton's poem is 'Such as the Heathen World were Incapable of by Infinite

Milton of course makes his own claim of religious purpose and truth in *Paradise Lost*, setting out to 'justify the ways of God to men', and distinguishing between his own 'higher argument' and the fictions of romance and epic tales of

> fabled knights
> In battles feigned.[12]

For many eighteenth-century readers and some editors *Paradise Lost* bore the scriptural warranty of truth, and might even be used as an exposition of, even an equivalent for, Holy Scripture. John Shawcross has penetratingly remarked that 'many people in England seem to have learned their Bible with *Paradise Lost* at hand, for it was considered an exposition of the orthodox creed' (Shawcross I. 25). *Paradise Lost* was, for example, a central text for John Wesley's project of education. In 1745 he arranged with his preachers for a small library, including copies of Milton, to be provided at headquarters in London, Bristol, and Newcastle. In 1746 he required that all his preachers should read *Paradise Lost*. In 1748 his curriculum for the seventh class at Kingswood School included the instruction: 'Transcribe and repeat select portions of Milton.'[13] Wesley published his own *Extract from Milton's Paradise Lost. With Notes* in 1763, a tiny duodecimo that might be carried around by the faithful, like a pocket Testament.

For the eighteenth century's greatest critic of English literary writing the scriptural character and authority of *Paradise Lost* was essential. Few eighteenth-century writers took more seriously than Samuel Johnson the notion of the true, and nowhere in Johnson's writing is the distinction between 'truth' and 'fiction' more important or more operative than in his 'Life of Milton'. 'The substance of the narrative is truth.' Though the ancient epic poets lacked 'the light of revelation', Milton as the poet of morality and belief began with the advantage of 'acquaintance with the sacred writings'. Notoriously Johnson finds that we are 'harassed and overburdened' by the exercise of reading *Paradise Lost*; the truths which it presents 'are too important to be new', 'too ponderous for the wings of wit'. It is, nevertheless, Milton's distinctive creative achievement that, confined within the circle of Christian truth, he could write his great epic without resort to falsehood: 'Whoever considers the few radical positions which the Scriptures afforded him will wonder by what energetick

Degrees, Such as None but the Noblest Genius could attain to, and That Assisted by a Religion Reveal'd by God Himself' (*Explanatory Notes and Remarks*, p. clii).

[12] *Paradise Lost* I. 26; 9. 30–1, 42. Where not from the text of editors under consideration, my quotations in this chapter are from Alastair Fowler's edition of *Paradise Lost*, in *The Poems of John Milton*, ed. John Carey and Alastair Fowler (London: Longmans, 1968).

[13] See Frank Baker's Introduction to his selection from Wesley's edition, *Milton for the Methodists. Emphasized Extracts from Paradise Lost Selected, Edited, and Annotated by John Wesley* (London: Epworth Press, 1988), p. viii.

operations he expanded them to such extent and ramified them to so much variety, restrained as he was by religious reverence from licentiousness of fiction.' Hence Johnson's profoundly equivocal response to the poem, his sense of awe and resistance. However new and various Milton made them, his 'few radical positions' are the sublime and fearful truths of Christian belief.[14] The 'Life of Milton' no doubt has complex intellectual and personal motives, but evidently one of the most significant is that, as a recent critic has convincingly argued, Johnson 'comes to *Paradise Lost*, as he would to a holy text'.[15]

Such an assessment of Milton's great work as a sacred or quasi-sacred text was never universal nor unqualified, but it evidently began early, and persisted as a significant element in Milton scholarship, criticism, and editing through the eighteenth century. It certainly lies behind the first full-scale commentary, Patrick Hume's *Annotations on Milton's Paradise Lost*, which were published in 1695, as part of Jacob Tonson's sixth edition of the poem.[16]

Hume broke new ground. His annotations have generally been considered one of the first systematic and scholarly commentaries on the text of a modern vernacular author.[17] In the absence of any clear model for such a project, Hume was considerably indebted, I would want to argue, to the most obviously appropriate genre at hand: that is, to the structures, substance, and methods of English commentary on the Bible.

English biblical commentaries, as I have shown, are commonly characterized by a twofold structure of explicating paraphrase, followed by a more discursive and learned annotation. Hume's *Annotations* on *Paradise Lost* offer no clear formal division of paraphrase and annotation, but these two modes of commentary are prevalent, and distinguishable, in the work. In Hume's subtitle the commitment to annotation, elucidating the poem's relation both to Christian Scripture and Greek and Roman epic, is spelt out, and the commitment to paraphrase is briefly but decisively stated: *Wherein the Texts of Sacred Writ, relating to the Poem, are Quoted; the Parallel Places and Imitations of the most excellent* Homer *and* Virgil, *Cited and Compared; All the Obscure Parts render'd in Phrases more Familiar; the Old and Obsolete Words, with*

[14] *Lives of the English Poets*, I. 174, 179, 182–4.

[15] Stephen Fix, 'Johnson and the "duty" of reading *Paradise Lost*', *ELH*, 52 (1985), 649–71 (p. 667).

[16] Hume's annotations were sometimes bound in with copies of the 1695 edition ('To which is added, Explanatory Notes upon each Book'). Hume is identified only as 'P. H.' in the title-page of the *Annotations*. Almost nothing is known about him, apart from his work on Milton (see *Dictionary of National Biography*, and Robert Chambers and Thomas Thomson, *A Biographical Dictionary of Eminent Scotsmen* (London: Blackie, 1875)). There is an important recent discussion of Hume in Howard Erskine-Hill, 'On historical commentary: the example of Milton and Dryden', in *Presenting Poetry*, ed. Howard Erskine-Hill and Richard A. McCabe (Cambridge: Cambridge University Press, 1995), pp. 52–74.

[17] By, for example, Wellek (*Rise of English Literary History*, p. 144) and Shawcross (I. 109).

their Originals, Explain'd and made Easie to the English Reader. By P. H. φιλοποιητης. Hume's paraphrase of Milton's poem is not continuous, but he offers nonetheless explanatory re-phrasing of a very large number of lines of his original. And he brings to the text a remarkable copiousness and diversity of information in the form of notes.

In his numerous passages of paraphrase Hume generally sought to elucidate Milton's meaning by putting it in other, more readily comprehensible, terms. Broadly speaking, his interpretative use of paraphrase conforms to the theoretical model which E. D. Hirsch describes, and which, I have suggested, lies behind English biblical commentary: 'the art of explaining nearly always involves the task of discussing meaning in terms that are not native to the original text . . . A translation or paraphrase tries to render the meaning in new terms.'[18] The changes in Hume's explanatory periphrases are usually minimal. Transpositions are ironed out, ellipses are expanded, allusions are made explicit, words of Greek or Latin origin are implicitly glossed. The following lines are part of Milton's invocation in the opening of Book 1:

> Sing heavenly Muse, that on the secret top
> Of Oreb, or of Sinai, didst inspire
> That shepherd, who first taught the chosen seed,
> In the beginning how the heavens and earth
> Rose out of chaos.
>
> (*Paradise Lost*, 1. 6–10)

Hume provides a carefully literal paraphrasing explanation: 'Inform me, Heavenly Muse, who didst instruct the Shepherd *Moses*, who first taught the Sons of *Israel*, how the Heavens and Earth were made, and how this Beauteous Universe arose in such bright various Forms out of confusion'. Such conservative renditions occur throughout Hume's commentary,[19] and they closely resemble in their method biblical paraphrases of Hume's time. Even where he ventures a little beyond the 'literal' meaning of his original, Hume frequently confines himself to reasonably legitimate implications. The shields of Satan's host, 'with boastful argument portrayed' (*Paradise Lost*, 6. 84), are, Hume explains, 'Painted with Vain-Glorious Boastings of what they now design'd'. God's 'invisible glory' is transformed into a brutish image,

> adorned
> With gay religions full of pomp and gold.
>
> (*Paradise Lost*, 1. 371–2)

[18] *Validity in Interpretation* (New Haven: Yale University Press, 1967), p. 136. Compare Henry Felton's formulations: '*Paraphrase* . . . gives the Meaning of an Author in the Way of Explication . . . the *Paraphrase* is indeed no more than the true *Translation*' (*A Dissertation on Reading the Classics, and Forming a Just Style. Written in the Year 1709* (4th edn, London, 1730), pp. 138–9, 143).

[19] For three of the many other possible instances, see Hume's notes on 4. 774–5; 6. 118; 6. 159–7.

Hume's paraphrase offers a rather more daring implied specification of the 'gay religions' aimed at: 'Decked and set out with Gawdy Rites and Shews, Solemn Processions and Copes wrought with Gold'.

To Ants Oras, who devoted a chapter to Hume in his study of Milton's early editors and commentators, Hume's paraphrases seemed clear evidence that he 'could not resist the temptation to reshape Milton after his own fashion'. 'There can be no doubt of Hume's endeavour to give more in [the paraphrases] than a mere sober account of the contents of Milton's text.'[20] Now it is true, as Oras alleges, that Hume very occasionally offers a brief passage of paraphrase in his own blank verse,[21] and true, too, that there are moments of rhetorical (especially alliterative) luxuriance, as well as of dubious wit. To concentrate on such freaks and idlings however is to misrepresent Hume's essential method and purpose. Hume does not set out to find fault with Milton's logic, taste, and expression, to read the poem in the context of his own, rather than Milton's, knowledge and culture. The purpose of Hume's paraphrase is generally not to offer, in substitution for Milton's meaning, a sense of his own, but to explicate, to unfold to his reader, Milton's meaning itself, with 'All the Obscure Parts render'd in Phrases more Familiar'. As contemporary biblical commentators used paraphrase to open the literal sense of Scripture to a wide readership, so Hume, using the same method, takes Milton's poem as a national scripture to be similarly made available.

To the second aspect of his project, annotation, Hume brought an enormously wide range of ancient and modern disciplines, including theology, rhetoric, philosophy, law, poetry, history, natural history, chemistry, architecture, astronomy, mythology, and philology. His *Annotations* are nonetheless dominated by methods and knowledges regularly used in learned biblical annotation: the identification of allusions to the text of the Bible, the citation of parallel texts of Scripture, and extensive resort to previous biblical exegesis of all dates and types, cabalistic, patristic, humanistic. Indeed the encyclopaedic character of Hume's work itself recalls that of many of the more learned biblical commentaries, such as I have illustrated in Henry Hammond's note on Matthew 9:23.[22]

Much of the basic original spadework of identifying Milton's use of the Bible was carried out by Hume, and was much exploited by later editors of *Paradise Lost*.[23] The sources of the great image of the 'chariot of paternal

20 *Milton's Editors and Commentators from Patrick Hume to Henry John Todd (1695–1801)* (Tartu: University of Tartu, and London: Oxford University Press, 1931), pp. 23, 26.

21 See for example his notes on *Paradise Lost*, 1. 230–7, 424–31; 6. 1ff., 58.

22 See above, p. 47.

23 Oras argues that, as far as Milton's biblical allusions are concerned, 'later commentators had only to fill in . . . the relatively slight gaps [Hume] left', and that 'more than half the biblical

deity' for example are found, in abundance and in detail, in Ezekiel and other scriptural prophecies.[24] The meaning and textual correctness of Milton's lines are often tested against their biblical parallels. So Hume wonders that on the sixth day of creation the earth should 'bring forth fowl living in her kind' (7. 451): ''Tis unaccountable how our Author, who has hitherto kept so close to the sacred Text, should deviate from it here, and make mention of *Fowl*, when there is no such in *Gen.* 1.24. where the Works of the Sixth Day are enumerated.' Here Hume proposes no correction, but his acute and detailed reference back to Scripture enables him at least to anticipate one of the two cogent emendations ('soul' for 'fowl') that Richard Bentley was later able to make.

Many of Hume's notes are, in both content and method, remarkably inclusive, combining wide biblical reference with other forms of knowledge. In commenting on the word 'Jehovah' (1. 386), for instance, Hume gives the Hebrew form; defines it as 'the peculiar and most expressive Name of God refers to Exodus 3:14 and 6:3, Isaiah 42:8, and Revelation 1:4 (quoting in the Greek); gives the Hebrew root; goes on to discuss the veneration of the Hebrews for this name, and its 'sacred Concealment'; identifies it as the *tetragrammaton*; and discusses cabalistic number mysteries deriving from it. Similarly, in his note on 'Moloch' (1. 392), Hume gives the Hebrew form; refers to Leviticus 18:21, 1 Kings 11:5, 2 Kings 23:10, Jeremiah 7:31, and other texts; points out that 'this Idol is by some thought the same with *Saturn*'; and describes the calf-headed idol itself and the child-sacrifice rites associated with it. Milton's invocation of the Holy Spirit (1. 17) calls forth from Hume a display of scholarship on the 'Divers . . . Opinions concerning the meaning of *Gen.* 1. 2. *The Spirit of God moved upon the Waters*'. Amongst the authorities cited are the Church Fathers Jerome, Basil, Theodoret, Tertullian, Chrysostom, and Athanasius; the 'Heathen Philosophers' Orpheus, Zoroaster, Heraclitus, and Plato; and 'the sublime *Virgil*'. Having offered so much Christian and pagan learning, the note triumphantly and orthodoxly concludes by insisting that Milton's meaning is conformable to two passages of Holy Writ, Job 26:13 and Psalms 104:30.

Clearly, Hume's copiousness of learning does not always serve to explicate or interrogate the poem. Oras asserts that Hume's annotations are full of valuable materials rarely related in any critically analytic way to the poem: 'details are usually heaped on details without any close connection with the context in Milton' (p. 23). The 321 pages of Hume's *Annotations* are certainly extraordinarily heterogeneous. In tone they are on some

references' found in Thomas Newton's notes on the first 500 lines of *Paradise Lost* had already been identified by Hume (Oras, p. 22). John Callander, in his Commentary on the first book of *Paradise Lost*, drew particularly heavily on Hume (see Oras, pp. 16, 254).

[24] 6. 749–59. Hume cites Ezek. 1:4, 13, 16, 18, 19, 20, 26, 27; 10:10, 12, 14; Isa. 66:15; Jer. 30:23; Amos 1:14; Dan. 10:16.

occasions flippant, or pedantic, or rhapsodic. Regularly, however, Hume's scholarship, and especially his biblical scholarship, is put to an interpretative use. Milton speaks of Nimrod in these terms:

> A mighty hunter thence he shall be styled
> Before the Lord, as in despite of heaven.
>
> (12. 33–4)

Hume explains by reference to past biblical exegesis of Genesis 10:9: 'Most Interpreters take the words, *Before the Lord* in the worst sense, as our Author does, *In despite of Heaven.*' Milton's notorious statement of the hierarchy of God, man, and woman, 'He for God only, she for God in him' (4. 299), is identified by Hume as the doctrine of St Paul, with appropriate reference to 1 Corinthians 11:3, 7, and 9. (Richard Bentley, by contrast, would amend to 'she for God *and* him', offering for explanation only 'the opposition' (with, presumably, the first half of the line) and the parallel with 4. 440.) The misleading irony of Satan's temptation of Eve depends partly on the grim impropriety of its Pauline phraseology:

> So ye shall die perhaps, by putting off
> Human, to put on gods, death to be wished.
>
> (9. 713–14)

Hume offers the parallel of 1 Corinthians 15:53: 'this mortal must put on immortality'. The 'secret top / Of Oreb' (1. 6–7), which Richard Bentley would later feel compelled to alter to 'SACRED top', is explained by Hume with reference to 'that thick Darkness which cover'd the Mount, when God spake there with his Servant *Moses*, as in private, *Exod.* 19. 16'.

Many of Hume's notes include philological and, especially, etymological elements. His etymologies include, as one would expect in biblical commentary, Hebrew, Greek, and Latin. Less familiar, but a logical result of applying the methods of biblical commentary to a vernacular poem, are etymologies in Anglo-Saxon, French, and Dutch. The effect can be curiously pedantic. Nonetheless, their provision often shows a detailed sensitivity to meaning and verbal suggestion. In his note to the second line of the poem Hume accurately and pertinently derives the 'mortal' taste of the forbidden tree from the Latin *mortalis*, 'deadly'. In his illicit entrance into Paradise, Satan 'at one slight bound high over-leaped all bound' (4. 181); Hume overcomes his usual dislike of verbal 'gingling' to illuminate Milton's play on the two opposed senses of 'bound' by reference to the French *bondir* and *bornes*.

Not infrequently Hume's notes aim at the doctrinal or moral function of biblical annotation. Oras has noted how Hume 'dwells on the moral importance of Milton's epic, very much as a commentator on the Bible tries to bring home the rules of conduct deducible from the stories of Scripture' (p. 24). Here too Hume's learning sometimes has an interpretative value.

The questions of God's fore-determination or fore-knowledge, of man's free-will or pre-destination, have always of course been central to the understanding and judgment of Milton's epic.[25] Hume provides a long note on God's assertion that his own 'Foreknowledge had no influence' on the fault of the rebel angels (*Paradise Lost* 3. 118), combining doctrinal and moral comment on the poem with an acute sense of a crucial interpretative issue:

> The Fore-knowledge of God does not determine the Minds of Men to good or bad Actions, thô that Fore-knowledge be infinite and infallible; nor does the commission of Good or Evil depend thereon: *But he that knoweth whereof we are made, and that searcheth the Hearts, and trieth the Reins, that knows all our Thoughts afar off*, clearly foresees all our Faults and Failings, which we should have committed undoubtedly, althô they had not been foreknown or foreseen by that infinite Eye . . . Good and Evil, Life and Death, therefore are in the Choice, and ballance the Wills of all Mankind; they have the Election of their Mischiefs and Miscarriages in their own Power; . . . they *Decree therefore their own Revolt*, that Defection from their Maker to his and their Enemy the Devil.

At such moments Hume goes beyond the literal sense to a conservative and critically apposite exploration of the moral sense of his text.

To Hume *Paradise Lost* was, more than a classic, a scripture. Milton had attempted 'a greater Undertaking' than either Homer, or Spenser, setting out 'to sing, not only of the Beauteous Universe, and all Created Beings, but of the Creator Himself, and all those Revelations and Dispensations He had been pleased to make to Faln Man through the Great Redeemer of the World, His Son'.[26] Milton's poem was, as Protestants thought the Bible, a work both requiring, and capable of, explication. To bring to bear upon *Paradise Lost* both explicatory paraphrase and learned annotation, the key instruments of biblical commentary, was implicitly to identify the poem as having a specially scriptural value and truth, and to privilege its author's meaning (not for nothing did Hume identify himself by the sobriquet φιλοποιητης, 'a friend of poets'). It was also, in an important sense, to initiate and give a first shape to a new genre, the secular literary commentary, which developed so rapidly, and diversified so much, as the eighteenth century progressed. Elements of the methods used by Hume would persist especially, as we shall see, in the work of later commentators on Milton.

'Knowing no real toad durst there intrude': Richard Bentley's edition of *Paradise Lost*

The orientations of Milton's next annotating editor are very much more complex. In Richard Bentley's notorious edition of *Paradise Lost*, published

[25] See, for example, Alastair Fowler's notes on *Paradise Lost* 3. 100–2, 113–23; 4. 66–70; 5. 529–34.
[26] Hume's note on *Paradise Lost* 1. 6.

in 1732, an extraordinary contest of authority takes place, between poet, text, and editor. Bentley's methods provoked profound disagreement in his own time, and have remained deeply suspicious ever since. Nonetheless he continues to be in some respects the most fascinating, and certainly the most discussed, of all eighteenth-century commentators on Milton. His giant figure casts a disproportionate and in many ways a distorting shadow over our view of the period's approach to Miltonic editing.

By 1732 Richard Bentley was entering the final decade of a long, tempestuous, and immensely distinguished life of learning and controversy. He established his reputation, European as well as British, as a classical scholar with his *Epistula ad Millium* (1691), a set of dissertations written to his friend John Mill, Principal of St Edmund Hall, arising out of the work of the Byzantine chronographer John of Antioch, or Malelas. This was followed by a devastating contribution to the quarrel of the Ancients and Moderns. Sir William Temple, arguing on the side of the Ancients, had celebrated the Epistles of Phalaris in his *Essay upon Ancient and Modern Learning* (1692); Bentley in his *Dissertation upon the Epistles of Phalaris*[27] demonstrated, with an overwhelming display of scholarship, that they were in fact spurious. In 1692, and again in 1694, Bentley was appointed to deliver the prestigious Boyle lectures in defence of the Christian religion. In 1700 he became Master of Trinity College, Cambridge, where he remained until his death in 1742. In the intervals of battles with the Fellows, his classical publications included significant new editions of Horace (1711), Terence, with Phaedrus and Publilius Syrus (1726), and Manilius (1739).[28] His theological scholarship included an answer to the deist Anthony Collins, *Remarks upon a Late Discourse of Free-thinking* (1713), and *Proposals for Printing a New Edition of the Greek Testament* (1721), promising a never-to-be-completed work of New Testament scholarship to rival his achievements in the classical field.

Why in the later years of such a career did Bentley set out on quite a new task, an edition of a vernacular epic by a recent English poet? The 1732 *Paradise Lost* has often been seen as a work of Bentley's dotage, an unfortunate and misguided attempt to apply the methods he had used in his classical scholarship to a vernacular literary work. Yet the very fact that the greatest scholar of his age should have chosen to turn his attention from Greek and Roman writers and from Holy Scripture to the poem that

[27] First published as an appendix to William Wotton's *Reflections upon Ancient and Modern Learning* (1697), and then expanded into a substantial volume (1699).

[28] For fuller accounts of Bentley's life and works, see R. C. Jebb, *Bentley* (London: Macmillan, 1882); Adam Fox, *John Mill and Richard Bentley* (Oxford: Blackwell, 1954); Rudolf Pfeiffer, *History of Classical Scholarship, from 1300 to 1850* (Oxford: Oxford University Press, 1976), pp. 142–58; Joseph M. Levine, *The Battle of the Books* (Ithaca and London: Cornell University Press, 1991), especially pp. 245–63.

was becoming the central English classic itself represents a significant transference of status and authority towards England, and English writing. His procedures and purposes in contributing to this transference raise the largest questions about the nature and development of early vernacular literary editing.

Bentley evidently brought to the text of *Paradise Lost* the attitudes of one whose editorial experience lay primarily in ancient texts. There are no autograph manuscripts of the classical Greek and Roman writers. Like other editors he had to work with manuscripts at a considerable and often uncertain degree of removal from the originals, often multiple, often corrupt, often incomplete. In such cases the authority of the documents was inevitably open to question. There could be no guarantee of 'correct' readings being found simply by the impartial collation of manuscripts, and the editor must on occasion resort to the divination of errors and to conjectural emendation. When dealing with Holy Writ, Bentley had been ready to accept the authority of the early manuscript witnesses, as a matter both of practice and of principle. With a significant awareness of the superior authority of earlier witnesses, he claimed, by the comparison of 'the Original Greek and Hierom's Latin', to be able to 'settle the original Text to the smallest Nicety', to a greater degree than was possible for 'any *Classic* Author whatever'. And he asserted his sense of the sanctity of the surviving documents, insisting that 'in the Sacred Writings there's no place for Conjectures or Emendations. Diligence and Fidelity, with some Judgement and Experience, are the Characters here requisite.'[29] In his classical editing however Bentley explicitly, and reasonably, asserts his preference for reasoned argument over the authority of the texts. Textual choices need to be made on the basis, not of a misplaced 'veneration' for the 'authority' of extant documents, but of thoughtful critical interpretation. In one of his notes on Horace he famously declares that reason and the sense itself are more persuasive than a hundred manuscripts: 'nobis et ratio et res ipsa centum codicibus potiores sunt'. In others he proposes readings witnessed by no extant codex, even insisting, on one occasion, that his suggested reading would indeed be found, were not all the codices corrupt.[30]

[29] *Proposals for Printing a New Edition of the Greek Testament* (1721), p. 4. Others shared Bentley's views on the danger of 'Emendation from Conjecture' in the text of Scripture without adequate documentary support. Compare Francis Hare, *The Clergyman's Thanks to Phileleutherus for his Remarks on a Late Discourse of Free-Thinking. In a Letter to Dr Bentley* (London, 1713), pp. 38–9. For a brief discussion of the debate on this issue in the eighteenth century and later see John Strugnell, 'A plea for conjectural emendation in the New Testament, with a coda on 1 Cor 4:6', *Catholic Biblical Quarterly*, 36 (1974), pp. 543–4.

[30] *Q. Horatius Flaccus, ex recensione & cum notis atque emendationibus Ricardi Bentleii* (Cambridge, 1711), Praefatio ad Lectorem, and notes on Odes I. 6. 3, I. 17. 14, 3. 27. 15; *The Odes of Horace in Latin and English* (2 vols., London: Lintot, 1712–13), I. 11–13. On Bentley's many proposed changes in

There has been consensus, from the beginnings of Milton editing, that the surviving early printed texts of *Paradise Lost* do not raise such problems. Probably Milton did not exercise supervision over the printing, but the first two editions of the poem, in ten books (1667) and twelve books (1674), were carefully and responsibly printed by the standards of their time, and contained very few significant errors, despite inconsistency in accidentals.[31] The second edition has generally been considered to offer an authoritative text for the twelve-book poem, though editors have differed about the treatment of the relatively small number of substantive variants from the first edition. Eighteenth-century editors were generally content to accept that the 1667 and 1674 editions adequately represented what Milton intended to write, whether they based their own text on those pristine documents, or took their turn in a process of linear textual inheritance running through Simmons's third edition of 1678, and the successive editions of the Tonson dynasty. Jonathan Richardson felt sure that, taking the first two 'Authentick Editions together, . . . we are in Possession of the Genuine Work of the Author As much as in Any Printed Book whatsoever' (there is a striking echo here of the arguments and phraseology of Anglican apologists for the reliability of the text of Holy Scripture).[32] Edward Capell, in his manuscript edition of *Paradise Lost* preserved in the Wren Library at Trinity College, Cambridge, expressed a confidence in the first textual witnesses typical of most eighteenth-century editors of Milton's poem: 'the great Author bestow'd no little attention upon the first impression of it; and sent it into the world in a state of perfection that is truly admirable, considering his condition'.[33]

For complicated reasons, some having to do with his assumptions and experience as a classical editor, Bentley took a very different view. In his brief but outspoken Preface he outlined with provocative clarity his understanding of the textual tradition of *Paradise Lost*, and his own editorial purposes. He begins with the presupposition that the early editions were, because of the circumstances of the poem's composition and transmission into print, radically faulty. Claiming to undertake 'a Restoration of the Genuine *Milton*', Bentley argued that the text of *Paradise Lost* had been subject to mistake or corruption in a number of ways. When Milton composed his great work he was not only blind, but also poor and friendless, and therefore at the mercy of the amanuensis, who, taking down the poet's dictation, was responsible for 'Errors in Spelling, Pointing, nay even in whole Words of a like or near Sound in Pronunciation'. The

the text of Horace, and their relation or lack of relation to manuscript support, see Harold R. Joliffe, 'Bentley versus Horace', *Philological Quarterly*, 16 (1937), 278–86.

31 See Moyles, *The Text of Paradise Lost*, especially p. 31.

32 *Explanatory Notes and Remarks*, p. cxxxiv.

33 'Dedication'. Capell Collection, MSS B.17.

bookseller and 'that Acquaintance who seems to have been the sole Corrector of the Press' were so negligent in overseeing the printing of the poem as to allow the first edition to appear 'polluted with such monstrous Faults, as are beyond Example in any other printed Book'. Worse than this, Bentley argues, Milton's 'Acquaintance' or 'suppos'd Friend' in fact behaved as an 'Editor', and, taking advantage of Milton's blindness, 'thought he had a fit Opportunity to foist into the Book several of his own Verses', which the blind and aged poet was in no position to reject. Finally, because of Milton's blindness, he was unable to revise the poem as a whole before its publication. In consequence, there are 'Inconsistencies in the System and Plan', which 'must be laid to the Author's Charge'.[34]

These statements are the basis for a major and characterizing shift in authority in Bentley's edition, from document and author towards himself as editor. Casting doubt on the status and dependability of the early physical witnesses, on the reliability with which authorially intended readings have been transmitted into print, and even on the coherence with which final authorial intentions were formed, Bentley establishes premises for a process of extensive editorial intervention. To use Peter Shillingsburg's taxonomy, Bentley undermines the possibility of documentary, sociological, and authorial approaches in order to justify what will appear to be an essentially aesthetic emphasis.

Bentley's doubts in the Preface are at least overstated. Milton was blind, but neither poor nor without friends. Bentley is properly aware that the textual problems of *Paradise Lost* are at least in part constituted by the circumstances of its original composition. To the usual questions regarding the accuracy of the press, of course, have to be added special questions about the effect of the poet's blindness and his use of an amanuensis. It seems, however, that Bentley's insistence that he is dealing with an extensively corrupt and adulterate text is aimed less at reinstating Milton's damaged authority against the first editor and printers, than to allow himself generous scope to query genuine readings, and to propose his own conjectural emendations. In particular, the device that gives Bentley his widest latitude, his assertion of editorial interpolation by Milton's 'acquaintance', has been thought an obvious stratagem. Bentley attempts in his Preface to deny that 'this *Persona* of an Editor' is 'a mere Fantom, a Fiction . . . to skreen *Milton* himself', but David Mallet accused him of 'calling *Milton* himself, in the person of this phantom, fool, ignorant, ideot, and the like critical compellations', and Samuel Johnson described Bentley's hypothesis as 'a supposition rash and groundless, if he thought it true; and vile and pernicious, if, as is said, he in private allowed it to be false'.[35]

[34] Preface, sig. a1^r–a2^v.

[35] Bentley, Preface, sig. a3^r; Mallet, *Of Verbal Criticism* (London, 1733), p. 10n.; Johnson, *Lives of the English Poets*, I. 181. It needs to be said that Bentley may have been led to his 'rash supposition'

Bentley himself describes his methods of emendation in his Preface. He aims to correct the faults introduced by the printer by 'retrieving the Poet's own Words', but he sets out to do so 'not from a Manuscript, (for none exists), but by Sagacity, and happy Conjecture' (Preface, sig. a2^{v}). This again seems a questionable assertion, playing down the authority and availability of documentary evidence: Bentley knew of the manuscript of the first Book of *Paradise Lost*, and in fact used it extensively himself.[36] Bentley insists nonetheless that his text of the poem itself remains unaltered.[37] The spurious nature of the 'Editor's Interpolations' in the text of the poem are drawn to the reader's attention 'by printing them in the *Italic* Letter, and inclosing them between two Hooks' (that is, in square brackets). Milton's 'own Slips and Inadvertencies' cannot be cured 'without a Change both of the Words and Sense', but all the conjectural changes Bentley proposes in restoring 'the Genuine *Milton*' are conscientiously confined to the margin of the text, or, in the case of longer passages, to the foot of the page, 'so that the Reader has his free Choice, whether he will accept or reject what is here offer'd him'. Changes made to Milton's 'Slips and Inadvertencies' are 'suggested, but not obtruded, to the Reader: they are generally in this Stile; *It* MAY *be adjusted thus; Among several ways of Change this* MAY *be one.* And if any Person will substitute better, he will deserve every Reader's Thanks' (Preface, sig. a2^{v}).

Bentley suggests, in his edition of the poem, more than 800 conjectural emendations, and around 70 conjectural deletions. The effect on the reader's eye is considerable. Even though, unlike Alexander Pope and William Warburton in their editions of Shakespeare, Bentley did not subject the body of the text itself to large-scale alteration, it is hard to escape the incessant effect of his hooks, italics, and remorseless questioning. Time after time the errors and impertinences of a 'bad printer' and a 'worse editor' are castigated. One example is Gabriel's accusing question,

> Why hast thou, Satan, broke the bounds prescribed
> To thy transgressions?
>
> (4. 878–9)

by his knowledge as a classical editor of the possibility of ignorant or intentional editorial intervention in the course of scribal transmission of such authors as Horace.

36 See Helen Darbishire's James Bryce Memorial Lecture, '*Milton's Paradise Lost*' (London: Oxford University Press, 1951), pp. 31–2; Moyles, *The Text of Paradise Lost*, pp. 18–20; and John K. Hale, 'Paradise purified: Dr Bentley's marginalia for his 1732 edition of *Paradise Lost*', *Transactions of the Cambridge Bibliographical Society*, 10 (1991), 58–74 (especially p. 58).

37 Preface, sig. a1^{v}. This too is a statement of rather dubious meaning. Bentley's text is based on Tickell's inconsistent 1720 revision of the considerably more impressive 1719 edition by John Hughes. He consults the first two texts only occasionally. He was by no means always aware of the provenance of his individual readings, and indeed silently incorporates a number of the emendations made by earlier editors. See Moyles, *The Text of Paradise Lost*, pp. 59–67, and the list of variant readings provided in *The Poetical Works of John Milton*, ed. W. A. Wright (Cambridge: Cambridge University Press, 1903), pp. 572–97.

PARADISE LOST I. 11

That ſparkling blaz'd; his other parts beſides
195 Prone on the flood, extended long and large,
Lay floating many a rood; in bulk *as huge* — *like that*
[*As whom the Fables name, of monſtrous ſize,*
Titanian, *or* Earth-born, *that warr'd on* Jove,
Briareos, *or* Typhon *whom the Den*
200 *By ancient* Tarſus *held, or that Sea-beaſt*]
* *Leviathan,* which God *of all his works*
Created hugeſt that ſwim th' Ocean ſtream:
Him haply ſlumb'ring on the *Norway foam,* — *flood*
The Pilot of ſome ſmall *night*-founder'd Skiff, — *nigh-*
205 Deeming ſome Iſland oft, as Sea-men tell,
With fixed Anchor in his *ſkaly* rind, — *skinny*
Moors by his ſide under the Lee; while night
Inveſts the Sea, and wiſhed morn delays.
† *So ſtretch'd out huge in length the Arch-fiend lay,*
210 Chain'd on the burning Lake: nor ever thence
Had ris'n or heav'd his Head, but that the Will

* *Leviathan, whom God the vaſteſt made*
Of all the Kinds, that ſwim the Ocean ſtream.
† *So vaſt, ſtretch'd out in length, th' Arch-rebel lay,*

And

ſolid Foam, that can ſupport a ſleeping Whale. Better therefore with plain Simplicity, FLOOD or DEEP.

V. 204. *Night-founder'd Skiff.*] *Foundering* in the Sea Phraſe is *ſinking* by a Leak in the Ship. So that *Night* alone never can founder. Beſides, *Night* is here ſuperfluous; for in the cloſe of this ſame Compariſon he has *Night* again, *While Night inveſts the Sea.* The Poet gave it thus,

The Pilot of ſome ſmall NIGH-*founder'd Skiff*;

Nigh-founder'd, almoſt founder'd. A good Excuſe, why in that Extremity, and in the Dark, they took a Whale for firm Land: ſo II. 940. ſpeaking of *Satan* caught in a ſort of Bog,

Nigh-founder'd *on he fares.*

Our Poet in VII. 412. deſcribes this *Leviathan* again, as ſleeping on the Deep like a *Promontory,* or ſwiming like a *moving Land:* Could he have reviſed his whole Work, he woud have avoided the Repetition.

V. 206. *In his* ſkaly *rind.*] SKALY *rind* is unlucky here; for it falls out contrary, that the Whale has no Skales; or if he had them; by Proportion with other Fiſh, they would be ſo large, thick, and ſolid, that no Seaman could *fix his Anchor* through them. But the Author gave it otherwiſe,

With fixed Anchor in his SKINNY *rind.*

'Tis truly a Skin, ſo ſoft and thick, as to make it not incredible, that a ſmall Anchor may be fix'd there without the Whale's feeling the Wound. They are ſtruck with Harping-Irons, which cannot pierce a *ſkaly* Crocodile.

V. 209. *So ſtretch'd out huge in length the Arch-fiend lay.*] Here *Arch-fiend* has the Tone in the firſt Syllable, diſagreeably; better above *v.* 156. *Th' Arch-fiend replied.* Beſides, *ſo ſtretch'd out,* that is, *as the Whale lies ſtretch'd out.* But that is improper; for the Whale cannot *ſtretch out* or contract any of his Joints: he is always of the ſame Length; whether his Tail be bent or ſtraight. Better therefore thus,

So vaſt, ſtretch'd out in length, th' Arch-rebel lay.

Arch-rebel, as *v.* 81. *Arch-enemy.* See VII. 414.

C 2 V. 218.

Figures 1 and 2 *Milton's Paradise Lost* (1732), edited by Richard Bentley, pp. 11, 266.

PARADISE LOST.

BOOK IX.

NO more of talk, where *God or* Angel Gueſt *ſocial*
With Man, as with his Friend, familiar us'd
To ſit indulgent, and with Him partake
Rural repaſt, permitting him the while
5 *Venial* diſcourſe unblam'd: I now muſt change *Menſal*
Thoſe notes to Tragic: Foul diſtruſt, and breach *My*
Diſloyal on the part of Man, revolt
And diſobedience: on the part of Heav'n
Now alienated, diſtance and diſtaſt,
10 Anger and juſt rebuke, and judgment giv'n:
[*That brought into this World a world of woe,*]
Sin and her ſhadow *Death*, and *Miſery* *Malady*
Death's Harbinger; Sad task, yet Argument
Not leſs but more Heroic, than the *Wrath*
15 *Of ſtern* Achilles [*on his Foe purſu'd* *or the Arms and Man;*
Thrice

V. 1. *Where* God or *Angel Gueſt.*] God did not *partake rural repaſt* with *Adam*. Rather thus, as perhaps the Author gave it;
Where SOCIAL *Angel Gueſt.*

V. 5. Venial *diſcourſe unblam'd.*] The Word *Venial* gives a Check to the Freedom of Diſcourſe, and leſſens the Familiarity and Condeſcenſion. I believe the Author gave it;
MENSAL *diſcourſe unblam'd.*
Table Talk, *Colloquia Menſalia.*

V. 11. *That brought into this World a world of woe.*] This Verſe is not genuine, but inſerted by the Editor. 'Tis falſe, that the *Judgment giv'n by Heav'n* brought Woe into the World. Woe was brought in before, by Man's Diſobedience in eating the forbidden Fruit; which, I, 3,
Brought Death into the world, *and all our* woe.
Would *Milton* have repeated this over again here, and added to it a ſilly Pun, which there he avoided?

V. 12. *And* Miſery *Death's Harbinger.*] *Harbinger* is he, that goes before ſome Potentate, to provide for his Reception. How then is *Miſery* the Harbinger of Death? There's manifold Miſery that does not uſher in Death, but invoke it in vain; beſides, there is Miſery after Death. The Author gave it,
Sin, *and her ſhadow* Death, *and* MALADY
Death's Harbinger.
Sickneſs is the proper Harbinger to Death, except a violent Death.

V. 15. *Than the* Wrath Of ſtern *Achilles.*] The Poet's Thought here, without Ornament, is this, That *Paradiſe Loſt*, even this latter part of it, *Adam's*

Here Bentley objects to the punning 'transgressions', preferring 'transcursions', and lamenting the case of the 'Poor Poet; in subjection to a saucy Editor, and an ignorant Printer' (p. 140). Milton's account of the Paradise of Fools (3. 444–98) is one of many passages placed in italics and hooks: 'I wish for the Poet and the Poem's sake, that the Reader would be of my Opinion, That all this long Description of the outside of the World, *the Limbo of Vanity*, was not *Milton*'s own, but an Insertion by his Editor' (p. 93). The comparison of Paradise with the fabulous gardens of Enna, Daphne, Nysa, and Amara (4. 268–85) is similarly dismissed with an impatience of tone appropriate in upbraiding an editor who will persist in spoiling Milton's great poem with the fabulous: 'Pray you, Sir; no more of your Patches in a Poem quite elevated above your Reach and Imitation' (p. 116). Out of all of Bentley's conjectures just two, both of them apparent errors of the press, have proved convincing to later editors.[38] '*Smelling* Gourd' (7. 321) is 'a mere Mistake of the Printer: The Author gave it . . . SWELLING' (p. 228). God's injunction on the sixth day that 'the earth bring forth foul living in her kind' (7. 451) appears, as Hume had already pointed out, to contradict the Scripture account of the Creation. Bentley goes beyond noticing the error to proposing a typographically and contextually credible emendation: 'SOUL living . . . So the Scripture, *living Soul. Fowl* were created the Day before this' (p. 234).

In such instances Bentley's suggestions might be represented as an attempt to recover Milton's own words from the inaccuracies of the press and the incursions of his 'hardy Editor'. In many notes however Milton himself is detected in error, and in some his logic is so defective as to impel Bentley himself to write new phrases and new lines. As he neared the end of the second book:

> our Poet's Memory fail'd him, or his Attention was wearied; and he had no Eyes to recover the Slip. Is *Chaos*'s Sceptre *weaken'd* by *Intestine Broils*? No: it is strengthen'd and subsists by them . . . So that here it should or might have been, or was,
>
> *Encroach'd on by Creations old and new.*
>
> And so the whole Passage will be duly connected; which at present is neither Syntax nor Sense. (*Paradise Lost*, 2. 1001; p. 74)

Two books later Bentley wonders that Ithuriel, knowing Eve's bower was 'sacred and sequester'd to *Adam* and *Eve* only', should not at once identify as Satan the toad at Eve's ear (4. 810), and therefore seeks to remedy the mistake:

> why may not I add *one* Verse to *Milton*, as well as his Editor add so *many*; especially, since I do not do it, as He did, clandestinely:

38 For an authoritative statement of how little emendation has historically proved necessary or convincing, see Moyles, *The Text of Paradise Lost*, pp. 142–4.

Him thus intent *Ithuriel* with his Spear
KNOWING NO REAL TOAD DURST THERE INTRUDE,
Touch'd lightly.

(pp. 136–7)

At the end of the poem Adam and Eve

hand in hand with wandering steps and slow,
Through Eden took their solitary way.

(12. 648–9)

Joseph Addison had found an unnecessary renewal of anguish in these lines and wished them away.[39] Bentley similarly considers that this distich 'contradicts the Poet's own Scheme', and in particular the assurance in the immediately preceding line that the pair were guided by Providence. Presuming somewhat further, therefore, he offers two concluding lines of his own, 'as close as may be to the Author's Words, and entirely agreeable to his scheme':

THEN hand in hand with SOCIAL steps their way
Through *Eden* took, WITH HEAV'NLY COMFORT CHEER'D.[40]

This new conclusion represents a final step in the Bentleian transference of authority. That process is enacted in the most striking way in the discourse of Bentley's commentary. Some of his notes, having identified what he takes to be non-authorial mistakes, tentatively suggest amendments: 'Perhaps it was given thus'. Many such textual decisions in favour of an inferred authorial intention over supposed readings of the first editor are more confidently stated: 'without question the Poet's Words were', 'no doubt the Author spoke it'. From correcting editorial error, Bentley moves on to give critical judgment on Milton's writing: 'he had better have said', 'he had better have given it thus', 'better thus'. In a highly significant change of tense, the author is kidnapped from his past context to be admonished in Bentley's present: 'he must give it thus', 'he must give it here'. Speculation at last, with an increasing degree of confidence, becomes the exercise of a retrospective authority, proposing such local re-writings as we have seen, where Bentley's voice takes over from Milton's.

Bentley's editorial decisions are regularly guided by an urge not only to correct but to improve, and even to create. In some notes at least, the criterion of authorial meaning is under pressure from the criterion of significance to the editor, Miltonic sense giving way to the Bentleian. Some of the operations of the speculative and creative impulse which lies behind Bentley's edition have been strikingly demonstrated in John Hale's fine

39 *Spectator*, 369. Addison, *Spectator*, III. 390.

40 Pp. 398–9. Other instances of Bentley's many proposed improvements on Milton may be found in his notes on 1. 39; 1. 169–70; 4. 177; 5. 200; 6. 299; 7. 239.

discussion of Bentley's marginal notes in his working copy of the poem, a first volume of Tonson's 1720 edition, now in Cambridge University Library. Hale paints a picture of Bentley working with his pen poised over the text, pursuing possible alternatives, 'following a heuristic associationism, as it were en route to real editing'.[41] Unhappy with the expression 'by their own recovered strength' (1. 240), Bentley jots down, one after the other, no fewer than six possible amendments. These speculations, and a number of others, do not survive into the printed edition itself. Nonetheless much of the exploratory spirit of the manuscript marginalia is preserved there, for instance in the note where Bentley rejects the description of Eve as 'marriageable' (5. 217):

> Why she was *wed, spous'd* already in the Verse before . . . He gave it MANAGEABLE; . . . But that will not please. Among several ways of Alteration, this may be one:
>
> *She spous'd about him twines Her Arms* LASCIVIOUS.
>
> (pp. 154–5)

A first guess purports to supply what the author wrote; a second frankly proposes Bentley's preferred reading. Such moments are not accidental tinkering, but part of a process by which Bentley subjected Milton's epic to an evaluative and interpretative process using standards of taste and horizons of knowledge different from Milton's own.

An outline of the aesthetic criteria by which Bentley judges and edits the poem can be readily drawn. Everywhere he finds offences against both local logic and larger consistency in the poem. 'Darkness visible', for example, 'will not serve to *discover Sights of Woe*' (1. 63; p. 4), and hell can hardly 'unfold . . . her widest gates' (4. 381–2; p. 120) when we know that, having already been opened by Sin (2. 883), they cannot be shut again.[42] Passages dealing with such 'Romantic trash' as Pandora, Grecian Pan, Lapland witches, and the stories of Arthur and Charlemagne, are sequestered by hooks.[43] Bentley's ideal of fit heroic style was of 'Grandeur' combined with 'Simplicity' (10. 1092n.; p. 347), of 'Propriety' controlling 'Magniloquence of Stile, and Sublimity of Thought' (6. 212n.; p. 189). Against these essentially classicist principles Milton often offends. To have 'th'Apostat Angel' speak 'though in pain' is 'low and vulgar'.[44] A regular and strict application of the Horatian test of the *usus loquendi* results in the purging of idiosyncratic usages: so Eve's question to the

[41] Hale, 'Paradise purified', pp. 60, 61. Bentley's working copy of the 1720 Tonson edition is CUL Adv. b. 52.12. Bentley's marginalia may also be found transcribed into one of the British Library copies (11626.h.6) of Bentley's edition.

[42] Other instances may be found in Bentley's notes on 1. 13–16, 690; 2. 55–6 (discussed by Christopher Ricks, *Milton's Grand Style* (Oxford: Oxford University Press, 1963), pp. 11–14); 4. 24, 299, 555.

[43] 1. 579–87; 2. 659–66; 4. 705–8, 714–19.

[44] 1. 125; p. 6. Compare Bentley's note on 6. 580.

serpent, 'How cam'st thou Speakable of Mute' (9. 563), is re-phrased 'How Thou cam'st VOCAL THUS', since '*Speakable*, in common Use, is not *What can speak*, but *What can be spoken*' (p. 288). At such moments it is apparent that Bentley is assessing the language of Milton's poem, and to some extent of Milton's age, by his own linguistic knowledge and tastes.[45] A revolution in attitudes to the proper wit of poetry lies between Milton and Bentley. Consistently Bentley reveals his distaste for what Addison would have called 'false wit' in Milton; verbal play, puns, equivocations. The 'affected Jingle' of 'at one slight bound high over-leap'd all bound' (4. 181), for instance, is remedied by the change 'high overleap'd all FENCE'.[46] Bentley regularly objects to manifestations of the figurative in *Paradise Lost.* Extended similes are hooked.[47] Metaphoric expressions are questioned. To call Proserpine a 'flower' (4. 270) is in Bentley's view 'but fit for a Madrigal' (p. 116); there is no allowance for the recurrent resonance of the flower image as applied to Eve, 'fairest unsupported Flour' (9. 432). Even such restrained modes of figuration as metonymy and transferred epithet – Satan's 'impious crest', for example (6. 188) – are rejected as 'irregular' (p. 188). The philosophy and natural philosophy of Milton's poem, in questions large and small, is similarly tested by Bentley against his own standards. Milton's reference to 'the Female Bee' (7. 490), for example, puzzles Bentley, who wonders whether the phrase refers to 'an *Amazonian* Race without Males, or . . . one Female, common Mother of all the Hive'. Neither explanation consists with Bentley's knowledge, and both are dismissed as 'idle and idiotical Notions, against the Course and stated Rule of Nature' (p. 236).

Amongst such judgments, Bentley's commentary makes little reference to Milton's other works (only *Paradise Regained* and *Samson Agonistes* are cited with any frequency), or to the works of other English writers. In discussing matters of linguistic usage, of style, of natural science, of the history of ideas, Bentley does not go far in relating Milton's poem to the state of culture and knowledge in its own time. Rudolf Pfeiffer has remarked that Bentley's edition of Horace 'was not controlled by knowledge of the writer'.[48] It is evidently possible to allege the same of his edition of *Paradise Lost.*

Whatever the limitations in Bentley's scholarship may have been in his editorial work on Milton, it is clear that he acted with a strong and conscious purpose. The character and distinctiveness of that purpose is already indicated in a remark by Lewis Theobald, in the Preface to his edition of Shakespeare which appeared in the year following Bentley's *Paradise Lost.* Bentley's editing, argues Theobald, was 'a Performance of

45 For similar instances, see 4. 264; 6. 93.

46 P. 112. Compare Bentley's notes at 4. 530; 9. 11.

47 As at 4. 499–501, 4. 714–19.

48 Pfeiffer, *History of Classical Scholarship*, p. 154.

another species'. Bentley did not give 'us his corrections as the Original Text of the Author'; rather, 'the chief turn of his Criticism is plainly to shew the World, that if Milton did not write as He would have him, he ought to have wrote so'.[49] The implications of Theobald's penetrating comment, and much else, are taken a good deal further in a recent study by Robert Bourdette, which presents a hypothesis so significant as to require summary.[50] Bourdette argues that Bentley's work on the New Testament is directly followed by his engagement with *Paradise Lost* and that, indeed, 'as the one prodigious project faded, its place was taken by the study of that other sacred text'. For Bentley *Paradise Lost* was a divine poem, a significant part of the body of religious literature by which orthodox Christianity might be defended, and a poem which stood in an 'ambivalent position as a classical yet modern, secular yet sacred text'. Bentley's later obsession with the poem that asserted 'eternal providence' is already prefigured in the arguments of the Boyle Lectures. Bentley accords the poem 'scriptural status', and Milton the poet is apotheosized in Bentley's words in the Preface, spatiating 'at large through the Compass of the whole Universe' and surveying 'all Periods of Time from before the Creation to the Consummation of all Things' (sig. a3^{v}). Just as Bentley had believed in the possibility that the New Testament might be restored from its state of textual chaos to its 'Original Beauty', so he believed, Bourdette argues, that Milton's other Scripture might be made whole again. To do so would require, he insisted, an editor of his own powerful scholarship, not such a blunderer as Milton's interpolating 'friend', nor such an ignoramus as Anthony Collins, who had famously and self-revealingly complained of the range of knowledges required to make sense of the holy books. As an editor Bentley equated *Paradise Lost* with Scripture, and amended the poem by Scripture's standards, testing its language for scriptural clarity, simplicity, and sublimity of style, using parallel places within the poem to elucidate difficult passages, and rejecting passages of the fabulous and mythological as inconsistent with the truths of Scripture.

This is a powerful and attractive hypothesis, which has the major virtue of providing a possible explanation of much that is deeply problematic in Bentley's work. Certainly many things make against Bourdette's argument: the extraordinary freedom, persistence, and tone of Bentley's conjectural emendations; the paucity, in comparison with other commentators on Milton, of his use of parallel passages in his author's works, and indeed his lack of the detailed knowledge of his author necessary to such a use; his resort to many stylistic criteria of judgment which would be hard to relate to an aesthetic derived from the Bible; and the weaknesses of his knowledge

[49] *The Works of Shakespeare* (7 vols., 1733), I. xxxix–xl.

[50] Robert E. Bourdette, Jr, 'A sense of the sacred: Richard Bentley's reading of *Paradise Lost* as "divine narrative"', *Milton Studies*, 24 (1988), 73–106 (quotations are from pp. 83–9, 94).

of Milton's cultural and linguistic horizons, in comparison with that of other editors of Milton, and his failure therefore to interpret *Paradise Lost*, as a learned biblical commentator might explain Scripture, in relation to its context. At the least, as Bourdette readily acknowledges, Bentley's revisions, according to a scriptural stylistic standard, 'emerge . . . from an aesthetic and historical understanding very different from Milton's'.

Yet Bourdette is surely justified in arguing that it is precisely in Bentley's apparently quixotic challenge to the authority of author and document that the scriptural basis of his edition is to be found, and this is most particularly because in Bentley the concept of authorial intention undergoes a sea-change. Bentley's editing is not orientated towards a determination of what the real author John Milton wrote and meant in the poem *Paradise Lost*, but, it can be credibly argued, towards an ideal Milton, who might and should have written the ideal poem that Bentley's emendations, and, at last, re-writings, seek to re-construct. The essentially theological ground of Bentley's re-alignment of intention is suggested by a remarkable passage in Bentley's eighth Boyle Lecture, delivered in 1692:

> the body of a man, which consists of an incomprehensible variety of parts, all admirably fitted to their peculiar functions and the conservation of the whole, could no more be formed fortuitously than the *Aeneis* of Virgil, or any other longer poem with good sense and just measures, could be composed by the casual combinations of letters . . . as it is utterly impossible to be believed, that such a poem may have been eternal, transcribed from copy to copy without any first author or original; so it is equally incredible and impossible that the fabric of human bodies, which has such excellent and divine artifice and, if I may so say, such good sense and true syntax, and harmonious measures in its constitution, should be propagated and transcribed from father to son without a first parent and creator of it.[51]

Here Bentley sets out to demonstrate God's divine authorship of the creation by an analogy between the fitness and harmony of the human body and an epic poem, but the analogy of course works also in the other direction. The good sense and organized form of Virgil's epic is, like God's creation, the product of an intending, originating author. If that original harmony has become untuned in the course of transmission it becomes, as Rudolf Pfeiffer has argued in relating this passage to Bentley's classical editing, the task of the textual critic to restore it.[52] If Bentley's sense of this analogy can be extended to his editing of Milton, it may be possible to explain or to defend his procedures in his edition of the great English epic of scriptural truth as an attempt to recover Milton's originating, harmonious, quasi-divine creative act.

[51] Bentley, *Works*, ed. Alexander Dyce (3 vols., London: Macpherson, 1836–8), III. 200.
[52] Pfeiffer, *History of Classical Scholarship*, pp. 146–7. See also Bourdette, 'Sense of the sacred', p. 84.

Defending the Ark: Bentley's answerers, and the development of Miltonic editing

In some particular respects Bentley's edition may be thought typical of his time. Some of his aesthetic criteria, and especially his stylistic criteria, bear a relation to principles of clarity, simplicity, and decorum of a kind found in some contemporary neo-classicist criticism. Several recent commentators have also made the case that his revisal of *Paradise Lost* might be compared with that general impulse towards re-creation that can be seen in Dryden's 'dramatic transversion' of *Paradise Lost* (*The State of Innocence and the Fall of Man* (1677)), in Dryden's Virgil and Pope's Homer, or (amongst many 'improvements' of Shakespeare) Nahum Tate's regularization of *King Lear* (1681).[53]

Yet Bentley's *Paradise Lost* must not be seen as representative of eighteenth-century attitudes to editing. His contemporaries reacted to his conjectural method as applied to Milton with profound suspicion and dissent. They did so, as John Hale has remarked in an important study of this issue, 'for the very reason that it seemed eccentric'.[54] They had many grounds of objection: the abrasive and often dismissive tone of Bentley's notes, the infrequency of reference to other writings by Milton, failures to refer to Scripture or alleged misuses of scriptural parallels, conjecture inadequately grounded in bibliographical or textual evidence, the flimsiness of Bentley's hypothesis of the editor, the discovery of innumerable textual blemishes which no one might have suspected before Bentley took the poem in hand.[55]

What is most striking and significant about contemporary reaction is how clearly Bentley's contemporaries recognized in his edition its radically destabilizing re-assessment of the nature of authorial intention, of the relation of poet's and editor's authority, and of the scriptural status of the text.[56] Bentley's project was seen to threaten a replacement of author's sense by editor's, or reader's, sense. The anonymous author of *Milton Restor'd, and Bentley Depos'd* (1732) lamented that Milton, falling into Bentley's amending hands,

[53] See, for example, Robert E. Bourdette, Jr, '"To *Milton* lending sense": Richard Bentley and *Paradise Lost*', *Milton Quarterly*, 14 (1980), pp. 41–2; Hale, 'Paradise purified', pp. 62, 72–3; and my own 'Bentley our contemporary: or, editors, ancient and modern', in *The Theory and Practice of Text-Editing*, ed. Ian Small and Marcus Walsh (Cambridge: Cambridge University Press, 1991), p. 167.

[54] 'Notes on Richard Bentley's edition of *Paradise Lost* (1732)', *Milton Quarterly*, 18 (1984), 46–50.

[55] See, for example, *Grub Street Journal*, 25 June 1730 (quoted by Hale, 'Notes on Richard Bentley's edition', p. 48), 27 January 1732, and 2 March 1732 (in Shawcross II. 51, 57).

[56] Robert Bourdette briefly hints that Bentley's work on Milton 'helped lay the groundwork for the postmodern formulations of the relations between text and critic' ('Sense of the Sacred', p. 102), a notion I have pursued more polemically, and at greater length, in my 'Bentley our contemporary'.

loses his own Beauties thro the Corrector's want of Taste: who, because at first Sight, his purblind Genius finds not out his Author's Meaning, Substitutes a new Reading . . . The same Liberty may be assumed by every Reader, as by you, Doctor; and so the whole of Milton's, or any other Poem, extinguished by degrees, and a new one set forth by Editors, challenge the Title not of Notes, but of a Text variorum. (p. vii)

In the course of a lengthy attack on Bentley, Jonathan Richardson *père* urged the reader not to presume 'on his Own Sense of a Passage' but rather 'to come Honestly to receive *Milton*'s Sense'. Benjamin Stillingfleet, in the letter preceding his manuscript notes on *Paradise Lost*, complained that Bentley's alterations 'often totally destroy the Author's meaning'. And David Mallet famously wrote, with a proper irony, of Bentley 'to *Milton* lending sense', making the English poet, as he had made Horace, 'write what never Poet writ'.[57]

Equally striking, and of course closely related, is the opinion amongst Bentley's contemporaries that he was guilty of the desecration of the sacred scripture which, as we have seen, *Paradise Lost* was so commonly taken to be. Bentley's edition, which so signally failed to treat Milton's poem with the reverence due to Scripture, was greeted with a sense of outrage which articulated itself in metaphors of profanation. The *Weekly Register* insisted on the sanctity of standard authors: 'The Name of *Milton* was become as venerable as *Homer* or *Virgil*; we deem'd it Sacrilege to treat his Work irreverently.'[58] The author of *Milton Restor'd, and Bentley Depos'd* similarly shuddered at the blasphemy of Bentley's conjectural method: 'this way of restoring, *i.e.* interpolating by Guess, is so sacralegious an Intrusion, that, as it had its Rise, so it is to be hoped it will have its Fall with you' (p. viii). This figure would become standard use amongst those who took up the priestly task of defending great poets and their scriptures against the depredations of irreligious amenders, in the case not only of Milton, but also, as we shall see, of Shakespeare.

Precisely because Bentley's edition was so generally unacceptable it concentrated minds wonderfully. Milton's defenders had to engage with Milton's words at least as penetratingly and as closely as Bentley had done, though they did so usually with principles and methods very different from his. If Bentley's editorial orientation by most criteria was primarily aesthetic, the orientation of most subsequent editors and commentators was, I shall attempt to show, largely authorial, though aesthetic elements of course persisted, as they must, and though a rather strictly documentary orientation to the establishment of the text is to be found in the work of Newton and Capell. A remarkably high proportion of notes by later editors

[57] Richardson, *Explanatory Notes and Remarks*, p. cxxxiv; Stillingfleet, fol. 1^r (see note 67 below); Mallet, *Of Verbal Criticism*, lines 135–6.
[58] *Weekly Register*, Sat. 12 February 1732, quoted in *Gentleman's Magazine*, 2 (February 1732), 601.

begin as answers to Bentley. Resisting his aesthetically orientated conjectural emendations, they set out to justify witnessed readings by explication of what they took to be authorially intended meaning. The most distinguished of Bentley's successors read with a rigorous closeness, and a growing sense of the intellectual richness and poetic suggestivity of Milton's poem, that makes them, in the judgment of Christopher Ricks, who was one of the first modern critics to appreciate their interpretative insight, 'still in many ways the best guide to Milton'.[59] Essentially continuing, with all their differences of emphasis and substance, the project of explanation by paraphrase and contextualizing annotation which had been initiated by Hume, they further formulated and developed techniques of textual interpretation which would allow them to 'illustrate the sense and meaning' (in Thomas Newton's phrase) of Milton's learned, difficult, and culturally distant poem for a contemporary readership.

The most impressive immediate reply to Bentley was the long and learned *Review of the Text of Milton's Paradise Lost* (1732–3) by Zachary Pearce.[60] Pearce, who was Vicar of St Martin in the Fields when he wrote the *Review*, and was installed as Bishop of Rochester in 1756, was distinguished even amongst Miltonic commentators by his classical and biblical learning. He published editions of Cicero's *De Oratore* (1716) and *De Officiis* (1745), and of Longinus on the sublime (1724). He was also, unsurprisingly and significantly, a biblical annotator and periphrast: his *Commentary* on the Gospels and Acts was posthumously published in 1777.[61]

Pearce's *Review* is an outstanding example of what can be found in the work of many eighteenth-century editors and annotators of Milton; careful reasoning, and extensive classical, modern, and biblical scholarship, in the service of detailed explication. Pearce throughout takes a sceptical view of conjecture, in note after note defending Miltonic readings against Bentley's emendations by careful interpretative argument. He offers some amendments of his own to *Paradise Lost*, but only either 'to propose words of like sound, which a blind Poet's Ear may be presum'd to have been sometimes mistaken in, when the Proof-Sheets were read to him', or to correct errors at points where 'it is not improbable that *Milton* trusted much to the Care of the Printer and Reviser' (pp. iv–v). Rejecting Bentley's notion that 'there was any such *Person of an Editor*, as made Alterations and added Verses at his Pleasure' (p. v), Pearce conscientiously sets out to recover Milton's sense from the text, preferring, and opposing, explication to alteration. Pearce was a perceptive and sensitive reader, able to interrogate the poem, and to understand it with attention to its own terms. In discussing matters of style

59 Ricks, *Milton's Grand Style*, p. 13.

60 Part I (1732) offers remarks on *Paradise Lost*, Bks 1–4; Part II (1732) on Bks 5–8; and Part III (1733) on Bks 9–12.

61 *A Commentary, with Notes, on the Four Evangelists and the Acts of the Apostles* (2 vols., London, 1777).

and lexis he is prepared to allow for, and often to illustrate, differences in usage between his own time and Milton's. His interpretations frequently are supported by an informed engagement with Milton's own horizon of knowledge, biblical, theological, literary, intellectual, or natural. His interpretative procedures regularly include, as we might expect, paraphrase and the use of parallel places.

Typical of Pearce's response to Bentley's complaints about the lexis and usage of *Paradise Lost* is his comment on Bentley's note on this line describing Abdiel's assault on Satan: 'So saying, a noble stroke he lifted high' (6. 189). 'Vulgar Use (says the Doctor) has long since made *Noble Stroke* base and unfit for Heroic. But how long since? was it base before *M*'s writing of this? unless it was, the Objection is frivolous' (pp. 202–3). Pearce's argument is that the linguistic standards of 1667, not those of 1732, are the true basis for evaluation. There is a telling disagreement with Bentley at *Paradise Lost* 5. 741, where Pearce, refusing to accommodate the poem to a classicist aesthetic, prefers Milton's poetic and peculiar 'be dextrous' to Bentley's prosaic and clear 'prove able' since, in poetry, 'a Metaphorical and more Remote word is often preferable to the Simplest and Nearest, because it throws the Diction still more out of Prose' (p. 187). Bentley rejects Satan's

> memory
> Of what he was, what is, and what must be,
>
> (4. 24–5)

complaining that one cannot have 'Memory of Future'; 'but no doubt, in stead of *Memory*, the Author gave it . . . THEORY' (p. 106). Pearce justifies Milton's word by comparing it with the familiar phrase 'remember that you must die', and with the Latin *recordatio*: 'the thinking and reflecting upon any thing, as well present and future as past' (p. 107).

Pearce is almost always more sympathetic to Milton's figurative methods. Where Bentley objects to 'fierce Ensigns' (6. 356), Pearce explains, with a weary irony, ''Tis a Figure call'd Metonymy of the Part for the Whole, well known among Poets and Orators.' Milton describes Satan's persuasive power in his call to rebellion in heaven:

> His countenance, as the morning star that guides
> The starry flock, allured them, and with lies
> Drew after him the third part of heaven's host.
>
> (5. 708–10)

Bentley points out that, if this is the true text, 'the Construction will be, *His countenance allured and drew them with Lies*', rejects the underlying metaphor, and suggests an alternative reading: 'He is the *Father of Lies* indeed, if not his Tongue, but his Countenance spoke them. The Author gave it, *And* HIS *Lies*' (p. 172). Pearce begins by suggesting that 'by . . . *His Countenance* is meant He himself', but goes on to clarify and defend the operation of the metaphor: 'if this will not be allow'd to be *M*'s meaning, yet it may be said that *Satan*'s *Countenance* seducing his followers by disguising the foul intentions of his heart, may be very properly said to *seduce* WITH *Lyes*' (pp. 184–5). Even where he finds Milton's expression unsatisfactory, Pearce does not reject the 'correct' for the 'good' reading; the quibbling 'high over-leaped all bound' (4. 181) is accepted as Milton's intention (against Bentley's 'fence' and Pearce's preferred 'mound') because of the confirmation offered by the corresponding phrase in the Argument for Book 4: 'overleaps the bounds' (pp. 114–15).

Pearce's notes are especially frequently informed by a sense of how far the language of the Authorized Version influences, and warrants, Milton's usage. When Bentley comes across Eve's 'Virtue and the Conscience of her Worth' (8. 502) he objects, as usual applying the Horatian principle of the *usus loquendi* rather narrowly, that '*Conscience* is here taken in a Signification unwarranted by Use', and changes the word to 'Consciousness' (p. 259); Pearce restores 'Conscience', on the grounds that 'in our English Version of the Bible the word is often us'd in this sense', citing 1 Corinthians 8:7 and Hebrews 10:2 (pp. 279–80). Similarly, where Bentley had objected to the

Rites
Mysterious of connubial Love,

(4. 742–3)

changing the 'threadbare' epithet 'mysterious' to 'solennious' (p. 134), Pearce restores the original reading, 'for [Milton] plainly alludes to St *Paul*'s calling Matrimony *a mystery*, Eph. v.32' (p. 140). Elsewhere, Milton refers to the golden calf of the Israelites with the phrase 'grazed ox' (1. 486), which Bentley found 'silly and superfluous' (p. 22); Pearce justifies Milton's usage by invoking the authority of the account of the worship of the golden calf in Psalms 106:20: 'Thus they changed their glory into the similitude of an ox that eateth grass' (pp. 33–4).

Pearce appreciates that Milton's natural science depended on the state of knowledge in his own day. When Raphael tells Adam '[the Moon's] spots thou seest / As Clouds' (8. 145–6), Bentley objects that '[the Spots] of the Moon are permanent; and have appear'd the same since the first Memorial of them; and therefore cannot be Clouds' (p. 247). Pearce answers by referring to Auzout's observations of change in the moon-spots reported in the *Philosophical Transactions* of 1666: 'and *M.* who wrote this Poem about that time, might approve of *Auzout*'s observation, tho' the Doctor and I do not' (p. 272). Similarly, Pearce defends Milton's description of bees as female and drones as male (7. 490), on the grounds that 'both those Opinions had been strenuously maintain'd by Mr *Charles Butler* in the 4th Ch. of his curious Treatise upon Bees, entitled the *Feminine Monarchie*, printed in 1634: and it seems to have been the prevailing doctrine in *M*'s days' (pp. 261–2). Elsewhere, Pearce explains an apparent oddity by reference to the Bible. Bentley objects to Leviathan's 'skaly rind' (1. 206), since 'the Whale has no Skales' (p. 11), but Pearce points out that '[Milton] does not mean a Whale. He meant what *Job* did by Leviathan in ch. 41. where by his Description he makes it as much a *Beast* as a Fish, and in *v.* 15 speaks of its *Skales*' (p. 21). Here the authority for a reading is not Milton's horizon of natural science, but the word of Scripture to which Milton's poem alludes, and on which its meaning depends.

Pearce resorts to parallel places within Milton's own works as a regular interpretative instrument. Pearce and his contemporaries not infrequently rise to a sense of how verbal and figurative connections might function within the poem's larger structures of meaning, but their kind of parallelism is of course distinct from such a modern conception of the shaping web of figuration as has been exploited, to the most powerful and illuminating effect, by such critics as Rajan, Ricks, Fowler, and Fish.[62] The concern of the eighteenth-century commentators was rather to explain a crux by reference to an analogous passage at another place in the scripture, in the manner of biblical commentators, using (to invoke Locke's comment on the subject once more) 'one part of the Sacred Text' to 'give light unto another'.

In some cases Pearce uses parallels to lend support to a particular reading by establishing Milton's idiolect. Such an explanatory function of parallelism is seen even in quite simple cases. 'Busiris and his Memphian *chivalry*' (1. 307) must be an error, according to Bentley, who prefers 'cavalry' (p. 16); Pearce argues that, in Milton's usage, '*Chivalry* . . . signifys not only Knighthood, but those who use Horses in fight' (p. 28), pointing both to *Paradise Lost* 1. 765 and *Paradise Regained* 3. 344. There is resort both to the logic of the local verbal context in *Paradise Lost*, and to a parallel expression in another poem, in Pearce's defence of the 'night-foundered skiff' of 1. 204 against Bentley's emendation to 'nigh-founder'd':

By *night-founder'd M.* means overtaken by the night, and thence at a loss which way to sail. That the poet speaks of what befel the Pilot by Night, appears from *v.* 207.

[62] This has been presented by Frederick M. Keener as a shortcoming in the work of the eighteenth-century commentators. Professor Keener considers that they were not much 'aware of parallels as inviting a distinct . . . approach to understanding the text', and that they had little sense that internal parallels could be 'central to author and readers' construction of the work' ('Parallelism and the poets' secret: eighteenth-century commentary on *Paradise Lost*', *Essays in Criticism*, 37 (1987), 281–302 (pp. 281, 282)). It is not however surprising that, having chosen to posit a very recent conception of parallelism as normative, Keener should find Pearce and his contemporaries wanting. Keener seems to me to underestimate the specifically interpretative function and value of their use of parallel places, and the similarity of their methods to those of classical and, more especially, biblical scholarship.

While Night invests the Sea &c. *Milton* [in *Comus* 483] uses the same Phrase: the two Brothers having lost their way in the wood, one of them says

for certain
Either some one, like us,
NIGHT-FOUNDER'D *here* &c.

(pp. 20–1)

Pearce's use of parallel places frequently involves not only perceptive interpretation of a particular passage, but also a sense of the poem's larger implications and resonances. Bentley objects to Eve's 'Matron lip' (4. 501), but Pearce thinks the expression 'the very properest that *M.* could have pick'd out: It is the opposite to *Virgin* Lip, and means more than *womanly*: it implies that she was married to him, and that therefore the Kisses, which he gave her, were lawful, pure and innocent: we have in XI. 136. *first* MATRON *Eve*' (p. 128). There is a similar awareness of predictions and relations in the poem's larger discourse in Pearce's comment on the account of Mammon's pioneering brigade in hell:

Soon had his crew
Opened into the Hill a spacious wound
And dig'd out ribs of Gold.

(1. 688–90)

Bentley objects to the logic: 'They could not dig out *Ribs* of Gold when presently *v.* 703. they melt the Ore . . . Better therefore thus, *Dig'd out* THE SEEDS *of Gold*' (p. 31). Pearce not only justifies the reading in terms of its immediate context – '[Milton] . . . meant veins of Gold-Ore, which are a sort of *Ribs* to the Earth' – but goes on to establish that Milton's choice of words opens the possibility of a suggestive metaphoric connection: 'I don't doubt but the Poet here . . . alludes to the formation of Eve VIII. 463. he *Open'd my Left, and took from thence a Rib: – wide was the wound.*'[63]

Interpretative parallels with other authors, ancient and modern, are used by Pearce to similar explanatory effect. The use of external parallels has long been suspicious to the Romantic and post-Romantic mind. Coleridge complained bitterly that the commentators on Milton were obsessed with sources, 'as if it was part of their Creed, that all Thoughts are traditional'.[64] The search for literary echoes can no doubt at its most mechanical turn into a mere exercise in 'literary reminiscence', in which memory is the faculty mostly employed, as Lawrence Lipking has judged it to do in the case of Thomas Warton's *History of English Poetry*.[65] Certainly

[63] Pearce, *Review*, p. 43. See Ricks's discussion of this passage (*Milton's Grand Style*, p. 141).
[64] In a letter to an unknown correspondent, December 1811, cited in Joseph A. Wittreich, Jr, ed., *The Romantics on Milton* (Cleveland and London: The Press of Case Western Reserve University, 1970), pp. 201–2.
[65] *The Ordering of the Arts in Eighteenth-Century England* (Princeton: Princeton University Press, 1970), pp. 388–9.

the eighteenth-century editors tracked Milton everywhere in the ancients' snow, and in the moderns' too, for purposes that were aesthetic as well as interpretative. 'When one good Poet imitates another' there arises, for many eighteenth-century minds, a second pleasure, additional to the primary pleasure of mimesis, 'from comparing the one Description with the other from which it was imitated'.[66] The energetic quest for precedents throughout eighteenth-century editing has also the important effect of claiming for the author a relation to distinguished literary forebears, a place in a literary history. For Pearce, however, and for many other eighteenth-century commentators on both Milton and Shakespeare, the identification of an author's literary allusions, and a rigorous analysis of how the author exploits, incorporates, and modifies particular allusions, is a necessary step towards understanding his sense. The point is articulated particularly explicitly in Benjamin Stillingfleet's manuscript notes on *Paradise Lost*.[67] Stillingfleet was persuaded that Bentley's persistent interpretative stumbles arose from his 'never once making use of the Advantage his Knowledge of the Greek & Latin tongues gave him'. Stillingfleet's own comments on *Paradise Lost*, which make especially extensive reference to classical sources, are rarely original, but they illustrate his conviction that the explication of Milton's sense is at least partly dependent on a knowledge of Milton's literary referents. Some of the most difficult passages, Stillingfleet tells us, 'I should never have been able to understand without recurring to [the] very same sources, from whence they were originally taken.'[68] The key word here is 'understand': the finding of sources, allusions, and parallels outside Milton's writing is seen by Stillingfleet, as by others, as having primarily an interpretative purpose. In the most intellectually rigorous of the eighteenth-century commentators on both Milton and Shakespeare, certainly including Pearce, the selection and application of literary parallels puts to a genuinely interpretative end the resources of formidably well-stocked minds.

One of Pearce's frequent uses of classical authors, or of their commentators, is his engagement with Bentley over the reading '*ridges* of grim war' in the account of the war in heaven (6. 236). Bentley had already suggested an

66 Anon., *An Essay upon Milton's Imitation of the Ancients, in His Paradise Lost* ([Edinburgh] 1741), in Shawcross II. 121.

67 Benjamin Stillingfleet, 1702–71, grandson of Edward Stillingfleet, Bishop of Worcester (1635–99), is described by the *Dictionary of National Biography* as 'naturalist and dilettante'; he intended an edition of *Paradise Lost* but Thomas Newton's *Proposals* for his edition prevented him. Stillingfleet's manuscript notes on *Paradise Lost* are interleaved in a copy of Bentley's edition now in the British Library (C.134.h.1). For a somewhat fuller account of Stillingfleet, see my 'Bentley our contemporary', pp. 173–4.

68 Letter to 'D___' [Dr Thomas Dampier, whose bookplate this copy bears], dated 27 April 1746, interleaved with the Arguments printed before the beginning of Book I in British Library, C.134.h.1, fol. 1^r.

echo of the Homeric phrase πολεμοιο γεφυρας (*Iliad*, 4. 371), by which, he suggests, the Greek poet refers to 'the open Intervals between Rank and File' (p. 190). However, Bentley knows that γεφυραι are, 'in common acceptation, *Bridges*', and therefore proposes to adopt that word in place of Milton's 'ridges', an expression he professes not to understand. Pearce, however, improving on Bentley's scholarship, is prepared to argue that it is the Homeric sense which underpins Milton's metaphor: 'The word *Ridge* signifies the space between two Furrows; and this acceptation of the word *M.* has transferr'd to the Spaces between Rank and File, when an Army is set in array' (p. 208). C. S. Lewis, two centuries later, remarks that this whole passage of the *Paradise Lost* 'is full of Homeric echoes', and refers 'ridges' to the same Homeric phrase – 'but what *they* were I do not know'.[69] Pearce's note not only answers Bentley, but provides a credible explanation of the witnessed reading, and an account of the working of Milton's figure, in its relation to a likely poetic source. Bentley's scholarly comment, and Pearce's interpreting reply, are instances of what at the best was possible to early commentators who could feel themselves at home in a world of classical letters and philology that they shared with Milton. But Pearce makes some use also of poets much nearer Milton's time, both in defending Milton's taste and in illuminating his sense. He defends 'larbord' (2. 1019), for example, a word which in Bentley's view 'in Heroic Stile is abominable' (p. 74), noting that it had been used by Dryden, in his translation of Virgil's *Aeneid*.[70] At greater length, Pearce explains the wording of Milton's claim to pursue 'things unattempted yet in prose or rhyme' (1. 16). Bentley had suggested the original reading, 'rhime', be changed to 'song', complaining that ''Tis very odd, that *Milton* should put *Rime* here as equivalent to *Verse*, who had just before declar'd against *Rime*, as *no true Ornament to good Verse*' (pp. 1–2). Pearce carefully explains that Milton here means 'not the *jingling sound of like Endings*, but Verse in general', arguing that the difference in spelling between Milton's Preface ('Rime') and poem ('Rhime') is intended and significant (pp. 4–6). Pearce justifies his preferred sense, not only by discussion of the source line in Ariosto, which Bentley had noticed ('Cosa, non detta in *Prosa* mai, ne in *Rima*'), but also by the use of 'rhime' for poetry in general in Spenser's Dedicatory Sonnet to Lord Buckhurst prefatory to the *Faerie Queene*, and of course in *Lycidas*:

> he knew
> Himself to sing, and build the lofty rhyme.
>
> (lines 10–11)

Paraphrase is a common explicatory strategy in Pearce's notes, as one

[69] Lewis's comment is the main gloss offered on Milton's line by Alastair Fowler.

[70] Pearce, *Review*, pp. 78–9. Addison also notes this parallel with Dryden (*Aeneis* 3. 526), and condemns both poets for it (*Spectator*, 297; Addison, *Spectator*, III. 63–4).

might expect of a biblical scholar. Bentley had invited any reader offended by Satan's 'Jingle', 'a chance but chance may lead' (4. 530), to 'alter it thus, or several other ways; SOME LUCKY *chance may lead*' (p. 125); Pearce suggests clarifying the line by parenthesizing 'but chance', and interprets with the paraphrase 'a *Chance*, and it can be only *a Chance*'.[71] The difficult syntax of Satan's complaint of his

foul descent! that I . . .
. . . am now constrained
Into a beast, and mix'd with bestial slime
This essence to incarnate and imbrute

(9. 163–6)

is defended against another Bentleian emendation ('am now constrain'd / INCLOS'D IN Beast', p. 272) by the simple expansion of an ellipsis and straightening of a transposition: 'but why may not the Construction be this? *Am now constrain'd into a Beast, and* (am) *mix'd with bestial Slime to incarnate and imbrute this Essence*' (p. 298). Somewhat more complex is Pearce's discussion of lines describing the creating act of the Holy Spirit:

Then founded, then conglobed
Like things to like, the rest to several place
Disparted, and between spun out the air,
And earth self-balanced on her centre hung.

(7. 239–42)

Bentley objects to almost everything in this richly suggestive passage, and proposes to re-write it almost entirely:

FOUR ELEMENTS THEN ROSE,
Like things to like, FIRE TO THE HIGHEST place
Disparted, and between spun out the Air,
And Earth TERRAQUEOUS on her Center hung.

(p. 225)

Pearce answers each of Bentley's many points of complaint at some length, but at the centre of his rebuttal is a careful paraphrase, which begins by placing the lines in their densely interwoven and syntactically extended poetic context, and goes on to elicit Milton's intentions by gloss and explanatory expansion:

M. had said that Messiah first purg'd downward the Infernal Dregs, which were adverse to Life; and that then of things friendly to Life he *founded and conglob'd* like to like, *i.e.* he caus'd them to assemble and associate together: the *rest*, i.e. such things as were not of the same nature and fit for composing the Earth, went off to other places, perhaps to form the Planets and fix'd Stars. This seems to be *M*'s meaning. (p. 245)

[71] Pearce, *Review*, pp. 129–30. Fowler paraphrases almost identically: 'It is only a chance; but chance *may* lead'.

Bentley's re-writing of Milton's poem here, as often, is effectively a proposal of improvement. By contrast, the purpose of Pearce's paraphrase, composed as a direct answer to Bentley, is to explain Milton's intended meaning as it is expressed in the words of the first witnesses.

Pearce's *Review* was shortly followed by one of the more remarkable eighteenth-century works of Miltonic commentary, the *Explanatory Notes and Remarks on Milton's Paradise Lost* (1734) by Jonathan Richardson, father and son. Most of this volume was in fact composed by Richardson senior, the portrait painter and art theorist, though he invites the reader to consider that, where he draws on scholarship possessed by his son but not by himself, he is to be understood as 'the Complicated *Richardson*' (p. cxli). Richardson's lengthy Preface is idiosyncratic as well as entertaining, yet it articulates with exceptional fullness and clarity some of the central theoretical ideas, particularly in the areas of intention and of the authority of poet and text, which were, I would wish to argue, generally shared by Bentley's successors.

In answer to Bentley's assumption of the careless or dishonest intervention of the poem's first editor, Richardson provides an extended account of the transmission from author's mind to print of the first two editions of *Paradise Lost*, concluding, as almost all his contemporaries had done or would do, that 'the Edition of 1674 is the Finish'd, the Genuine, the Uncorrupted Work of *John Milton*' (pp. cxxv ff., cxxxviii). Richardson is not concerned simply with justifying the care of the first printers however; rather he insists that the editions of 1667 and 1674 adequately convey the intended meaning of their author, 'the True Thought of the Poet'. Any 'Intelligent Reader', who does not, with Bentley, presume 'on his Own Sense of a Passage, and Then Blames the Words or Points as not Expressive of That', will find in these first two editions '*Milton's* Sense' (pp. clxvii, cxxxiv–cxxxv). Using an imagery which was already becoming familiar in Shakespearean as well as Miltonic editing, Richardson states his unwillingness to lay sacrilegious hands upon the first textual witnesses: 'We have Reverenc'd our Text, have handled it as Somthing which it would be a Sort of Prophaneness, as well as a Ridiculous Presumption in Us to Aim at Improving, by Adding or Diminishing . . . 'tis his Author's Thoughts, not his Own, which the Publick Expects from an Expositor, and Such Only We pretend to be' (pp. clxxiii–clxxiv). The text is sacred not merely as a text, but because it embodies the author's meaning. It is the business of the 'expositor' to communicate the author's meaning to the reader. In pointed response to the Bentleian claim of authority for the editor, Richardson subordinates his authority to that of the author and of the text he produced. The text is the author's scripture or testament. Richardson's warning against 'Adding or Diminishing' echoes, perhaps deliberately, both the 'main Precept' of the Father's Will in Swift's *Tale of a Tub* – not to 'add to, or diminish from' the coats which represent the Christian religion – and Swift's own source, St John's injunction in Revelation against textual omissions and additions:

If any man shall add unto these things, God shall add unto him the plagues that are written in this book:
And if any man shall take away from the words of the book of this prophecy, God shall take away his part out of the book of life.[72]

Richardson's volume is not of course an edition, but he promises that the passages selected for comment in the body of the Explanatory Notes 'are Printed just as we find them in the Authentick Edition of 74'.[73] Avoiding textual alteration, he announces unequivocally his purpose of explicating Milton's intended meaning, even postulating, something William Rushworth had rejected as impossible in the case of the penmen of Scripture, a resurrected Milton come back to life to explain his own words: 'we have had but One Single Point in View, That Important One, to give Our Author's Sense, as we Conceiv'd He would have Explain'd Himself, had he risen from his Urn and Dictated to Us' (p. clxxii). Somewhat more conventionally, and in words that recall the Protestant principle of explaining Scripture by itself, Richardson undertakes to arrive at Milton's sense in *Paradise Lost* in the light of 'what he has said in Other Parts of his Work, or in Other Works of His, and brought him to be his own Expositor' (p. clxxii).

Few were more alert than Richardson to Milton's linguistic richness, density of suggestion, and economy of expression. A strikingly eloquent passage in his Preface urges upon his reader, as upon himself, the consequent necessity of information and attention if we are to fulfil our obligation to interpret the author's meaning:

a Reader of *Milton* must be Always upon Duty; he is Surrounded with Sense, it rises in every Line, every Word is to the Purpose; . . . [Milton] Expresses himself So Concisely, Employs Words So Sparingly, that whoever will Possess His Ideas must Dig for them, and Oftentimes pretty far below the Surface . . . if a Good Writer is not Understood 'tis because his Reader is Unacquainted with, or Incapable of the Subject, or will not Submit to do the Duty of a Reader, which is to Attend Carefully to what he Reads. (pp. cxliv–cxlv)

Richardson attends very carefully to what he reads, in over 500 pages of explanatory notes, and is always concerned with making out his author's sense. The account of Adam and Eve in the fourth book (4. 321ff.) is

[72] *A Tale of a Tub*, ed. A. C. Guthkelch and D. Nichol Smith (2nd edition, corrected, Oxford: Oxford University Press, 1973), p. 81; Revelation 22:18, 19. It may be a coincidence that the note identifying Swift's source was first added to *A Tale of a Tub* in the edition of 1734.

[73] Richardson provides a list of minor errors in his transcriptions of the text: *Explanatory Notes and Remarks*, pp. 537–41.

written in intelligible words, but nonetheless, if we are fully to take in Milton's intended meaning, requires exposition: 'to Understand an Author is to have a clear and Distinct Idea, the Same That Author Has, and would communicate. What Images were Intended to be set before us?' (p. 156). Richardson's concern in this note is partly with the 'Delightful Picture' that Milton would draw for us, and which Richardson proceeds to set out at length. There could hardly, however, be a more explicit statement than he offers here of his (essentially humanist) theoretical assumption, almost universally shared with his contemporaries, that meaning is intended by an author and communicated by his poem to the reader; and that it is the editor's duty to facilitate that communication.

Richardson is everywhere sensitive to verbal implication, and especially to the resonances of etymological with derived senses. In his listing of the rebel angels, Milton refers to those who would become the idols of heathen religion, profaning God's feasts, and daring to 'affront his light' (I. 391). Taking the object of his interpretation as usual to be the meaning intended by the author, and supporting his reading by the local verbal logic, Richardson explains the etymological derivation and force of 'affront': 'This Word Carries a Stronger Sense than what is commonly intended by it, though it also has That; it is from the *Italian Affrontare*, to Meet Face to Face; an Impudent Braving. the Context shews This was the Authors Idea' (p. 29). He discerns, too, a more poignant equivocation, in Eve's words persuading Adam to join her in the first crime:

> Were it I thought death menaced would ensue
> This my attempt, I would sustain alone
> The worst, and not persuade thee rather die
> Deserted, than oblige thee with a fact
> Pernicious to thy peace.
>
> (9. 977–81)

Richardson points out, supporting his assertion both by reference to a parallel place within the poem, and to an analogy in classical usage, that

> the Word *Oblige* here is capable of a Double Sense. Either to Tie to, to Drag Along With, or After, or to make Guilty, and Punishable, to Devote to Death, as *v.* 901. *Obligare Morti.* So *Hor.* Od. II. 8, 5.
>
> – Sed tu simul Obligasti
> Perfidum Votis Caput.
>
> Both Senses are Included.
>
> (p. 432)

Comparison of places is used regularly by Richardson, often with a striking interpretative intelligence, and some feeling for the larger structures and arguments of the poem. Adam wakes early in Paradise,

for his sleep
Was airy light from pure digestion bred,
And temperate vapours bland.

(5. 3–5)

Pausing only to gloss 'bland' as 'Pleasing, Chearful', from the Latin *blandus*, Richardson goes on to explore the implications of this account by contrasting it with Milton's very different account of post-lapsarian sleep:

the Sleep of a Happy Man; the Sleep of Nature, the Sleep of Temperance, Innocence and Contentment. the Sleep of Paradise; in Opposition to

Grosser Sleep
Bred of Unkindly Fumes, with Conscious Dreams
Encumberd.

(IX.1049) and from Whence the Sleeper Arises *as from Unrest*, and finds the Morning, *all Unconcern'd* at That, has begun *her Rosie Progress Smiling*. XI. 173. (pp. 192–3)

There are also frequent explicatory uses of parallels outside *Paradise Lost*, especially in the classics. It is 'the Complicated *Richardson*', presumably, who explains by reference to Virgil that, in the depiction of Satan facing the forces of heaven, while 'on his crest / Sat Horror plum'd' (4. 988–9), 'Horror is Personiz'd, and is made to sit on the Cone of the Helmet, as the Ancients plac'd Sphynxes, Dragons, *&c.* there Horror sits shaded with a Plume of Feathers, as the Chimaera on the Helmet of *Turnus*, Aen. VIII. 785' (p. 186). Parallels too are invoked from Milton's other writings. Some of the possible spiritual resonances of Adam's waking in Paradise, his heart overflowing 'with fragrance and with joy' (8. 265–6), are suggested by Richardson's comparison, in the course of a long explanatory note, with a similar expression in the *Reformation of Church Discipline*: 'Methinks a Sovereign and Reviving Joy must needs Rush into the Bosom of him that Reads or hears; and the sweet Odour of the Returning Gospel Imbath his Soul with the *Fragrance* of Heaven.'[74]

The most persistently employed of all Richardson's modes of interpretation, however, as in Hume and Pearce, is paraphrase. A very high proportion of his notes set out to clarify obscurities by reversing transpositions and filling in ellipses, often in a very straightforward way. The trees of Paradise bear golden fruit,

Hesperian fables true,
If true, here only, and of delicious taste.

(4. 250–2)

Richardson explains: 'What is said of the *Hesperian* Gardens is True Here only; if all is not Pure invention This Garden was meant. and Moreover

[74] P. 368. The reference is to *Of Reformation Touching Church-Discipline in England* (1641), p. 6.

these Fruits have a Delicious Taste, Those There had None' (p. 150).[75] At a number of points Richardson provides a rather different kind of outline account of more extended passages in Milton's poem. The dialectical twists and turns of Satan's anguished account of his fall, and commitment of himself to evil (4. 32ff.), are a natural candidate for such Richardsonian summary, a freely periphrastic sketch or argument, set off by quotation marks, to guide the reader:

''tis Address'd to the Sun who appearing Alone in the Heavens he Imagines seems the God of this New World, tells him he Hates his Beams which put him in mind of the Glory Himself had, 'till he Lost it by his Pride and Ambition; Reproaches his own Ingratitude and Malice, Disdaining Subjection, and Presuming One Step higher would Discharge the Debt, and Ease him of the Burthen of it, Fancy's he had not Fell had he been an Inferior Angel, but soon sees, the Folly of That Thought'.[76]

Elsewhere, paraphrase or near paraphrase articulates the closest and most penetrating discriminations and disentanglings of verbal sense, as in Richardson's extended discussion of the lines describing Adam's first waking in Paradise:

all things smiled,
With fragrance and with joy my heart o'erflowed.
(8. 265–6)

Richardson explains his preference for this, the punctuation of the two editions of Milton's lifetime, over later editions which moved the comma to follow 'fragrance':

In the One *Adam* says, All things Smiling, his Heart overflow'd with Fragrance and Joy; in the Other, that All things Smil'd with Fragrance, and his Heart o'erflow'd with Joy: Both are Beautyful, but we will Adhere to the First, not only because 'tis as in *Milton*'s Own Editions, . . . but This Sense is the Best; it takes in the other, and with an Additional, and more Noble Idea. All things Smile, not with Fragrance Only, but in Every respect. (p. 367)

So Richardson's use of paraphrase allows him to argue, as Pearce had so frequently done, for the less conventional, more difficult, and more suggestive reading, as recorded in the first editions.

Richardson's extensive use of paraphrase is substantially a response to the 'peculiarity' of Milton's poetic language. Richardson points in his Preface to Milton's adventures with word order, to his daring and elliptical syntax, and to what he and most of his contemporaries took to be the persistently Greek and Latin idiom of his poetry:

[75] P. 150. Such simple paraphrasing explanations are everywhere: compare, for example, Richardson's explanations of 1. 93–7 (pp. 16–17), 1. 589 (p. 39), 4. 381 (p. 162), 4. 944 (p. 184).
[76] Pp. 139–40. For another example, see Richardson's note on 1. 156 (p. 19).

Words Seldom or Not at all Us'd in English, or not in the Sense *Milton* Understands them, which is generally That in which Those from whence they were derived to us were taken by the People who Originally made use of them; . . . His Transpositions and Syntax are more Bold and Masterly than English Readers are Us'd to; and Lastly, he is a Notable Oeconomist of his Words, he leaves it to his Reader to Supply Some which a Common Writer would have furnish'd them with. (pp. clxvi–clxvii)

These are qualities which had already been investigated, and defended against Bentley's criticisms, by Pearce. Increasingly, eighteenth-century commentators recognized, appreciated, and described Milton's peculiar poetic methods. In his 'Examination of *Milton*'s Stile', notably, Francis Peck provides a numbered account of the particular features of Milton's linguistic 'singularity', including archaism, ellipsis, repetition, Graecisms, Latinisms, technical terms, a number of varieties of change of part of speech, and several kinds of transposition.[77] The difficulties of comprehension caused by Milton's language were a regular and central concern amongst editors and annotators of his poetry, and paraphrase continued to be persistently employed as a key method of elucidation.

The attempt to explicate meaning by resort to terms other than those of the poem itself offends of course against that Romantic and post-Romantic orthodoxy which is expressed in Coleridge's celebrated claim 'that it would be scarcely more difficult to push a stone out from the pyramids with the bare hand, than to alter a word, or the position of a word, in Milton or Shakspeare . . . without making the author say something else, or something worse, than he does say'.[78] Post-Romantically, we understand how far the organic uniqueness of Milton's poem is bound up with its distinctive rhetorical methods, amongst them its manipulations of normal syntactical ordering. Stanley Fish for example has taught us the importance of Milton's strategies of entrapment and surprise, so dependent on his extended periods, equivocal syntax, and deferred resolutions.[79] To cite just one amongst his many detailed analyses of the poem which opened up new worlds of interpretative possibility, Christopher Ricks has shown how, in the opening of Milton's epic, the delaying of the predicator 'sing' allows Milton both to state and to contain 'the magnitude of the poem's subject'.[80]

Eighteenth-century writers persistently reworded Milton, and twentieth-century literary historians have often blamed them for it. John Shawcross names a number of redactions and laments 'the lack of perception of

[77] *New Memoirs of the Life and Poetical Works of Mr John Milton* (1740), pp. 105–32.
[78] *Biographia Literaria*, ed. James Engell and W. Jackson Bate (2 vols., London: Routledge, and Princeton: Princeton University Press, 1983), p. 23.
[79] *Surprised by Sin* (London: Macmillan, and New York: St Martin's, 1967).
[80] *Milton's Grand Style*, pp. 28–9.

achievement, the assumption of "correctness"' manifested by such eighteenth-century re-writings.[81] I would wish to argue, however, that neither lack of understanding, nor the wish to improve, lies behind the greater part of eighteenth-century paraphrase. Most commentators employed paraphrase as Hume had done in its interpretative, rather than its evaluative, function, setting out to clarify Milton's meaning by putting it in other, more readily comprehensible, terms. They did not, on the whole, do so in order to flatten and homogenize the particularities of Miltonic expression: many eighteenth-century commentators had a sophisticated sense of the poem's rhetoric, and often an extraordinarily energetic and penetrating insight into the detailed movements of its meaning. Many of them nonetheless took the severely practical view that Milton's syntax, and in particular his alterations of 'a natural or plain *English Prose-Order*',[82] created difficulties for all but the most practised readers. Such an attitude may imply a different understanding of what poetry is and how it operates. It is also however part of a project to use paraphrase, not to supplant Milton's poem, but to make available what was taken to be its literal meaning, just as a biblical paraphrase would.

The extreme case of redaction is represented by George Smith Green's full-length prose version, which was printed in 1745 together with the notes of Nicolas de St Maur.[83] Green's periphrastic methods and purposes are worth brief examination. These are the opening lines of Milton's poem:

> Of man's first disobedience, and the fruit
> Of that forbidden tree, whose mortal taste
> Brought death into the world, and all our woe,
> With loss of Eden, till one greater man
> Restore us, and regain the blissful seat,
> Sing heavenly Muse, that on the secret top
> Of Oreb, or of Sinai, didst inspire
> That shepherd, who first taught the chosen seed,
> In the beginning how the heavens and earth
> Rose out of chaos:

This, in slightly edited form, is the beginning of Green's paraphrase:

> Heavenly Spirit of Truth and Harmony assist me! to write of Man's first Disobedience, and of the Fruit of that forbidden Tree, the Tasting of which brought Death and all our Woe into the World, and occasion'd the Loss of Paradise, till JESUS CHRIST, a Man far greater than ADAM, restore and redeem, and once more regain a Paradise for us. THOU, who from the thick Clouds on the secret

[81] Shawcross II. 4.
[82] James Paterson, *A Complete Commentary . . . on Milton's Paradise Lost* (London, 1744), p. vi.
[83] *The State of Innocence* (London: T. Osborne and York: J. Hildyard, 1745). There are later editions of 1755 (London), 1765 (London or Scotland), 1767 (London), 1770 (Aberdeen), 1770 (London).

Top of Mount OREB, . . . or, perhaps, SINAI . . ., didst inspire MOSES when a shepherd there, who first taught the Children of ISRAEL, how Heaven and Earth were created from the Elements, which were till then nothing but a mix'd and confus'd Heap, and without Form. (*State of Innocence*, pp. 2–3)

Whatever we have in Green's prose version, of course, it is not Milton's *Paradise Lost.* Some of the changes certainly reflect altered cultural perspective. Some of Milton's senses are lost, and some new ones are created. The resonantly poetic 'mortal taste' disappears, and 'sing' becomes the less figurative 'assist me to write'. 'Heavenly Muse' is de-hellenized and expanded into 'Heavenly Spirit of Truth and Harmony', and the Christian message is made more emphatic: Christ not only restores but also 'redeems'. Most of the alterations, however, amount to explication, designed to make this passage more comprehensible for the common reader. There are a number of re-orderings of the difficult transpositions: the adjunct 'into the world' in line 3 no longer separates the components of the compound object, 'death and all our woe', and, of course, the suspended predicator 'sing' from line 6 is moved to its normal position. Allusions are clarified. 'One greater man' is identified, for the reader whose recollection of Paul is imperfect, as Christ, and 'that Shepherd' is identified as Moses. Explanation, however, goes further than this. Green's introduction of the phrase 'thick clouds', and retention of the epithet 'secret' for the top of Mount Oreb, for instance, provides the reader with a succinct response to a small skirmish in the eighteenth-century debate about the poem's meaning. Green implicitly rejects Bentley's emendation to '*sacred* top', accepting the explanation offered by commentators from Hume onwards, that 'secret' refers to the privacy of Moses's meeting with God, and alluding more specifically to the account in Exodus 19:16 of a 'thick cloud upon the mount'.

Reductively, Green's prose version might be taken for a crib, and a crib may be used as an alternative, rather than an aid. The way in which his paraphrase unfolds, expands, and glosses the original might suggest however that it is intended to be read with, and not instead of, Milton's poem. The formal resemblance of Green's book to the biblical paraphrase with commentary, Green's prose version running in parallel with St Maur's scholarly, detailed, and lengthy annotations, is compromised only by the absence from his page of the scriptural text itself.[84] The frequent reprintings of Green's work suggest that eighteenth-century readers found it as helpful, and as necessary, as they found the popular guides to sacred Scripture. Green set out neither to replace nor to improve *Paradise Lost* but to explain it. He asserts in his Preface that 'this Work is not done to

[84] This might be explained on grounds of economy and bulk, or some residual nervousness about Tonson's hold, in practice if not in law, of copyright.

insinuate that it is superior to or in any Way equal to the Poetry of *Paradise Lost*; but, on the contrary, design'd only to make it more intelligible'. What Green claimed for his full prose version might have been claimed, *a fortiori*, on behalf of the more selective uses of explanatory paraphrase by other Miltonic editors and commentators.

A new edition: Thomas Newton's variorum

A highly significant and in many respects representative indication of the directions of mid eighteenth-century editing of Milton may be found in Thomas Newton's great variorum *Paradise Lost* of 1749.[85] Like Pearce, Newton was a rising Churchman when he turned to Milton, occupying from 1744 the rectory of St Mary le Bow, and in 1760 becoming Bishop of Bristol. His edition of *Paradise Lost* is, like Pearce's *Review*, recognizably the work of a biblical scholar. Newton is a rare case of an editor who undertook all the three functions of editing as the eighteenth century understood the science: establishing the text, explaining difficulties, and pointing out beauties and defects. His text is based on a rigorous examination and use of the original documents, which he took to be an adequate record of Milton's intentions. His commentary has marked evaluative tendencies, but it is characterized also by the application and development of many of the distinctive interpretative techniques of authorially based editing which we have already seen in Hume and Pearce.

Newton begins his Preface with a clear statement of his view of the function of his work:

> To publish new and correct editions of the works of approved authors has ever been esteemed a service to learning . . . It is not material whether the author is ancient or modern. Good criticism is the same in all languages. Nay I know not whether there is not greater merit in cultivating our own language than any other . . . My design in the present edition is to publish the Paradise Lost, as the work of a classic author cum notis variorum. (I. sig. a2^{r})

The canon of authors who are worthy of learned editing has now expanded to include modern and vernacular authors. To publish Milton in a variorum edition is to insist quite explicitly on his status as a classic. Newton's was the first Miltonic variorum, and certainly distinctive in annotational fullness and coherence. The handsome Royal Quarto format reinforces the claim of prestige. The poetic text is broadly leaded and set in

[85] *Paradise Lost* (2 vols., London, 1749). The edition of *Paradise Lost* was followed by *Paradise Regain'd. A Poem, in Four Books. To which is Added Samson Agonistes: and Poems upon Several Occasions. A New Edition with notes of Various Authors* (London, 1752), constituting the third volume of Newton's complete edition of the *Poetical Works of John Milton*.

a large type, with generous margins. The notes, set at the foot in a smaller type in double columns, and often occupying half the page, include the remarks both of Newton himself, and of previous and contemporary commentators. Newton cites a number of authorities on a regular basis. Addison is particularly fully represented, providing a body of evaluative criticism congruent with Newton's own. Extracts from Addison's *Spectator* papers which relate to particular passages in Milton's poem appear in the appropriate place in the notes, while his more generalized remarks are printed before the text. Bentley is quoted on many occasions, usually accompanied by the replies of Zachary Pearce. Other regular sources are Hume, the Richardsons, Heylin, and Jortin. In addition there are occasional citations of comments by Warburton, Lauder, Benson, Upton, and Onslow. The notes of Mr Thyer, 'librarian at Manchester', received late by Newton, are printed in an extended Appendix. Newton's variorum can be represented as a cooperative exercise, in which Newton's own notes take their place in a community of commentary. There are in particular similarities of approach and method, as might be expected, with that other learned clerical Miltonist, Zachary Pearce, whose *Review* 'is not only a most complete answer to Dr Bentley, but may serve as a pattern to all future critics, of sound learning and just reasoning'. It was Pearce, Newton tells us, who 'first engaged me in this undertaking, and . . . has kindly assisted me in it from the beginning to the end' (I. sig. a3^{r}). Newton claims that his notes are 'intended for general use' (I. sig. b1^{r}), but the list of subscribers to his edition has some predictable bias to the Church, to the University, and to gentleman-amateur scholarship, including such names as William Warburton, Benjamin Hoadly, Charles Jennens, Joshua Barnes (the editor of Homer), and, of course, Pearce.

Newton produced what R. G. Moyles has described as a 'securely definitive' text of *Paradise Lost*,[86] based scrupulously and faithfully on the editions of 1667 and 1674, which Newton, with almost all of his contemporaries, considered authoritative:

> the first care has been to print the text correctly according to Milton's own editions . . . we have an authentic copy to follow in the two editions printed in his own lifetime, and have only to correct what may be supposed to be the errors of the press, or mistakes occasioned by the author's blindness. These two editions then . . . are proposed as our standard: the variations in each are noted; and we never deviate from them both without assigning, as we think, a substantial reason for it. (I. sig. a2^{r}–a2^{v})

Newton carefully collated the 1667 and 1674 editions, which served as the 'standard' (or, as we would say, base text) for his own, and was aware of

[86] See Moyles's discussion of Newton's textual policies and procedures, *The Text of Paradise Lost*, pp. 73–5.

6 PARADISE LOST. Book I.

Sing heav'nly Muſe, that on the ſecret top
Of Oreb, or of Sinai, didſt inſpire
That ſhepherd, who firſt taught the choſen ſeed,
In the beginning how the Heav'ns and Earth
Roſe out of Chaos: Or if Sion hill 10
Delight

judgment the whole Earth would be made a Paradiſe XII. 463.

-------- for then the Earth
Shall all be Paradiſe, far happier place
Than this of Eden, and far happier days.

It ſhould ſeem that the author, ſpeaking here of *regaining the bliſsful ſeat*, had at this time formed ſome deſign of his poem of *Paradiſe Regain'd*. But however that be, in the beginning of that poem he manifeſtly alludes to the beginning of this, and there makes Paradiſe to be regain'd by our Saviour's ſoiling the tempter in the wilderneſs.

I who ere-while the happy garden ſung,
By one Man's diſobedience loſt, now ſing
Recover'd Paradiſe to all mankind,
By one Man's firm obedience fully try'd, --
And Eden rais'd in the waſte wilderneſs.

6. -------- *that on the ſecret top*
Of Oreb, or of Sinai, -----]

Dr. Bentley ſays that Milton dictated *ſacred top*: his reaſons are ſuch as follow: The ground of Horeb is ſaid to be *holy*, Exod. III. 5. and Horeb is called the *mountain of God* 1 Kings XIX. 8. But it may be anſwer'd, that tho' that place of Horeb, on which Moſes ſtood, was *holy*, it does not follow that the top of the mountain was then *holy* too: and by the *mountain of God* (Dr. Bentley knows) may be meant only, in the Jewiſh ſtile, a very great mountain: Beſides let the mountain be never ſo *holy*, yet according to the rules of good poetry, when Milton ſpeaks of the *top* of the mountain, he ſhould give us an epithet peculiar to the *top* only, and not to the whole mountain. Dr. Bentley ſays farther that the epithet *ſecret* will not do here, becauſe the top of this mountain is viſible ſeveral leagues off. But Sinai and Horeb are the ſame mountain, with two ſeveral eminences, the higher of them called Sinai: and of Sinai Joſephus in his Jewiſh Antiquit. Book 3. Chap. 5. ſays that *it is ſo high, that the top of it cannot be ſeen without ſtraining the eyes*. In this ſenſe therefore (tho' I believe it is not Milton's ſenſe) the top of it may be well ſaid to be *ſecret*. In Exod. XVII. it is ſaid that the Iſraelites, when incamp'd at the foot of Horeb, could find no water; from whence Dr. Bentley concludes, that Horeb had no clouds or miſts about its *top*; and that therefore *ſecret top* cannot be here meant as *implying that high mountains againſt rainy weather have their heads ſurrounded with miſts*. I never thought that any reader of Milton would have underſtood *ſecret top* in this ſenſe. The words *of Horeb or of Sinai* imply a doubt of the poet, which name was propereſt to be given to that mountain, on the top of which Moſes receiv'd his inſpiration; becauſe Horeb and Sinai are uſed for one another in Scripture, as may be ſeen by comparing Exod. III. 1. with Acts VII. 30. but by naming Sinai laſt, he ſeems to incline rather to that. Now it is well known from Exod. XIX. 16. Ecclus. XLV. 5. and other places of Scripture, that when God gave his laws

Figures 3 and 4 *Paradise Lost: New Edition, With Notes of Various Authors* (1749), edited by Thomas Newton, I. 6–7.

Delight thee more, and Siloa's brook that flow'd
Faſt by the oracle of God; I thence
Invoke thy aid to my adventrous ſong,
That with no middle flight intends to ſoar
Above th' Aonian mount, while it purſues 15
Things

laws to Moſes on the top of Sinai, it was cover'd with *clouds*, *dark clouds*, and *thick ſmoke*; it was therefore *ſecret* at that time in a peculiar ſenſe: and the ſame thing ſeems intended by the epithet which our poet uſes upon the very ſame occaſion in XII. 227.

God from the mount of Sinai, whoſe *gray top*
Shall tremble, he deſcending, *&c.*

Dr. Bentley ſhows that *ſacred hill* is common among the poets in ſeveral languages; from whence I ſhould conclude that *ſacred* is a general epithet: whereas *ſecret*, in the ſenſe which I have given it, is the moſt peculiar one that can be: and therefore (to uſe Dr. Bentley's words) *if, as the beſt poets have adjudg'd, a proper epithet is to be preferr'd to a general one, I have ſuch an eſteem for our poet, that which of the two words is the better, That I ſay (viz. ſecret) was dictated by Milton.* Pearce.

We have given this excellent note at length, as we have met with ſeveral perſons who have approved of Dr. Bentley's emendation. It may be too that the poet had a farther meaning in the uſe of this epithet in this place; for being accuſtomed to make uſe of words in the ſignification that they bear in the learned languages, he may very well be ſuppoſed to uſe the word *ſecret* in the ſame ſenſe as the Latin *ſecretus*, *ſet apart* or *ſeparate*, like the *ſecretoſque pios* in Virgil, Æn. VIII. 670. and it appears from Scripture, that while Moſes was with God in the mount, the people were not to come near it or touch it, till after a ſignal given, and then they were only to approach, and not to aſcend it, nor paſs the bounds ſet for them upon pain of death. Exod. XIX. So that upon all accounts *ſecret* is the moſt proper epithet, that could have been choſen.

8. *That ſhepherd, who firſt*, &c.] For *Moſes kept the flock of Jethro his father-in-law.* Exod. III. 1. And he is very properly ſaid to have *firſt taught the choſen ſeed*, being the moſt ancient writer among the Jews, and indeed the moſt ancient that is now extant in the world.

9. *In the beginning how the Heav'ns and Earth*] Alluding to the firſt words of Geneſis.

11. *and Siloa's brook*] Siloa was a ſmall river that flow'd near the temple at Jeruſalem. It is mention'd Iſai. VIII. 6. So that in effect he invokes the heavenly Muſe, that inſpir'd David and the Prophets on mount Sion, and at Jeruſalem, as well as Moſes on mount Sinai.

15. *Above th' Aonian mount,*] A poetical expreſſion for ſoaring to a highth above other poets. The mountains of Bœotia, anciently called Aonia, were the haunt of the Muſes, and thus Virgil, Ecl. VI. 65.

Aonas in *montes* ut duxerit una ſororum,

And again Georg. III. 11.

Aonio rediens deducam *vertice* Muſas;

though afterwards, I know not by what fatality, that country was famous for the dulneſs of its inhabitants.

16. *Things*

almost all significant variants between the first two editions.[87] He also collated the subsequent editions, and was hence conscious not only of the readings of the texts printed in Milton's lifetime, but also of where errors and changes had been introduced in the course of subsequent linear transmission. Newton is silent regarding the grounds of many of his choices between the readings of the first two editions, but in several cases he offers clear interpretative statements of his reasons for preference, as in this cogent use of gloss and paraphrase:

– a second multitude
With wondrous art founded the massy ore,]
The first band dug the metal out of the mountain, *a second multitude on the plain hard by founded* or melted it; for *founded* it should be read as in the first edition, and not *found out* as it is in the subsequent ones; *founded* from *fundere*, to melt, to cast metal.[88]

Persuaded of the authority of the first editions, Newton distinguishes the editorial procedures proper for Milton from those required in Shakespeare's very different case:

For the first editions of Shakespear's works being printed from the incorrect copies of the players, there is more room left for conjectures and emendations . . . But we who undertake to publish Milton's Paradise Lost are not reduced to that uncertainty; we are not left floting in the wide ocean of conjecture, but have a chart and compass to steer by. (I. sig. a2r)

Indeed Newton is extremely resistant to the introduction into his text of any substantive reading not witnessed in the authoritative first two editions, refusing even the most cogent conjectural emendation. So he does not admit the Bentleian proposal of '*swelling* gourd' for '*smelling* gourd' (*Paradise Lost*, 7. 321), despite the force of bibliographical and literary evidence in its favour: 'The mistake was easy of *w* for *m*: and Dr Bentley's emendation is certainly right; and to the authority which he has brought from Propertius, we may add another from Virgil [*Georgics*, 4. 121]. But we have not alter'd the text, as the common reading makes sense, tho' not such good sense as the other' (II. 32–3). This is a significant moment at which, in Newton's edition, documentary considerations take precedence over the authorial or interpretative.[89] Newton writes of his determination 'to establish the true

[87] But not of the variants at 2. 375, 2. 631, 7. 322, 10. 397.

[88] *Paradise Lost* I. 702 (Newton, I. 66). Compare *Paradise Lost*, 7. 366, where Newton prefers on interpretative grounds the 1674 reading, '*her* horns' (1667 *his*), 'which is certainly properer for the planet Venus' (I. 36); and *Paradise Lost*, 4. 705, where he prefers, on bibliographical as well as interpretative grounds, the 1667 reading '*shadier* bower', noting that in 1674 'we read *In shadie bower*, but with such a space as is not usual between two words, as if the letter r had occupy'd the room, and by some accident had made no impression', and that '*In shadier bower* marks more strongly the shadiness as well as the retiredness of the place, and the shadiness is a principal circumstance of the description, and the bower is seldom mention'd but it is call'd *shady bower*, III. 734. V. 367, 375. *shady lodge*, IV. 720. *shady arborous roof*, V. 137.'

[89] Similarly, Newton's text has 'He for God only, she for God in him' (*Paradise Lost*, 4. 299), though

genuin text of Milton' (I. sig. a4v), but it is clear in his practice that he thinks that genuine authorial text to be adequately witnessed in the surviving early documents, whose authority therefore overrides any attempt to penetrate by conjecture to some imagined pre-textual intention.

Newton's commentary on *Paradise Lost* is to a significant degree concerned with matters of aesthetic judgment. A number of his annotations aim 'to point out the beauties and defects of sentiment and character, and to commend or censure the conduct of the poem' (I. sig. a4v). He frequently judges or defends *Paradise Lost* by referring both to modes of procedure and to particular modes of expression in classical poetry, and, more especially, in the epic. Anthony Blackwall, in *The Sacred Classics Defended and Illustrated* (1725), had set out to vindicate the apparent stylistic oddities of the Bible by finding analogies, with considerable ingenuity, in Greek and Roman writing. With a not dissimilar motive, Newton aimed to justify the poetic ways of Milton to eighteenth-century men, by appeals to the same sources. A significant part of the critical and evaluative element in Newton's commentary is made up of extended citations from Addison's *Spectator* passages, whose arguments and attitudes fit almost seamlessly into Newton's discourse. Most of Newton's note on Adam's speech to Eve before the two take sexual 'solace of their sin' (*Paradise Lost*, 9. 1029ff.), for example, is made up of a long quotation from Addison, in which he suggests an echo of the *Iliad*, applauds Milton's Homeric knowledge, and finds in the resemblance to the Greek epic both a ground of greatness and a defence of the English poet's methods:

> 'Adam's converse with Eve, after having eaten the forbidden fruit, is an exact copy of that between Jupiter and Juno in the fourteenth Iliad . . . As no poet seems ever to have studied Homer more, or to have more resembled him in the greatness of genius than Milton, I think I should have given a very imperfect account of his beauties, if I had not observed the most remarkable passages which look like parallels in these two great authors . . . The greater incidents . . . are not only set off by being shown in the same light with several of the same nature in Homer, but by that means may also be guarded against the cavils of the tasteless or ignorant.' (II. 198–9)

In his own voice, Newton defends the verbal quibbles of Satan's mockery of God's angelic forces before the war in heaven (*Paradise Lost*, 6. 568ff.). At such rare moments we may suppose that Milton 'sacrific'd to the taste of his times, when *puns* were better relish'd than they are at present in the learned world'. Perhaps, Newton surmises, 'we are . . . grown too delicate and fastidious in this particular', particularly as such ancients as Cicero and Aristotle gave such devices their approval. The final justification is the

he prefers Bentley's '*and* him': 'this is so much better, that we cannot but wish it was admitted into the text' (Newton, I. 251).

demonstration that 'our author seems to have been betray'd into this excess in great measure by his love and admiration of Homer. For this account of the Angels jesting and insulting one another is not unlike some passages in the 16th book of the Iliad.'[90] Newton's constant reference of the poem to classical epic implies of course a judgment analogous to a central tenet of Addison's *Spectator* papers: that Milton resembled the Greek and Roman heroic poets, and at the same time had an overwhelming advantage over them, in that his subject was truth, and his source Holy Writ. The claim becomes explicit, for example, in his note on the exchange between God and the Son (*Paradise Lost*, 3. 344):

> If the reader pleases to compare this divine dialogue with the speeches of the Gods in Homer and Virgil, he will find the Christian poet to transcend the Heathen, as much as the religion of the one surpasses that of the others. Their deities talk and act like men, but Milton's divine Persons are divine Persons indeed, and talk in the language of God, that is in the language of Scripture. (I. 188)

A high proportion of Newton's notes relate passages in *Paradise Lost* to the Bible, the book which, more than the pagan classics, lends Milton's poem its moral and religious as well as its literary authority. Newton's concluding note chooses to celebrate Milton as 'a most critical reader and a most passionate admirer of holy Scripture', indebted more to Holy Writ than to Homer or Virgil 'and all other books whatever', and finally invites his reader to learn from the example of Milton and his poem 'to reverence those sacred Writings' (II. 432).

Broader evaluative tendencies are to be found in the provision in Newton's edition of an Index of Topics. This lists characters (and, under each character, particular actions, and speeches), subjects, poetic *topoi*, and other themes. So, under 'Adam' are listed such topics as 'his discourse with Eve on the prohibition of the tree of knowledge', and 'Invites the Angel Raphael to his bower'. Such moral and theological topics as reason and free will, charity, conscience, election, fame, fate, hypocrisy, and reprobation, also appear. This topic index is a guide to the use of the poem, presupposing an audience and operating within given aesthetic, moral, and theological assumptions; it naturally moves from meaning to significance, offering guidance through *Paradise Lost* as a scripture which contains both information and instruction suited to the readership for whom the editor mediates the text. To some extent such a topic index as Newton's is specific to its own moral, religious, and cultural horizon. The point might perhaps be made most clearly by a representative extract:

[90] Newton, I. 430. But contrast the somewhat less approving tone of the note to the line 'That brought into this world a world of woe' (*Paradise Lost*, 9. 11), which Newton compares with 'The world erelong a world of tears must weep' (11. 627): 'in these instances Milton was corrupted by the bad taste of the times, and by reading the Italian poets, who abound with such verbal quaintnesses' (Newton, II. 120–1).

Woman, conjugal obedience her happiness, &c.	iv.635
Man's love towards her, how consistent with his superiority	viii.657
Two of her loveliest qualities	ix.232
The effect of leaving her to her own will	ix.1182
His superiority over her, given him by God	x.145, 195.
A novelty, defect of nature, &c. (sarcastically)	x.888
The advantage of her social, over her artificial accomplishments	xi.614
Every way the cause of man's misery (sarcastically)	xi.632.[91]

Because we use the poem in quite different ways now, we would not produce a topic index quite like this. If we did, the headings would be different, because our concerns and our preconceptions are different. I leave to the interested reader the exercise of imagining the different topic indexes that might have been constructed in 1970, or 1980, or 1990.

Such features of Newton's commentary may be thought to confirm a tendency in some modern studies to consider the eighteenth-century editors as substantially or even primarily engaged in accommodating writings of the past to their own literary and cultural values. Most of John Shawcross's selections from Newton's edition in his *Critical Heritage* volume, for example, are of critically evaluative remarks, naturally enough in an anthology which sets out to represent critical response. Shawcross includes relatively few examples from Newton of notes which serve as gloss, explanation, periphrasis, or textual comment.[92] It needs to be stressed however that Newton's commentary on *Paradise Lost* is not only 'critical' in this sense, but also persistently 'explanatory', and more interesting for this reason, perhaps, than Shawcross's particular choice of extracts makes it appear. In a great many of his notes Newton sets out not to judge but to interpret the poem, 'to illustrate the sense and meaning' (I. sig. a4^{v}). Some of the notes, Newton explains in his Preface, are intended 'to remark the peculiarities of stile and language, to clear the syntax, and to explain the uncommon words, or common words used in an uncommon signification; . . . some to show his imitations and allusions to other authors, whether sacred or profane, ancient or modern' (I. sig. a4^{v}). In fact Newton's variorum displays the full range of explanatory methods that had been applied to *Paradise Lost* in the eighteenth century – whether exploited by Newton himself or the community of commentators whom he cites – including paraphrase, parallels within and beyond Milton's own writings, and the interpretative application of a wide variety of knowledges.

Newton uses paraphrase, his own or that of others, and notably of Hume and Richardson, as one of his most insistent interpretative methods, and is

[91] Newton, II. sig. Ddd2^{v}. [92] Shawcross II. 153–68.

entirely self-conscious about doing so. A rather closely literal paraphrase of the account of Paradise on Satan's first approach (*Paradise Lost*, 4. 132–7, 178–9) is concluded with the succinct remark that 'this account in prose may perhaps help the reader the better to understand the description in verse' (I. 236). Newton uses and develops paraphrase in powerful and sophisticated ways. Some passages of paraphrase straighten out transpositions, and incorporate glosses, explanatory expansions, and illumination from learned sources, as in this careful explication of the comparison of Satan's first experience of the 'native perfumes' of Paradise with mariners coming upon 'the spicy shore / Of Araby the blest' (*Paradise Lost*, 4. 162–3):

> The north-east winds blowing contrary to those who have doubled the *Cape of Good Hope*, and are past the iland *Mozambic* on the eastern coast of Africa near the continent, and are sailing forwards, they must necessarily *slack their course*; but yet they are well enough *pleas'd with such delay*, as it gives them the pleasure of smelling such delicious odors, *Sabean odors*, from Saba, a city and country of Arabia Felix *Araby the blest*, the most famous for frankincense. (I. 238)

The exercise of paraphrasing regularly leads Newton, as it led other eighteenth-century editors, into a close and perceptive engagement with Milton's poetry. In none of the natural delights of Paradise can Satan 'find place or refuge' (*Paradise Lost*, 9. 119). Bentley preferred the conjectural emendation 'place *of* refuge', and 'another learned gentleman' proposes 'find *peace* or refuge'. Newton however, sensitive both to Milton's choice of words and to their context, elicits in his paraphrase the more suggestive double meaning:

> it may be understood thus, *but I in none of these find place* to dwell in *or refuge* from divine vengeance. And this sense seems to be confirm'd by what follows.
>
> But neither here seek I, no nor in Heaven
> *To dwell.* (II. 132)

Paradise can be to Satan neither a refuge from his personal hell, nor a place in which he could live.[93] In some notes, as in Hume, close periphrastic explanation of the literal sense of Milton's words makes a distinct shift into moral application, for instance in Newton's long discussion of Satan's cormorant perching on the tree of life (*Paradise Lost*, 4. 196):

> Satan . . . sat upon it, but did not thereby regain true life to himself, but sat devising death to others who were alive. Neither did he think at all on the virtues of the tree, but used it only for the convenience of prospect, when it might have been used so as to have been a pledge of immortality. And so he perverted the best of things *to worst abuse*, by sitting upon the tree of life devising death, or *to meanest use*, by using it only for prospect, when he might have applied it to nobler purposes.

[93] Newton is partly anticipated by Jonathan Richardson's explanation of 'place or refuge' as 'a Habitation, or Security from Divine Wrath' (*Explanatory Notes and Remarks*, p. 399). Newton's paraphrasing explanation is discussed by Ricks, *Milton's Grand Style*, p. 85.

But what use then would our author have had Satan to have made of the tree of life? . . . What . . . use . . . could he have made of it, unless he had taken occasion from thence to reflect duly on life and immortality, and thereby had put himself in a condition to regain true life and a happy immortality. (I. 241–2)

The concern with moral and theological usefulness is reminiscent of Hume, but at such moments Newton the clergyman-editor is especially close to the forms and purposes found in the biblical paraphrase with annotation of, for example, Richard Baxter.

Newton, like Richardson, is everywhere acutely perceptive about the derivations, uses, and implications of particular words. An awareness of Latin etymology might be expected. So Satan's fall from heaven, 'with hideous ruin and combustion down' (*Paradise Lost*, 1. 46), is explained as drawing on Latin *ruo*, which 'includes the idea of falling with violence and precipitation' (I. 12). Noting an especially telling local effect in the description of Satan reduced to a serpent,

till supplanted down he fell
A monstrous serpent on his body prone,
(*Paradise Lost*, 10. 513–14)

Newton draws attention to an important and more general tendency in Miltonic metaphor:

We may observe here a singular beauty and elegance in Milton's language, and that is his using words in their strict and litteral sense, which are commonly apply'd to a metaphorical meaning, whereby he gives peculiar force to his expressions, and the litteral meaning appears more new and striking than the metaphor itself. We have an instance of this in the word *supplanted*, which is deriv'd from the Latin *supplanto*, to trip up one's heels or overthrow, a planta pedis subtus emota: and there are abundance of other examples in several parts of this work. (II. 252)

Newton's alertness to etymological implication, and to the frequency with which Milton 'uses words in their proper and primary signification', extends to other languages, as in his note on Beelzebub's urging an attack on the 'puny habitants' of God's new-created world (*Paradise Lost*, 2. 365–7), where he follows Hume in suggesting a derivation from French *puis né*.[94] More rarely, Newton's notes ground his reading of the poem in the materials of an English historical lexicography. Hurled from heaven, Mulciber could not escape 'by all his *engines*' (*Paradise Lost*, 1. 750). Drawing on the observation of an unnamed 'ingenious gentleman', Newton glosses the word by reference to its use in a statute of Edward I: 'this word in the old English was often used for devices, wit, contrivance; so in the glossary to Chaucer and in the Statute of Mortmain, 7 Edw. I. the words aut alio quovis modo, arte, vel *ingenio*, are English'd in our statute books, or by any

[94] Newton, II. 104–5. Newton's notes on *Paradise Lost*, 10. 512–13 and 2. 365–7, are discussed by Ricks, *Milton's Grand Style*, pp. 64–5.

other craft or *engin*' (I. 71). In such moments Newton turns to interpretative purpose historical linguistic evidence of a kind which was already being exploited in Shakespearean editing by Lewis Theobald, and would be developed further by Edward Capell.

Notes demonstrating Milton's 'imitations and allusions to other authors' form a very substantial part of the commentary. Newton's use of parallels in Scripture, and in the ancient classics, as well as in more modern authors, is generally more interpretative than aesthetic. A sentence in Newton's Preface states this purpose clearly: 'I would not produce every thing that hath any similitude and resemblance, but only such passages as we may suppose the author really alluded to, and had in mind at the time of writing' (I. sig. a4^{v}). Newton sets out on a quest in fact not for mere likeness or analogy, for literary nostalgia or mechanical reminiscence, but for the purposeful allusions that may be argued to have shaped the intended meaning of the author's words.[95]

Some of Newton's scriptural parallels are very simple: that 'the serpent subtlest beast of all the field' (*Paradise Lost*, 9. 86) alludes to Genesis 3:1, for instance, or that there is a reference to Genesis 2:16–17 in 'this one, this easy charge' (*Paradise Lost*, 4. 421) laid on Adam not to eat from the tree of knowledge. 'These things are so evident', remarks Newton, a cleric editing Milton for a biblically literate readership, 'that it is almost superfluous to mention them. If we take notice of them, it is that every reader may be sensible how much of Scripture our author hath wrought into this divine poem.'[96] In some notes the biblical allusion is a good deal less obvious, and the editor's demonstration of its implications is consequently the more enlightening and suggestive. Before what he imagines will be his triumphant return to the hall of Pandemonium, Satan urges his commission on his new-made plenipotentiaries on earth:

> If your joint power prevails, the affairs of hell
> No detriment need fear, go and be strong.
>
> (*Paradise Lost*, 10. 408–9)

Here Newton remarks that 'Satan encourages Sin and Death in much the same words as Moses does Joshua. Deut. xxxi. 7, 8',[97] revealing new and disturbing ironic possibilities, just as Hume had noticed a similarly

[95] A sense of the relative rigour which Newton brings to allusion tracing might be gained by contrast with the very much weaker criteria used by Francis Peck; see, for example, his notes on *Paradise Lost*, 2. 586 and 7. 438, which assert sources in Shakespearean passages on the most general grounds (*New Memoirs*, pp. 174–5, 184).

[96] Newton's note on *Paradise Lost*, 4. 430–2 (I. 261).

[97] II. 244. Deuteronomy 31:7–8 reads: 'And Moses called unto Joshua, and said unto him in the sight of all Israel, Be strong and of a good courage: for thou must go with this people unto the land which the LORD hath sworn unto their fathers to give them; and thou shalt cause them to inherit it. / And the Lord, he it is that doth go before thee; he will be with thee, he will not fail thee, neither forsake thee: fear not, neither be dismayed.'

resonant parodic misappropriation of the language of Paul in Satan's temptation of Eve.[98] At *Paradise Lost*, 9. 1027, Newton cites a note by Hume which opens up a significant equivocation in Adam's post-lapsarian words to Eve by tracking them to their biblical source:

> – Now let us play,
>
> As meet is after such delicious fare;] He seems to allude to Exod. XXXII.6. I Cor. X.7. *And the people sat down to eat, and to drink, and rose up to play*; understanding the word *play* with several commentators, not of dancing after the sacrifices as it ought probably to be understood in these texts, but of committing uncleanness, as when we say to *play the whore*, and as the word is often used in the learned languages. (II. 198)

It might of course be said that this is an English sense of 'play' which was knowable without recourse to the English Bible,[99] but this note is striking both as an application of biblical exegesis to the understanding of Milton, and as an explicit invocation of biblical commentary. Newton's annotations frequently reveal an editor as familiar and learned in the Bible as the poet whose work he is explaining. Milton's phrase 'the tree of prohibition' (*Paradise Lost*, 9. 644–5) is described and justified as 'An Hebraism for the prohibited or forbidden tree'.[100] The apparent tautology in Eve's comment on the beasts, 'whom God on their creation-day / Created mute' (*Paradise Lost*, 9. 556–7), which Bentley had rejected as 'mere fillings', is explained as 'exactly in the stile of Scripture', and compared with Genesis 2:4: 'These are the generations of the Heavens and of the Earth when they were created; in the day that the Lord God made the Earth and the Heavens' (II. 166). Here Newton echoes a tendency in mid eighteenth-century biblical scholarship, pointing out one of the kinds of repetition that Robert Lowth had explored in his Oxford Lectures on the Hebrew sacred poetry, delivered between 1741 and 1750.[101]

Tracing parallels in classical literature had been a tradition of Milton editing from Hume onwards, and it plays a significant part in Newton's variorum. Partly this is, as we have seen, evaluative, a judgment of Milton's epic by classical heroic standards. Frequently however specific parallels allow Newton to defend the readings of the first documentary witnesses. Bentley had objected to the 'jejune' repetition in Eve's sweetness bereaving Satan's 'fierceness of the fierce intent it brought' (*Paradise Lost*, 9. 462);

[98] See above, p. 61.

[99] In Leontes's words in the *Winter's Tale*, for example: 'Go play boy, play: thy mother plays' (I. 2. 188).

[100] Compare Hume's note on 'son of despite' (9. 176), cited by Newton: ''Tis a Hebraism by which wicked men are termed *sons of Belial* Deut. XIII.13. valiant men, *sons of courage* 2 Sam. II.7. untameable beasts, *sons of pride* Job XLI. 25. the disciples, *sons of light* Luke XVI. 8.' (II. 135).

[101] *De sacra poesi Hebraeorum praelectiones* (London, 1753); translated into English by G. Gregory (2 vols., London, 1787).

Newton's answer is to find an analogue in the *Aeneid*: 'Et nostro *doluisti* saepe *dolore*' (I. 669). Many classical parallels noticed in Newton are frankly interpretative, illustrating and explaining the particular Miltonic usage. As Satan leaves the 'Stygian Council',

> . . . him round
> A globe of fiery seraphim enclosed
> With bright emblazonry, and horrent arms.
>
> (*Paradise Lost*, 2. 511–13)

Newton's commentary explains 'globe' as 'a battalion in circle surrounding him', with a corroborating illustration from the *Aeneid* ('qua *globus* ille virum / densissimus urget', 10. 373), and 'horrent' as including 'the idea both of terrible and prickly, set up like the bristles of a wild boar', with two further illustrations from the same source (I. 114).[102] The snake is described in the prelapsarian Paradise:

> close the serpent sly
> Insinuating, wove with Gordian twine
> His braided train, and of his fatal guile
> Gave proof unheeded.
>
> (*Paradise Lost*, 4. 347–9)

Newton points here, as he often does, to the radical Latin sense: '*Insinuating*, wrapping, or rolling up, and as it were imbosoming himself. Virgil frequently uses the words *sinuosus* and *sinuare* to express the winding motions of this animal' (I. 255). 'Insinuating' has a familiar fallen meaning, but Newton's note alerts us to a poignantly innocent, and primary, sense.

The contextualization of the poem in Newton's variorum locates it also, if much less frequently, within a modern European and English poetic discourse. That the word 'worm' at *Paradise Lost* 9. 1068 means 'serpent' is confirmed by appeal to Shakespeare's use of the phrase 'the mortal worm'.[103] Bentley rejects the 'sparkling *orient* gems' of the gate of heaven (*Paradise Lost*, 3. 507), as an expression appropriate only to an earthly context, and prefers '*ardent* gems'; part of Newton's defence of the reading is Thyer's comparison with lines from Spenser's 'Hymn of Beauty':

> the blossoms of the field
> Which are array'd with much more *orient* hue.[104]

The use of adverbs as verbs in Satan's reflections on his own fate, 'who aspires, must down as low / As high he soar'd' (*Paradise Lost*, 9. 169–70), is recognized by Pearce as a familiar Miltonic grammar (by comparison with *Paradise Lost*, 10. 503), and compared by Newton with 'a most beautiful instance' in Shakespeare:

[102] Newton, I. 114. The Virgilian phrases cited are '*Horrentia* Martis arma', and 'densos acie atque *horrentibus* hastis'.

[103] II. 202–3; the reference is to *2 Henry VI*, 3. 2. 265.

[104] Appendix, II. 437.

Henry the fifth is crown'd: *up*, Vanity!
Down, royal state![105]

Newton regularly puts to interpretative use the principle of parallel places within the poem. The hirelings who climb into the church (*Paradise Lost*, 4. 193) are 'lewd' in a wider sense than Newton's contemporaries might think; the word 'signified profane, impious, wicked, vicious, as well as wanton: and in this larger sense it is employ'd by Milton in the other places where he uses it, as well as here'.[106] Bentley had rejected the wording of Adam's resolve to die with Eve:

How can I live without thee, how forgo
Thy sweet converse and love so dearly join'd.
(*Paradise Lost*, 9. 908–9)

Newton however supports Pearce's periphrastic explanation of the elliptical syntax of the line, 'the *sweet converse and love* of thee *so dearly join'd* to me', by claiming that this is 'a common way of speaking in Milton, and the reader may see more instances of it in IV. 129. and VIII. 423', as well as by finding an echo of Adam's sentiment in Eve's later appeal to their being 'linked in love so dear' (*Paradise Lost*, 9. 970).

The importance of parallel places as a principle of understanding is attested also by Newton's provision of a very extensive 'Verbal Index'. This is essentially a concordance to Milton's poem, occupying 112 double-column pages, and containing some 8,000 words. For many of the words dozens of references are provided. This verbal index, together with the thematic index, makes it possible for the reader to use *Paradise Lost* as though it were a Bible, by providing the reader with just those indexical helps that users of the Bible already had.[107] The topic index, whose evaluating or appropriative effect I have already illustrated, arguably belongs as a genre to an early phase in eighteenth-century editing; before the relatively conservative Newton it is found, for example, in Pope's Shakespeare. Later scholars and critics turned more and more to the verbal index, and sometimes also to the glossary. A glossary has an obvious interpretative purpose. A verbal index has a similar purpose, which is also obvious once it is appreciated that, like a concordance, it not only gives verbal clues to finding known places, but also allows the comparison of places where the same word is used, permitting the explication of one passage by reference to another, or even the pursuit of an image through the poem. A reader wishing for example to investigate

105 II. 134–5; the reference is to *2 Henry IV*, 4. 3. 248–9.

106 Newton's examples are *Paradise Lost*, 1. 490 and 6. 182. Modern editors would add the senses 'ignorant' or 'untrained'.

107 Newton is anticipated here by Alexander Cruden's *Verbal Index to Milton's Paradise Lost* (London, 1741).

the implications of Milton's figuring Eve as 'fairest unsupported flower' (*Paradise Lost*, 9.432) by tracking other uses of the image in the poem would find 12 references for 'flower' in Newton's Verbal Index, and 43 further references for the plural and related forms. By this date the verbal index was becoming established in secular editing. The very presence of so comprehensive an example of the genre in Newton's edition in itself makes the method of comparison of places possible and easy.

The variety of interpretative techniques on which Thomas Newton was able to draw in his edition of *Paradise Lost*, both his own and those of his predecessors in Milton editing, will be apparent. Newton's fullest single application of the range of those techniques might be found not in his work on *Paradise Lost*, but in his lengthy note on the most famous and contested interpretative crux in *Lycidas*:

> Besides what the grim wolf with privy paw
> Daily devours apace, and nothing said,
> But that two-handed engine at the door,
> Stands ready to smite once, and smite no more.
>
> (*Lycidas*, 128–31)

After explaining the 'grim wolf' by invoking the parallel of Spenser's similar image for 'popish priests' in his ninth Eclogue,[108] and noting the replacement in Milton's manuscript of 'nothing' by 'little', Newton proceeds to this lengthy discussion of the 'two-handed engine' itself:

> that is, the ax of reformation is upon the point of smiting once for all. It is an allusion to Mat. III. 10. Luke III. 9. *And now also the ax is laid to the root of the trees.* An ax is properly *a two-handed engin. At the door*, that is, this reformation is now ripe, and at hand; *near, even at the doors.* Mat. XXIV.33. *Behold the judge standeth before the door.* James V. 9. And it was to be a thorough and effectual reformation, *Stands ready to smite once, and smite noe more*, in allusion to the language of Scripture, 1 Sam. XXVI. 8. *Let me smite him, I pray thee, with the spear, even to the earth at once, and I will not smite him the second time.* This explanation is the more probable, as it agrees so well with Milton's sentiments and expressions in other parts of his works. His head was full of these thoughts, and he was in expectation of some mighty alteration in religion, as appears from the earliest of his prose-works, which were publish'd not four years after this poem. In the second book of his treatise of Reformation in England, he employs the same metaphor of *the ax of God's reformation, hewing at the old and hollow trunk of papacy*, and presages the time of the bishops to be but short, and compares them to a wen that is going to be cut off. Vol. I. p. 17, 18. Edit. 1738. And in his Animadversions upon the Remonstrants Defense, addressing himself to the Son of God he says – *but thy kingdom is now at hand, and thou standing at the door.* Come forth out of thy royal chambers, O Prince of all the kings of the earth, – *for now the voice of thy bride calls thee, and all creatures sigh to be renew'd.* p. 91. The reading of these treatises

[108] 'September', lines 156–61.

will sufficiently make appear what his meaning must be, and how much about this time he thought of lopping off prelatical episcopacy.[109]

This seems to me a *tour de force* of the mid eighteenth-century editor's art. It will be apparent that the primary purpose of the note is exegetical. Newton goes beyond the poem to base his interpretation on a number of sources: Spenser, Milton's other writings, the Scriptures. Newton's assumptions are patently intentionalist: the value of reference to *Of Reformation* and *Animadversions* is that they show 'what his meaning must be', demonstrating the thoughts of which his head was full. The identification, or postulation, of scriptural allusion, Newton's primary interpretative evidence, aims to define meaning. The choice of substantiating reference is confidently decisive. The 'engine' *is* the axe of reformation referred to in Matthew 3:10, which will hew down those trees that do not bear good fruit; the imminence and finality of that reformation is expressed in two biblical idioms, 'at the door', echoing Matthew 24:33, and 'ready to smite once, and smite no more' echoing 1 Samuel 26:8. There lies behind this an assured familiarity with the Bible and biblical ideas, and a closeness at least in time if not wholly in spirit to Milton's own knowledge and thinking about the Bible, that entitles Newton's arguments here to some respect. In such moments, and there are many in his work, he might be seen as an unsuspected ancient, closer to the cultural horizon of the scripture upon which he comments than we can be.

Twenty pages of discussion of this crux in *Lycidas* in the *Variorum Commentary* prove of course that Newton scarcely settled the matter; many other possible scriptural echoes and sources, and some non-scriptural ones, have been found, and many other alternative interpretations have consequently been advanced.[110] More radically, the two-handed engine of *Lycidas* is for Stanley Fish a representative example of a kind of interpretative crux which is in its nature beyond solution by the traditional methods employed in editorial exegesis, by the editors of the *Variorum Commentary* particularly, and by their forebears. Since it appears to Fish that no satisfactory or agreed answer to this and other such problems can be found, he concludes that 'the commentators and editors have been asking the wrong questions'.[111] Certainly in Fish's terms Thomas Newton is

[109] Thomas Newton, ed., *Paradise Regain'd*, pp. 492–4.

[110] *A Variorum Commentary on the Poems of John Milton, Volume Two: The Minor English Poems*, ed. A. S. P. Woodhouse and Douglas Bush (Part II, London: Routledge and Kegan Paul, 1972), pp. 686–706. The most significant eighteenth-century commentary on the passage after Newton is in the edition by Thomas Warton the Younger of Milton's *Poems upon Several Occasions* (London, 1785), pp. 22–3. A briefer discussion by William Warburton is cited by Newton in his note on *Paradise Lost*, 6. 251.

[111] 'Interpreting the Variorum', in Fish's *Is There a Text in this Class? The Authority of Interpretive Communities* (Cambridge, Mass., and London: Harvard University Press, 1980), pp. 147–73 (p. 149).

asking the wrong questions. Newton asks, and posits answers to, such questions of course because, like the *Variorum* editors, he worked self-consciously from the very different premise that *Paradise Lost* and Milton's other poems, difficult and distant though they might appear, bore intended and determinate meaning, which could in principle be explained by the sufficiently energetic application of rational argument and pertinent information. In this he owed something to past exegetical theory and practice especially in the field of interpretation of the Bible, was substantially representative of the preconceptions and methods of most of the Miltonic editors of his time, and arguably anticipated some at least of the theoretical assumptions of Milton editors, and some at least of their evidential and rational procedures, for the next two centuries.

4

Making sense of Shakespeare: editing from Pope to Capell

Issues in the editing of Shakespeare

For the eighteenth-century public, and for eighteenth-century editors and scholars, Shakespeare was, like Milton, a figure of *auctoritas* and quasi-sacred status. He was the most widely known of all English writers. With Milton (and sometimes with Spenser) he would achieve a central symbolic importance for a sense of English literary identity and English literary history. Shakespeare raised, however, for eighteenth-century editors and scholars some problems rather obviously distinct from those presented by Milton. Firstly, whereas Milton wrote for publication in print, Shakespeare was a dramatist, writing for the stage, and even the first of the eighteenth-century editors were aware that this had implications both for the nature of the artistic object he produced, and for its transmission. Secondly, despite Bentley's fiction of a licentious first editor and a grossly altered text, and despite the inclination of editors in the eighteenth century to introduce many changes, the textual problems raised by *Paradise Lost* were few; there was consensus that the first two editions of 1667 and 1674 were generally reliable texts, the obvious bases for any responsible edition, adequately representing the author's intentions despite the special problem posed by his blindness. Shakespeare, however, seemed to have paid relatively little attention to the publication of the text of his plays, whose first collected edition, published after his death by the 'player editors', was thought by most in the eighteenth century to bear the marks of carelessness and impertinent non-authorial alteration. Thirdly, though Milton raised his own problems of reference and expression, Shakespeare seemed appreciably more remote in both linguistic and cultural terms, to some eighteenth-century minds even 'barbarous', his texts inevitably therefore more in need of mediation and explication.

Such issues of course continue in our own time to make Shakespeare a battleground for many of the central questions of editorial and bibliographical theory. In few areas of English studies has so much research effort been expended, and in few has the theoretical war been more intense. From the elevated vantage ground recently gained the work of the eighteenth-century editors has seemed in a number of ways deficient. In comparison with modern scholars, they had a very incomplete understanding of the early textual history of Shakespeare's plays. They knew relatively little about Shakespeare's language and culture, or printing-house or theatre practice in Shakespeare's time. Finding much to baffle or offend them in Shakespeare's words, they resorted, it is alleged, to editing on the basis of 'subjective and impressionistic literary "taste" and "judgment"', making emendations 'governed by the literary, grammatical, and linguistic standards of their time'[1]. Further, they failed to understand that Shakespeare's plays were written for performance, in particular producing editions of *Lear* and *Hamlet* which conflated the distinct Quarto and Folio texts. 'There is no evidence', writes Professor George Hibbard, the latest Oxford editor, 'that Shakespeare ever envisaged, much less wrote as one piece, a *Hamlet* such as Theobald's is, and none to show that such a *Hamlet* was ever staged prior to the closing of the theatres in 1642.'[2]

Some of these accusations are at least in part true. Some of the areas of knowledge to which they relate, the bibliography of early modern secular literary texts in particular, might credibly be thought of as evolutionary sciences, and the eighteenth-century editors clearly came at a very early stage of that evolution. They could not benefit from Lachmannian stemmatics or the discoveries of the New Bibliography. They had for descriptive bibliographies only what they were able to construct for themselves. They lacked scholarly libraries of the scale of the Folger or the British Library. None of them had access to all the early texts of independent authority, and some such texts (Q1 *Hamlet* is an example) were not known to them at all. In this chapter however I shall be concerned to show that some of the most distinguished of the eighteenth-century editors, in particular Theobald and Capell, worked on the basis of informed and by no means untheorized choices amongst a range of possible editorial orientations. They could of course make those choices only in the light of the knowledge available to them, of their own theoretical orientations, and of the cultural circumstances in which they worked. In judging the nature and value of their achievement we might heed the words of F. A. Wolf, who insisted at the end of the eighteenth century, with reference to Aristarchus and the other early editors of Homer, that 'we must thoroughly abolish the opinion by which we model the critics of that period to match

[1] Margreta de Grazia, 'The essential Shakespeare and the material book', *Textual Practice*, 2 (1988), 69–86 (p. 69); Norman Sanders, 'Shakespeare's text', in *Shakespeare: a Bibliographical Guide*, ed. Stanley Wells (new edition, Oxford: Oxford University Press, 1990), p. 20. Compare Gary Taylor, in Stanley Wells and Gary Taylor, with John Jowett and William Montgomery, *William Shakespeare: a Textual Companion* (Oxford: Oxford University Press, 1987), p. 55.

[2] *The Oxford Shakespeare: Hamlet*, ed. G. R. Hibbard (Oxford: Oxford University Press, 1987), p. 23.

the modern rules of the art'.[3] If Theobald made other editorial decisions than those of Professor Hibbard he may have done so for reasons worth our seeking.

In discussing the work of some of the eighteenth-century editors I shall take *Hamlet* as my chief example text.[4] *Hamlet* was already in the eighteenth century the most discussed and the most performed of all Shakespeare's plays. There were no fewer than 601 recorded performances of *Hamlet* during the eighteenth century,[5] and the play was, as we shall see, repeatedly reprinted individually, as well as in successive collected editions. Rich and interesting dialogues about the play's many well-known textual and interpretative difficulties appear in scholarly discourses from very early in the century. *Hamlet* has a complex and still fiercely disputed textual history, surviving as it does in three substantive texts: a first, 'bad' Quarto (1603), some 2,154 lines long, which is probably a corrupt memorial reconstruction, but also is very possibly based on an abridged acting version deriving from a 'good' text; a substantially longer 'good' second Quarto (1604–5) of some 3,674 lines, probably deriving from Shakespeare's 'foul papers', and reflecting many of the inconsistencies of that source; and a Folio text (1623), which may derive from the theatre company's prompt-books, or from a fair copy of the play perhaps made by Shakespeare, with some influence perhaps from Quartos 3 and 4, and perhaps incorporates Shakespeare's own revisions.[6] These textual complexities raise editorial questions concerning the choice and use of the surviving textual witnesses. The possible answers to those questions for any editor depend on assessments of, particularly, the relationships amongst the different texts, the nature of authorial and of non-authorial involvement in them, and the relationship of the surviving textual witnesses to the play as acted; and these in turn depend at least to some extent on the theoretical presuppositions from which the editor starts. *Hamlet* is a play that demonstrates particularly clearly the theoretical positions that lie behind the various decisions made by eighteenth-century, as by modern, editors.

In assessing the theoretical options available to the eighteenth-century editors, and the nature of the editorial choices they made, it might be

[3] *Prolegomena to Homer (1795)*, trans. and ed. Anthony Grafton, Glenn W. Most, and James E. G. Zetzel (Princeton: Princeton University Press, 1985), p. 157.

[4] My source for act, scene, and line references, and quotations where not taken from named eighteenth-century editions, is the Oxford Shakespeare *Hamlet*, edited by George Hibbard. For other Shakespearean plays I quote from and refer to the *Complete Works*, ed. Stanley Wells, Gary Taylor, J. Jowett, and W. Montgomery (Oxford: Oxford University Press, 1988).

[5] See Charles Beecher Hogan, *Shakespeare in the Theatre 1701–1800* (2 vols., Oxford: Oxford University Press, 1952, 1957), II. 716.

[6] For some of the most recent of the many accounts, see *The New Cambridge Shakespeare: Hamlet*, ed. Philip Edwards (Cambridge: Cambridge University Press, 1985), pp. 8–32; Hibbard, ed., *Hamlet*, pp. 67–130; Wells and Taylor, *Textual Companion*, pp. 396–402; Barbara Mowat, 'The form of *Hamlet*'s fortunes', *Renaissance Drama*, 19 (1988), 97–126.

useful to draw once more on Peter Shillingsburg's exemplary statement of the four possible orientations of editing: aesthetic, sociological, historical (or documentary), and authorial.

Editors working on the basis of the aesthetic orientation make their decisions by reference to some standard of correctness, whether of the author or the editor, or the author's or editor's time. It was natural that the first editors of Shakespeare in the eighteenth century should have operated by aesthetic criteria. Shillingsburg restates a familiar definition of the aesthetic principle: 'to search out those words that the editor either does not understand or does not like and replace them with words which he does'.[7] Jocular though this is, it accurately states the two pressures of incomprehension and distaste operating on at least the earliest of the eighteenth-century editors in the face of dramatic works whose language was often colloquial or demotic or indecorous, and whose references were often rendered alien or obscure by the passage of time. The early editors were concerned to mediate and explain to their contemporaries a writer who, however much revered, was perceived (in Samuel Johnson's words) to have written at a time when 'the English nation was yet struggling to emerge from barbarity'.[8] Naturally enough they wished to present Shakespeare, the earliest representative of a characteristic and quasi-divine English genius, in the best possible light to a more refined and knowledgeable age. They set out, in fact (to borrow once more F. A. Wolf's account of the 'first emenders' of Homer), 'to make him appear nowhere inconsistent or unworthy of himself, often removing many verses, and elsewhere adding polish where there was none'.[9] It is true that Pope overtly, and Warburton more or less covertly, adopted an aesthetic orientation, as I shall go on to illustrate. No doubt elements of an aesthetic orientation continued to be more or less present in editions of Shakespeare throughout the eighteenth century (they have not disappeared in our own time). I shall wish to argue, however, that as the century wore on aesthetic considerations became less and less important.

Sociologically orientated editing thinks of literary production, to use Jerome McGann's phraseology, as 'a social and an institutional event' rather than 'an autonomous and self-reflexive activity'.[10] The important shift in modern editorial practice and theory from an authorial to a sociological orientation has already been noted in chapter 1. In the

[7] *Scholarly Editing in the Computer Age* (Athens, Ga., and London: University of Georgia Press, 1986), p. 21.

[8] *Johnson on Shakespeare*, ed. Arthur Sherbo (New Haven: Yale University Press, 1968), VII. 81. *Johnson on Shakespeare* (so abbreviated hereafter) is volumes VII and VIII of the Yale University Press edition of the *Works* of Samuel Johnson.

[9] Wolf, *Prolegomena*, pp. 157–8.

[10] *A Critique of Modern Textual Criticism* (Chicago: University of Chicago Press, 1983), p. 100.

Shakespearean field that shift has been based not on a merely theoretical tendency, but on a growing understanding of the nature of dramatic text as 'the most socialized of all literary forms',[11] and in particular a detailed understanding that Shakespeare's plays, like those of his contemporaries, were produced by a 'collaborative process' within the playhouse, in which the author was only one participant.[12] There is also now a general consensus that, in the case of works printed in Shakespeare's time – the early Quarto editions of Shakespeare's own plays, for instance – an author had relatively little effective control, and that final authority as well as ownership in such published texts normally lay with the publisher. New knowledge in these areas, then, has led modern editors and bibliographers of Shakespeare in an essentially sociological direction. To eighteenth-century editors of Shakespeare, however, such an editorial orientation was simply not available, lacking as they did not only a modern theory of socialized text production, but also a modern knowledge of the circumstances of composition, revision, production, and collaboration. They had not formulated, and on the basis of their understanding of these things could not have formulated, anything like a modern notion of the diffused intention lying behind the printing or performance of a play in Shakespeare's time.

In the historical or documentary orientation editors locate authority primarily in the historical document, resisting the eclectic mixing of discrete texts, or, in the strong form, seeking to reproduce a single document. Editors in few fields of eighteenth-century editing felt sufficient confidence in the textual tradition as they knew it to put their faith in single witnesses and resist eclectic and conjectural correction, still less to adopt anything resembling the stronger form of the orientation. I have already noticed in chapter 1 the objections by Richard Bentley and Alexander Pope to what they considered to be slavish and pedantic adherence to the readings of particular surviving manuscripts. Eighteenth-century editors of Shakespeare generally thought the early textual witnesses of Shakespeare especially unreliable. No 'authentic Manuscript' survived, as Theobald amongst others pointed out.[13] The first printed copies, more especially the Folio, were published by the players, who, having appropriated Shakespeare's works, altered or 'improved' them in the light of their own gothic ignorance and printed them without care or responsibility. Pope, in the Preface to his edition, notoriously rejected out of hand the authority of the

[11] Gary Taylor, in Wells and Taylor, *Textual Companion*, p. 15.

[12] See G. E. Bentley, *The Profession of Dramatist in Shakespeare's Time 1590–1642* (Princeton: Princeton University Press, 1971). For a summary statement of the argument, see Stephen Orgel, 'What is a text?', *Research Opportunities in Renaissance Drama*, 24 (1981), pp. 3–6.

[13] Theobald, Preface to *The Works of Shakespeare* (7 vols., London, 1733), I. xlv.

Folio.[14] Johnson stated the general case, with a particular eye to the early 'stol'n and surreptitious copies', in his *Proposals* of 1756:

> To have a text corrupt in many places, and in many doubtful, is, among the authours that have written since the use of types, almost peculiar to Shakespeare . . . the works . . . were immediately copied for the actors, and multiplied by transcript after transcript, vitiated by the blunders of the penman, or changed by the affectation of the player; . . . and printed at last without the concurrence of the authour, without the consent of the proprietor, from compilations made by chance or by stealth out of the separate parts written for the theatre.[15]

Not all editors in the period shared this relatively extreme view, and Johnson himself would change his mind in his edition. Nonetheless the attitude of the eighteenth-century editors in general contrasts with the much more optimistic judgment of the early printed texts established by the New Bibliography, particularly by Pollard and Greg,[16] and naturally led them to resort to eclecticism and emendation.

In the fourth of Shillingsburg's possible editorial orientations, authority 'resides . . . with the author' (*Scholarly Editing*, p. 24), and editors seek to recover authorially intended words and meanings. In recent times, as the concept of authorship has come under theoretical challenge, so a theory of editing based on authorial intention has become increasingly problematized, and nowhere more than in the field of Shakespearean editing. In this chapter I shall attempt to show that we can only make sense of, and do justice to, the eighteenth-century editors of Shakespeare if we understand that most of their work was guided by the authorial orientation. They generally assumed that they were in the business of establishing what Shakespeare intended to write and what Shakespeare intended to mean. The choice of an authorial orientation was underwritten by their assumptions or understandings, often explicit and often sophisticated, concerning some issues which we continue to regard as central to the theory of editing in general, and Shakespearean editing in particular. In the remainder of this section I shall make some initial suggestions regarding eighteenth-century editorial positions on five such issues: the nature and status of an author; the role and nature of editorial conjecture; the possibility of establishing valid grounds of interpretation; the possibility of a stable and determinate text; and the play in the theatre and on the page.

I have already made the point that authors become the proper subject of editorial attention when they are invested with authority, and this was particularly true for Shakespeare and Milton, the two writers perceived as

[14] *The Works of Shakespear* (London, 1723–5), I. xvi, xxi.

[15] *Johnson on Shakespeare*, VII. 51–2.

[16] See especially W. W. Greg, *The Editorial Problem in Shakespeare* (Oxford: Oxford University Press, 1942), pp. vii, 7, 18, 156, and compare A. W. Pollard, *Shakespeare's Fight with the Pirates* (2nd edn revised, Cambridge: Cambridge University Press, 1920), pp. 95ff.

the pillars of an identifiably English tradition. This had a fundamental effect on the assumptions upon which the eighteenth-century editors operated. The eighteenth-century worship of Shakespeare as Bard reached its zenith in the Stratford Jubilee of 1769, where, in David Garrick's Jubilee ode, Shakespeare was spoken of as 'the god of our idolatry'. The divinization of the figure of Shakespeare was common however throughout the century. Pope, with the scepticism of familiarity, notes that Shakespeare is styled 'the divine' in 'ev'ry Play-house bill'. Lewis Theobald refers to Shakespeare as 'so divine an Author' in the Preface to his edition. William Collins, in an imagery common amongst those poets of the mid-century who found in Shakespeare a model of creative genius, speaks of 'the sacred seat of Shakespeare's breast'. In editorial discourse throughout the eighteenth century, the texts of Shakespeare are insistently figured as sacred, reverend, scriptural, worthy of the pious respect that a scripture demands. William Warburton insisted, however implausibly, that in the text of his edition 'I have religiously observed the severe Canons of literal Criticism'; Thomas Edwards, in his attack on Warburton in *The Canons of Criticism*, represents him as a Satan figure who attacks Shakespeare's 'godlike page', incited by the 'o'erweening pride' that takes authority from the 'sacred Dead' and appropriates it for the commentator himself. Eighteenth-century editors at least claimed to reverence Shakespeare's sacred words and to believe in the notion of the true and sacred text. It is important to understand, however, that they more or less universally located that sacred text not in the surviving physical textual witnesses, but in an original authorial text or texts, now lost, that lay behind the first printed texts, and which embodied what Shakespeare intended to write and what Shakespeare intended to mean. Theobald promises, for instance, in the Preface to his edition, that 'his genuine Text is religiously adher'd to . . . Nothing is alter'd, but what by the clearest Reasoning can be proved a Corruption of the true Text; and the Alteration, a real Restoration of the genuine Reading.' Warburton similarly speaks of 'restoring the Poet's genuine Text'. The use of the definite article – 'the true text', 'the genuine reading' – and the imagery of 'restoration' of the sacred original, which has been lost or corrupted, are significant of editorial assumptions which Theobald and Warburton for all their differences shared with each other, and indeed with most other editors of their time and of subsequent decades.[17]

The belief in the scriptural authority of the original authorial text underlies some of the characteristic procedures of eighteenth-century

[17] Pope, 'The First Epistle of the Second Book of Horace Imitated', lines 69–70 (*Poems*, ed. Butt, IV. 199); Theobald, *Works of Shakespeare*, I. xxxvi, xl; Collins, 'Ode to Fear', line 65 (*The Poems of Thomas Gray, William Collins, Oliver Goldsmith*, ed. Roger Lonsdale (London: Longmans, 1969), p. 423); Warburton, *Works of Shakespear* (8 vols., London, 1747), I. xiv; Edwards, *The Canons of Criticism* (7th edn, London, 1765), p. 24.

editors. It at least partly explains, for example, the conflation of Quarto and Folio texts of *Hamlet*, a process already evident in Rowe's edition of 1709, and essentially completed in Theobald's edition in 1733.[18] In his conflation of the texts Theobald knew very well what he was doing. He had personal experience of writing for the stage, adapting for the stage, and writing promptbooks. There were numerous performances of *Hamlet* in the London theatres during his literary career, including some dozens after 1715 at Lincoln's Inn Fields, the theatre with which he had a close professional association.[19] Theobald certainly knew therefore that the form in which *Hamlet* appeared on the stage in the first decades of the eighteenth century resembled neither the text as it appeared in his own edition, nor, for that matter, the complete second Quarto or first Folio text. It was his purpose not to approximate the play as performed either in his age or in Shakespeare's, but to provide a text which fully reported all of the holy writ constituted by Shakespeare's own words.[20] Theobald especially objected to the first Folio text because, in his view, it omitted genuinely authorial passages on the whim of the players. Theobald re-instates from the 'good' Quarto text some eight verses following *Hamlet* 3. 4. 72 – 'Sense, sure you have, / Else you could not have motion' – noting that they were left out in performance for 'the Ease of the Actor', and omitted from the Folios because 'they were printed from the *Playhouse* castrated Copies'. The lines 'carry the Style, Expression, and Cast of Thought' peculiar to Shakespeare, and there 'can be no Authority for a modern Editor to conspire in mutilating his Author' (*Works of Shakespeare*, VII. 313). Theobald is not prepared to accept the Folio edition as an adequate basis for his text, because he sees it as a playhouse text, in which the authority of the author has been damaged. His conflated text restores those parts of the scripture which the impertinence of the player editors omitted. Conflation is therefore not a consequence of mere bibliographical ignorance (though of course Theobald knew less than modern editors do), but of a conscientious choice of the authorial orientation in his editing.

The tendency of eighteenth-century editors to conjectural emendation

[18] For a detailed account of the process, see Mowat, 'The form of *Hamlet*'s fortunes', especially pp. 99–111.

[19] See Peter Seary, *Lewis Theobald and the Editing of Shakespeare* (Oxford: Oxford University Press, 1990), pp. 18–27; Charles Beecher Hogan, *Shakespeare in the Theatre 1701–1800*, I, pp. 109ff. For comments by Theobald reflecting his awareness of the stage traditions of *Hamlet*, see, for example, *Shakespeare Restored* (London, 1726), pp. vii, 13.

[20] It is possible to argue that Theobald's now contemned conflated text is after all more faithful to a Shakespearean original than modern editions based on Q2 or F1. Barbara Mowat asserts that 'since we cannot know what preceded Q2 and F *Hamlet*, we cannot determine whether the complex Q2/F text is an out-and-out creation of editorial combining or whether editors have, in fact, re-created a document that once existed as Shakespeare's "complete" *Hamlet* (an "original" of which both Q2 and F represent modifications)' ('The form of *Hamlet*'s fortunes', p. 98).

needs also to be understood in the light of their editorial orientations. Certainly some aesthetically orientated editors – especially Pope and Warburton – set out to 'correct' Shakespeare by standards of taste of their own time. Most editors however, as I shall attempt to show, resorted to conjectural emendation in an attempt to restore Shakespeare's original intention, now lost because of the absence of any evidently authorial original copy. The wide-ranging debate in eighteenth-century Shakespeare editing about the necessity, methods, and proper limits of conjectural emendation, and the different ways in which it was practised, is one of the central loci of interpretative as well as textual theory in the period.

In chapter 1 I have already made the familiar argument that all textual editing is inevitably conjectural, with the sole exception of rigorously conservative diplomatic editing or facsimile reproduction. Some text-editorial judgments involve choices between readings found in one or more surviving textual witnesses. Some may involve the proposal of new readings without support in any textual witness. Gary Taylor has argued eloquently that the Shakespearean textual situation requires that editors must at least occasionally resort to conjectural emendation in the latter sense: 'An editor, in emending, decides that a text is diseased; such decisions may be mistaken. But we know that every early printed edition of Shakespeare's plays is more or less diseased.'[21] At genuine textual cruces, where none of the surviving textual witnesses provides a reading that makes sense, 'the editor's responsibility is to make sense of them for the reader and the actor, by emendation if necessary'.[22]

The point had been made with equal intelligence, in the terms of the eighteenth-century theoretical debate, in a striking exchange between Pope and Theobald. In the Preface to his edition, in 1725, Pope insisted that he had piously observed the sanctity of the Shakespearean text: 'I have discharg'd the dull duty of an Editor . . . with a religious abhorrence of all Innovation, and without any indulgence to my private sense or conjecture' (I. xxii). Lewis Theobald, in *Shakespeare Restored* (1726), the response to Pope's edition that would make him the hero of the *Dunciad*, questioned what he took to be Pope's unthinking use of the metaphor: 'I cannot help thinking . . . that what he is pleased to call a *religious Abhorrence* of *Innovation*, is downright *Superstition*: neither can I be of Opinion, that the Writings of *SHAKESPEARE* are so *venerable*, as that we should be excommunicated from good Sense, for daring to *innovate properly*' (p. iv). Theobald had a proper reverence for the sanctity of what Shakespeare wrote: the difference from Pope is Theobald's belief that sacred authority is not located in the surviving printed texts, which were known or thought to be corrupted, but

[21] Wells and Taylor, *Textual Companion*, p. 60.

[22] 'Inventing Shakespeare', *Deutsche Shakespeare-Gesellschaft West Jahrbuch 1986*, p. 44.

in the 'genuine text', the 'true reading', which was to be found in a now lost original and must be restored. Because original textual authority has been lost in transmission, Theobald's argument runs, the intelligent textual critic must supply an extra-textual authority to restore sense in the place of fortuitous nonsense. Pope had grudgingly admitted that, in *Shakespeare Restored*, Theobald had found a 'glimmering of sense' in the 'Heavy-headed revel' passage in *Hamlet* (I. 4. 17), but had complained that 'it is purely *conjectural* and founded on no *Authority* of *Copies*'. 'But', Theobald replied in his edition in 1733,

> is this any Objection against Conjecture in *Shakespeare*'s Case, where no Original Manuscript is subsisting, and the Printed Copies have successively blunder'd after one another? And is not even a Glimmering of Sense, so it be not arbitrarily impos'd, preferable to flat and glaring Nonsense? If not, there is a total End at least to this Branch of Criticism: and Nonsense may plead Title and Prescription from Time, because there is no direct Authority for dispossessing it. (VII. 247n.)

Theobald's assertion of course still leaves some questions. How readily may an editor permit himself to diagnose 'nonsense' or (to use Taylor's metaphor) 'disease' in a text? As the century wore on, editors increasingly sought to explain what they found in the old copies before they turned to conjecture. As Shakespeare's scriptural authority became more and more established, so editors became more and more unwilling to touch the Ark. In his 1721 *Proposals* for an edition of the Greek New Testament Bentley himself had insisted that 'in the Sacred Writings there's no place for Conjectures or Emendations'.[23] That sense of caution in respect of the sacred Scripture increasingly was applied to secular scriptures, and especially the sanctified and canonic writings of Shakespeare.[24]

This shift in emphasis, however does not in itself answer the theoretical problem of conjecture. It was easy to identify and reject extreme and subjective licence. Conjecture, however is a necessary part of any editorial process that aspires to do more than transmit the errors of a single inadequate witness. Of course there is a long and respectable history of scepticism about the possibility of considering conjecture to be in any way a science. 'That a conjectural critick should often be mistaken,' insists Johnson in the Preface to his edition of Shakespeare, 'cannot be wonderful . . . if it be considered, that in his art there is no system, no principal and axiomatical truth that regulates subordinate positions.'[25] Gary Taylor, in his Introduction to the Oxford *Textual Companion*, having suggested that

[23] *Proposals for Printing a New Edition of the Greek Testament* (1721), sig. A2^{v}.

[24] William Dodd, comparably, in his *Beauties of Shakespeare* (1752), claims that 'the text of an author is a sacred thing: 'tis dangerous to meddle with it' (Brian Vickers, ed., *Shakespeare. The Critical Heritage* (6 vols., London: Routledge and Kegan Paul, 1974–81), III. 465. Hereafter abbreviated as Vickers).

[25] *Johnson on Shakespeare*, VII. 109.

recent editors of Shakespeare have been too unwilling to use conjecture, nonetheless goes on to distinguish between bibliography, which 'aspires to the status of a science' and can at least claim to be an 'archaeology', and emendation which is 'all too obviously an art', dependent on 'an individual assessment of probability and a subjective inference about intention' (pp. 58–9, 60). Taylor here raises a question the answer to which seems to me critical. If conjecture is not to be thought merely individual and subjective, if in fact it can aspire to the condition of a science, it has to be shown that validatable criteria for assessing authorial meanings and authorial readings are available. In my Introduction I have briefly traced some modern arguments for that position. I shall attempt to argue in the course of this chapter that in the explicit statements and editorial practice of such eighteenth-century scholars and editors as Theobald, Upton, Johnson, and Capell there is an attempt to establish and develop criteria for valid conjecture, that is, criteria for valid interpretation. Those criteria, some deriving from classical editing and many from biblical editing and commentary, for the most part, I shall suggest, had to do with ascertaining the possibilities and horizons of authorial meaning. They included such interpretative procedures as the comparison of places, the explicatory use of verbal paraphrase, and the resort to a wide range of historical, cultural, and linguistic knowledges.

The story of editing in the eighteenth century as we shall see becomes, as the century goes on, more and more an attempt to interpret the text. Early editions, such as Pope's, which bear very little marginal gloss, give way to a lineage of editions – Theobald, Warburton, Johnson, Capell, Steevens – characterized by a growing variorum commentary aimed at the detailed establishment or restoration of the author's original words, and explication of his intended meaning. This eighteenth-century development was in many vital aspects of form and method a foundation of the familiar modern project of the editing of secular literary classics. We are now, however, thoroughly aware of the problematic nature of both textual identity and authorial intention in the case of a dramatist writing at a time when non-authorial textual determinants were so important. Many recent enquiries into the Elizabethan and Jacobean stage, and into the processes of Elizabethan and Jacobean book-making, have made it impossible for us to forget just how collaborative was the process by which an author's script became the play in performance or on the page.[26] We know that the author's original text would be extensively altered in production and in the printer's shop, with or without reference to the original author. We

[26] See especially E. A. J. Honigmann, *The Stability of Shakespeare's Text* (London: Arnold, 1965); G. E. Bentley, *The Profession of Dramatist in Shakespeare's Time 1590–1642*; Stephen Orgel, 'What is a text?'; T. H. Howard-Hill, 'Playwrights' intentions and the editing of plays', *TEXT*, 4 (1988), 269–78.

understand that in such conditions authority as well as property in the text passes to some degree out of the hands of the originating author, and that the concept of a unitary final authorial intention becomes at least problematic. Further, we have witnessed the division of the kingdoms, the success of the hypothesis that Shakespeare revised. We have learnt to think of *Lear* as not one play but (at least) two, the 1608 Quarto *History of King Lear* and the 1623 Folio *Tragedy of King Lear*; and to believe that a number of other plays, including *Othello* and *Hamlet*, may well bear the marks of authorial revision.[27]

These are arguments from bibliographical and historical evidence, credible new hypotheses arising within an evolutionary science as data increases and is better understood. They are advances, certainly, on the state of knowledge reached in the eighteenth century. Some of the radical textualizing conclusions which have been drawn from the new bibliographical discoveries, however, represent a position different in principle from those entertained by editors in that time. Margreta de Grazia and Peter Stallybrass for instance argue that recognition of the multiplication of *texts* casts in doubt 'the self-identity of the work', that the plurality of texts of *Lear* requires us 'to reconceptualize the fundamental category of a *work* by Shakespeare'.[28] It is possible to suggest that the existence of two discrete texts of *Lear* is evidence of two, discrete, acts of final authorial intention; this argument has been familiar enough in such analogous cases as the *Prelude*. Jonathan Goldberg however insists that the historical multiplicity of the text 'means that there is no text itself; it means that a text cannot be fixed in terms of original or final intentions'. Goldberg goes on to argue the 'radical instability . . . of the Shakespearean text', in terms which, if cogent, would raise serious questions about the function of editing in general, and the assumptions and purposes of eighteenth-century editing in particular: 'no word in the text is sacred. If this is true, all criticism that has based itself on the text, all forms of formalism, all close reading, is given the lie.'[29]

This is of course a familiar manoeuvre of modern radical scepticism: to conclude that, because objective certainty is not attainable, no valid interpretative knowledge can be reached. Goldberg's radical textual scepticism is also, however, arguably analogous to the textual scepticism of

[27] See especially Steven Urkowitz, *Shakespeare's Revision of King Lear* (Princeton: Princeton University Press, 1980); Gary Taylor and Michael Warren, eds., *The Division of the Kingdoms* (Oxford: Oxford University Press, 1983); Grace Ioppolo, *Revising Shakespeare* (Cambridge, Mass.: Harvard University Press, 1991).

[28] 'The materiality of the Shakespearean text', *Shakespeare Quarterly*, 44 (1993), 255–83 (p. 255). The emphasis on *work* is by De Grazia and Stallybrass. For a significant response to scepticism about the literary work, see Ian Small, '"Why edit anything at all?" Textual editing and postmodernism: a review essay', *English Literature in Transition*, 38 (1995), 195–203.

[29] 'Textual properties', *Shakespeare Quarterly*, 37 (1986), 213–17 (pp. 214, 215).

Roman Catholic writers of the late seventeenth century. His position is the polar opposite of Richard Bentley's insistence that variation is an inevitable consequence of all textual transmission and may be found 'in all Classicks whatever', and neither renders the text of the Scriptures 'precarious', nor substantially darkens its meaning. Such robust tolerance in the face of textual fragmentation and multiplicity offers a remarkable contrast to Goldberg, particularly as the uncertainties of the biblical canon and text are no doubt greater than those of the Shakespearean. That the doubts of such modern thinkers as Goldberg concerning the status, determinacy, self-identity, and authority of the Shakespearean text were not shared by eighteenth-century editors is not due to ignorance on their part about possible sceptical arguments. Belief in the coherence and transmissibility of texts and the intended meanings of their authors, and conscious rejection of textual scepticisms, at least partly for reasons I have explained in chapter 2, were tenets so deeply rooted in eighteenth-century English letters as to be almost beyond debate, though certainly not beyond sophisticated theoretical understanding. Belief in the possibility of constructing Shakespeare as the author of coherent and meaning-bearing texts was an enabling condition for the eighteenth-century project of editing his dramatic works.

The eighteenth-century scholarly editions that I shall be examining in this chapter (there were, as we shall see, editions of another kind), in attempting to restore a now lost authorial written original, are designed for the closet, not the theatre. In this respect they raise questions which a more theatrically orientated modern scholarship would answer rather differently. Did Shakespeare write for the stage, with no care for publication? Or did he have readers at least partly in mind? What light is cast on this issue by Heminge and Condell's emphatic advice to 'the great Variety of Readers', in the first Folio, to 'Reade him . . . againe, and againe'? Does the sheer length of most of Shakespeare's surviving play texts suggest that, as Greg argues, he 'had some sort of publication in mind'?[30] Shakespeare's writings are characterized by a distinctive verbal difficulty, and suggestiveness, which has made them seem to many at least as appropriate to the study as to the theatre. This feature, which Harry Berger cogently describes as 'the richness and complexity of a text which is overwritten from the standpoint of performance and the playgoer's limited perceptual capacities',[31] raises significant questions about authorial purposes and the role of editorial interpretation.

For Samuel Johnson the book precedes performance. In the most theoretically powerful passage of his Preface, the discussion of the nature of

[30] *The Editorial Problem in Shakespeare*, p. viii.

[31] *Imaginary Audition* (Berkeley: University of California Press, 1989), pp. 29–30.

mimesis, he insists that 'a dramatick exhibition is a book recited with concomitants that encrease or diminish its effect'.[32] Where Berger argues for 'an attempt to reconstruct text-centered reading in a way that incorporates the perspective of imaginary audition and playgoing',[33] Johnson seems at first sight more unequivocally book-centred: a play is 'a book recited', and, famously, 'a play read, affects the mind like a play acted'. This emphasis has sometimes been seen as idiosyncratically Johnsonian, but it might be suggested, and should become clear in the course of this chapter, that Johnson's words are a representative statement of a more general eighteenth-century phenomenon: the growth of a literary and scholarly tradition of Shakespearean editing independent of a dramatic tradition, embodying a concern for the values of the printed book as against oral tradition and the spoken word. This concern is humanist and, arguably, Protestant. It celebrates Shakespeare as a literary hero, as an English literary classic, as a *poet*: a poet whom critics and scholars wished to see as an embodiment of natural genius, a brilliant individual, rather than as a social function. It sees his plays as constituting a body of literary work, within a literary context, recoverable and interpretable by the scholarly study of that context.

The eighteenth-century literary editors of Shakespeare were not of course exclusively book-centred. Theobald, as I noted earlier, had close links with the theatre, and Edward Capell was Deputy Inspector of Plays from 1737, though Pope, by contrast, had a fine contempt for many aspects of the theatre, and was happy to boast that 'the Play'rs and I are, luckily, no friends'.[34] Capell produced for Garrick a cut and re-arranged version of *Antony and Cleopatra* specifically for performance; published in October 1758, it was first acted on 3 January 1759.[35] It is possible to argue that in a number of ways eighteenth-century literary editors of Shakespeare attempted to create a reader's text that approximated to, or substituted for, the theatrical experience of the plays. Lists of *dramatis personae*, act and scene divisions, and some stage directions entered the text, mostly via Rowe's edition. It has been claimed that Samuel Johnson's emendations of the text are intended, by clarifications, emphases, and condensations, to 'compensate in the closet for the sound of the stage', to bring the vividness of stage performance 'to the pages of the script'.[36] Edward Capell's otherwise bare 1768 text of the plays offers the reader a set of marks with a similar function: a hyphen ranging with the

32 *Johnson on Shakespeare*, VII. 79. 33 *Imaginary Audition*, p. xiv.
34 *Epistle to Dr Arbuthnot* (1735), line 60.
35 See George Winchester Stone, Jr, 'Garrick's presentation of *Antony and Cleopatra*', *Review of English Studies*, 13 (1937), 20–38.
36 Arthur M. Eastman, 'Johnson's Shakespeare and the laity: a textual study', *PMLA*, 65 (1950), 1112–21 (p. 1120).

bottom of the printed line indicates 'a change of the address' ('Welcome, *Horatio*; _ welcome, good Marcellus'); a dagger or 'cross' indicates 'a thing shown or pointed to' ('Will you play upon this †pipe?'); a cross with two bars, 'a thing deliver'd' ('Give him this ‡money, and these ‡notes'); double quotation marks, an aside ('"Though this be madness, yet there is method in't." _ Will you walk out of the air my lord?'); and a point ranging with the top of the printed line, irony (Capell remarks no instances of irony in *Hamlet*).[37]

There was of course a tradition in the eighteenth century of editions of individual Shakespearean plays, including especially *Hamlet*, as theatre texts. This was, however, essentially separate from the tradition of literary editing, even though the 'Players' Quarto' of 1676, which was the chief root of the eighteenth-century playhouse *Hamlet*, had a significant initial influence on eighteenth-century literary *Hamlet* through Rowe's edition.[38] Theatre texts represent, or may represent, the changes necessitated by public performance. In the 1676 Quarto we are told that: 'This Play being too long to be conveniently Acted, such places as might be least prejudicial to the Plot or Sense, are left out upon the Stage.'[39] As Hibbard points out:

> The Players' Quarto recognizes that by 1676 there were two *Hamlets* not one. On the one hand, there was the play script, a kind of quarry from which the theatre manager might extract whatever he thought most suitable to make up an evening's entertainment . . . On the other hand, however, there was the Shakespearean text, already establishing itself as a literary masterpiece, which no reader of the play would forgo. (*Hamlet*, ed. Hibbard, p. 20)

During the eighteenth century a succession of editions of *Hamlet*, in quarto and sometimes in duodecimo, published by a variety of booksellers, recorded (or claimed to record) the text of the play as acted, at the Theatre Royal, Drury Lane or Covent Garden, sometimes marking passages omitted on the stage, sometimes actually omitting those passages from the printed text.[40]

I shall be concerned here, rather, with editions which consider Shakespeare's plays not as texts to be endlessly remade in theatrical performance,

[37] Capell's explanation is offered in the Preface to his *Prolusions* (London, 1760), pp. v–vi; I take my examples from Capell's 1768 text of *Hamlet*.

[38] See Mowat, 'The form of *Hamlet*'s fortunes', pp. 106–7.

[39] Address 'To the Reader', sig. A2. These passages (amounting to over 800 lines) are not in fact omitted, but picked out in quotation marks. On the 1676 Quarto see Hazelton Spencer, *Shakespeare Improved* (Cambridge, Mass.: Harvard University Press, 1927), pp. 174–5.

[40] For a list of the small-format editions of *Hamlet* printed in the first part of the century, see H. L. Ford, *Shakespeare 1700–1740* (Oxford: Oxford University Press, 1935), pp. 70–6. A few survivals of printed texts annotated as promptbooks provide a more detailed account of stage practice, including Garrick's 1773 production of *Hamlet*: see Edward A. Langhans, *Eighteenth-Century British and Irish Promptbooks* (New York: Greenwood Press, 1987), illustration 9 and pp. 148–9; G. W. Stone, Jr, 'Garrick's long lost alteration of *Hamlet*', *PMLA*, 49 (1934), 890–921.

but as works, the product of a human author, bearing his intended meaning. The eighteenth-century theatre texts are functional reprints rather than works of scholarship, assimilating Shakespeare to the practical and various requirements of the eighteenth-century theatre and the tastes of eighteenth-century play-goers, and bearing virtually no signs of editorial intervention in terms of commentaries, glossaries, or introductions. (Alexander Pope's much amended and thinly annotated edition might be thought, paradoxically, a similar assimilation of Shakespeare to the tastes of eighteenth-century readers.) The editions of Lewis Theobald, Samuel Johnson, and Edward Capell, however, and the writings of John Upton, Thomas Edwards, and other contributors to Shakespearean scholarship and understanding, evidently represent a different project, which was sharply, and often self-consciously, differentiated from the forms and purposes of theatrical adaptation.[41] In the following three parts of this chapter I shall set out to illustrate from these writers the beginnings and development of a literary tradition of Shakespeare editing, book-centred, primarily authorial in its orientation, seeking to develop techniques and knowledges which might make possible the interpretation of the works of Shakespeare in their own terms, rather than accommodating them to the different tastes and values of a later age.

Pope and Theobald

It is certainly true that 'taste' was accorded a great deal of prestige at the beginning of the century, before the rise of editorial scholarship which we associate with Theobald. Pope's approach (and, as we shall see, Warburton's) was primarily if not wholly aesthetic rather than interpretative. His note to the first line of his translation of the *Iliad* (1715) explicitly privileges evaluative criticism over either textual or exegetical scholarship, complaining that, though many of the commentators explain at length Homer's knowledge of the various sciences that appear in his poem, 'there is hardly one whose principal Design is to illustrate the Poetical Beauties of the Author'. Pope goes on to pour cold water on over-ingenious interpretations. The 'common understanding' of such works as Homer's is available by taking their words in the 'usual acceptation', without recourse to pedantic or scholastic ingenuity: 'Men of a right Understanding generally see at once all that an Author can reasonably mean.'[42] Interpretation is seen here by Pope as relatively unproblematic, an activity more or less intuitive to men of taste and common sense, and the editor or commentator

[41] For a suggestive formulation of this point, see Simon Jarvis, *Scholars and Gentlemen* (Oxford: Oxford University Press, 1995), p. 8.

[42] *The Twickenham Edition of the Poems of Alexander Pope*, vol. VII: *The Iliad of Homer*, Bks I–IX, ed. Maynard Mack *et al.* (London: Methuen, and New Haven: Yale University Press, 1967), p. 82.

or translator is not therefore required to provide either elaborate historical contextualizing research or extended exegetical comment. On the surface Pope's comment may seem to privilege authorial meaning – 'all that an Author can reasonably mean' – but what Pope has in mind does not include anything like the attempt at validation of authorial meaning by reference to the author's own culture and language, the author's own meaning horizon, to be found either in late eighteenth-century German Homeric scholarship, or in most of the English editions of Shakespeare which followed his own.

Pope's aesthetic conception of the editor's task led him to devote a significant part of his energies to pointing out both the fine and the faulty in Shakespeare's writing. In the Preface to his edition he claims that 'the pointing out an Author's excellencies' is 'the better half of Criticism'. Within Pope's text of the plays the 'most shining passages' are pointed out by marginal quotation marks, or preceded by an asterisk.[43] In *Hamlet*, for example, Polonius's speech to Laertes, 'Give thy thoughts no tongue', and most of Claudius's prayer are so distinguished, Polonius's speech no doubt for its apopthegmatic moral guidance, Claudius's speech perhaps because of its themes of spiritual agony and perverted justice.[44] In allocating his marks of approval, Pope was probably influenced by the tastes of previous writers in a predominantly neo-classical line: Dryden, Dennis, Addison, Gildon (who compiled the unauthorized seventh volume of Rowe's edition, including Gildon's own 'Remarks on the plays of Shakespeare'). Partly, however, Pope's decisions were based on his own taste, and in particular, it has been suggested, his own inclination to the moral and satiric.[45]

Pope makes disapproving as well as approving judgments, with a significant effect on his text of the plays: 'Some suspected passages which are excessively bad, (and which seem Interpolations by being so inserted that one can intirely omit them without any chasm, or deficience in the context) are degraded to the bottom of the page' (*Works of Shakespear* (1723–5), Preface, I. xxii). The degraded passages, which add up to a fairly small proportion of the whole, are mostly from the comedies, and are often characterized by verbal quibble or conceit or banter.[46]

[43] *Works of Shakespear* (1723–5), I. xxiii.

[44] *Hamlet*, I. 3. 59–69, 3. 3. 36–64; Pope, *Works of Shakespear* (1723–5), VI. 362, 418–19.

[45] On these issues, see Peter Dixon, 'Pope's Shakespeare', *Journal of English and Germanic Philology*, 63 (1964), 191–203; J. M. Newton, 'Alexander Pope on Shakespeare's best passages: a check-list', *Cambridge Quarterly*, 3 (1968), 267–73.

[46] For example, the dialogue between Mote and Costard and Armado in *Love's Labour's Lost*, 3. 1; the dialogue between the Princess and the Forester in *Love's Labour's Lost*, 4. 1. 11–40; Arthur's speech, *King John*, 4. 1. 60–7; *Taming of the Shrew*, 5. 2. 181–94. R. B. McKerrow gives a total of 1,560 degraded lines, and calculates this as about 1.5 per cent of the total: 'much less than has been rejected by many more recent writers' ('The treatment of Shakespeare's text by his earlier editors, 1709–1768', *Proceedings of the British Academy*, 19 (1933), 89–122; p. 108).

A further significant aspect of the aesthetic orientation of Pope's edition is the extensive 'Index of the Characters, Sentiments, Speeches and Descriptions in Shakespear', which appeared in the sixth volume. The Index was probably assembled by Fenton,[47] but it is in every way consistent with Pope's evaluative approach to Shakespeare. It was evidently designed to accompany a literary text regarded as a thing both of beauty and of use. Section II is an index of gnomic or moral sayings in Shakespeare, instructive and valuable passages on such topics as 'ambition', 'love' (in twenty-eight sub-divisions), or 'gravity affected, to be thought wise'. Section IV is an Index of 'Thoughts, or Sentiments', including such *topoi* as 'bastardy, defended', 'marriage', 'power', and so on. Section VI is an 'Index of Descriptions, or Images', of places ('bank, flowry'; 'Dover Cliff'; 'Pisa'), of persons ('a Foppish courtier'; 'Irishmen'; 'Trojans'), of things, and of times and seasons. Section VII is an 'Index of some Similies and Allusions' ('Authority compared to a Farmer's Dog'; 'Opportunity, to the Tide'). This is an Index which presents Shakespeare as a writer worth reading because he offers both moral instruction and poetic beauty. It is designed to guide the reader to striking or sententious passages, and treats Shakespeare as a storehouse of thoughts and images. In both format and purpose it has some similarity with Edward Bysshe's *Art of English Poetry*, the second part of which was 'A Collection of the most Natural, Agreeable, and Noble *Thoughts* . . . to be found in the best *English Poets*', arranged alphabetically according to theme,[48] or with such later guides to poetic *topoi* and descriptions as John Newbery's *Art of Poetry on a New Plan* (1762). This Index implies a reader looking for instruction, images, and ideas, wishing to find profit and pleasure rather than to be puzzled by interpretative problems. It is appropriate to an edition aimed at a readership in the gentry and aristocracy, male and female, rather than at the scholar or the critic.

In contrast to the extent that aesthetic considerations affect his editorial choices, and to the efforts he makes to provide his reader with assessments of beauties and faults, there is in Pope's edition rather less obvious evidence of interpretative effort in textual choices, or in explication. Many editorial decisions are made without any discussion of the grounds of judgment. In his text of *Hamlet* Pope prints 'mobled queen', and notes the F1 reading 'enobled' (in fact, 'inobled'), but gives no reason at all for the textual choice

[47] See George Sherburn, *The Early Career of Alexander Pope* (Oxford: Oxford University Press, 1934), pp. 235–6. A very short glossary of hard words is offered in the spurious seventh volume edited by Dr George Sewell (1725).

[48] Bysshe's *Art* was first published in 1702, and revised and enlarged in its subsequent editions. It is possible that Pope's selection of passages in Shakespeare may in some cases have derived from Bysshe: see Peter Dixon, 'Edward Bysshe and Pope's "Shakespear"', *Notes and Queries*, 209 (1964), 292–3.

(beyond the presumption that Q2 is the better text). There are a number of silent emendations. Some conjectures appear at the foot of the page: 'Nature is *fire* in love', for example, for '. . . *fine* in love', though neither the necessity nor the justification of the emendation is argued.[49] In his second edition of 1728 Pope adopts several of the emendations that Theobald had urged in *Shakespeare Restored*, including '*canon* 'gainst self-slaughter' and 'sanctified and pious *bawds*', but without acknowledgment or explanation.[50] Explanatory notes are extremely rare, in marked contrast to the variorum editions of later in the century. In the case of *Hamlet* almost half the pages have no notes, and 21 consecutive pages pass without any note of any kind.[51] There are about 65 notes in total, in 127 pages. Many of the notes are one-word glosses. A rare example of an explanatory note is on the 'airy of children, little yases': 'Relating to the playhouses then contending, the *Bankside*, the *Fortune*, &c. – play'd by the Children of his majesty's chappel' – but even here such difficulties as 'yases' are not explained.[52] Pope's second edition (1728) remains thinly annotated, though it does include some new materials in response to, or borrowed from, *Shakespeare Restored*. So widely informed a later editor as Edward Capell, determined to illuminate Shakespeare's expression by reference to Elizabethan and Jacobean usage, might still, as I shall suggest, err simply because the lexicographical aids available to him were not adequate. Pope by contrast very rarely attempts detailed lexical examination; if he does not refer to what was known about Shakespeare's language it is normally through choice.[53]

Pope's Shakespeare certainly involves some significant advances in textual scholarship over that of Rowe, advances that seem, and to some extent are, in an authorial direction.[54] Rowe's edition had been mainly based on the fourth Folio. Pope however consulted the Quartos extensively, assembling 'Parties of my acquaintance ev'ry night, to collate the several Editions of Shakespear's single Plays'.[55] For Pope, reliance on the

[49] *Hamlet*, 2. 2. 493, 4. 5. 163; Pope, *Works of Shakespear* (1723–5), VI. 394, 440.

[50] *Hamlet*, 1. 2. 132, 1. 3. 130; Pope, *The Works of Shakespear* (2nd edn, 8 vols., London, 1728), VIII. 216, 224.

[51] *Works of Shakespear* (1723–5), VI. 441–61.

[52] *Hamlet*, 2. 2. 335; *Works of Shakespear* (1723–5), VI. 390.

[53] One of the very rare exceptions is Pope's explanation of 'blote king' (*Hamlet*, 3. 4. 171) by reference to Skinner's *Lexicon*.

[54] For discussions of Pope as an editor, see, in addition to Dixon's 'Pope's Shakespeare', Thomas R. Lounsbury, *The First Editors of Shakespeare* (London: Nutt, 1906); McKerrow, 'Treatment of Shakespeare's text'; James R. Sutherland, 'The dull duty of an editor', *Review of English Studies*, 21 (1945), 202–15; John A. Hart, 'Pope as scholar-editor', *Studies in Bibliography*, 23 (1970), 45–59; Joseph M. Levine, *The Battle of the Books* (Ithaca and London: Cornell University Press, 1991), pp. 226–32; A. D. J. Brown, 'The little fellow has done wonders', *Cambridge Quarterly*, 21 (1992), 120–49.

[55] Pope to Jacob Tonson, Jr, 16 or 23 May 1722 (*The Correspondence of Alexander Pope*, ed. George Sherburn (5 vols., Oxford: Oxford University Press, 1956), II. 118).

Folio as sole authority was made impossible by his belief that it was an interpolated and corrupted text, riddled with the errors and arbitrary omissions and additions of the player-editors. It appears from his 'Table of the Several Editions of *Shakespear*'s Plays, made use of and compared in this Impression'[56] that Pope had access to at least one Quarto edition of every play published in Shakespeare's own lifetime, with the exception of *Much Ado*, as well as to copies of the first and second Folios, a more complete set of original copies than any other editor before Capell or Jennens would have available. For *Hamlet*, for instance, Pope had Q2 and Q3 as well as the first two Folios. It seems clear that Pope made use of all his Quarto copies in collating the text of the plays, though he probably did not use his Folio copies at all extensively; he seems to have collated his Quartos against Rowe.[57] Pope at a number of points claims that, where the Folio was defective, its readings 'unintelligible' or its sense 'not compleat', he has 'restor'd it to sense from the old edition'. Pope, however, does not always adopt Quarto readings in cases of variance, nor, in contrast to the practice which would be adopted by Theobald, does he restore all the Quarto passages omitted in the Folio edition. In the case of *Hamlet*, for instance, though he restores most of the Quarto passages, Pope relegates to the foot of his page the 'heavy-headed revel' passage, commenting, 'these 21 lines following are in the first edition, but since left out, perhaps as being thought too verbose'.[58]

It is clear that many of Pope's text-editorial decisions were made for essentially aesthetic reasons, rather than to reconstruct an original authorial text. He used Quarto readings not as a matter of course, but where it seemed to him to make better poetry or better drama. Pope set out, in fact, to present a 'best' text. He resorted at times to a process of elaborate selection and alteration amounting to poetic, and dramatic, rewriting.[59] Pope was by no means alone amongst his contemporaries in believing that Elizabethan English was, as compared with the English of his own time, inelegant and incorrect, and that Shakespeare's writings had become foreign not only to the taste but also to the comprehension of early eighteenth-century readers. In a letter to Pope of August 1721 Francis Atterbury wrote that 'in a hundred places I cannot construe [Shakespeare], I don't understand him . . . I protest that Aeschylus does not want a Comment to me more than he does.'[60] By no means unreasonably therefore Pope understood his editorial task to be largely one of mediating

56 Following the Index in volume VI, sig. Oooo1r.
57 See especially Hart, 'Pope as scholar-editor', pp. 50–1.
58 *Hamlet*, A. ii. (following I. 4. 16); *Works of Shakespear* (1723–5), VI. 365–6.
59 See Hart, 'Pope as scholar-editor', and, especially, A. D. J. Brown's analysis of Pope's radical reconstruction of the beginning of *Romeo and Juliet* 4. 5 ('The little fellow has done wonders').
60 Pope, *Correspondence*, II. 78–9.

Shakespeare to the taste as well as to the understanding of readers in his own time. The text of Shakespeare required not only transmission but improvement. What was barbarous in his language needed refinement, what was obscure needed clarification, not, usually, by explicatory gloss, but by modernization and amendment of the text itself. Such a procedure came naturally to a poet who, as J. R. Sutherland has pointed out, had spent much of his life correcting and polishing his own writings and those of other men.[61]

Pope's choice of an aesthetic orientation was wholly reasonable within his historical context. He conceived his business as the mediation of Shakespeare, the author of a past and less cultivated age, to readers in his own. This is a form of modernization more liberal and extensive than that found in recent modernized text editions, but not essentially different in motive. There seems little point in asking whether his judgments are consistent with aesthetic criteria that Shakespeare might have used. They are not, because Pope's orientation is not authorial.

A number of recent commentators have explained Pope's methods in the light of his historical and cultural position.[62] One in particular has made larger claims for the general coherence and utility of Pope's 'poetic response'. A. D. J. Brown gives an account of Pope's editorial procedure in *Romeo and Juliet* 4.5, detailing his very extensive alterations, and demonstrating that Pope *constructs* a text by a series of eclectic decisions based on *aesthetic* criteria. Brown goes beyond a justification of Pope's edition, however, to make a general argument for aesthetic, or 'poetic', editing, at least for Shakespeare:

> The poetic approach, rather than the scholarly one, puts the case that we only have corrupt texts of *Romeo and Juliet*, and that editing the play is not a matter of minor emendation or restoration, but a job which requires major reconstruction by a craftsman with a sensitivity and skill comparable with Shakespeare's . . . For the texts attributed to Shakespeare, only a tiny proportion of the recognisable textual problems can be solved by 'scientific' evidence. Consequently even the most apparently unartistic editor must present a text informed by critical judgments and subjective decisions, even if they are dressed in the language of science.[63]

In these statements Brown begins with the position, prevalent in the eighteenth century, and cogent in any, that, where textual evidence is incomplete, conjectural emendation, on some ground, is inevitable. From that he proceeds however to declare a preference for 'poetic', or aesthetic, grounds of judgment, and concludes by denying any practical distinction

61 Sutherland, 'Dull duty of an editor', p. 213.
62 See especially Hart, 'Pope as scholar-editor', and Sutherland, 'Dull duty of an editor'.
63 Brown, 'The little fellow has done wonders', p. 149; 'Pope's Shakespeare', *Cambridge Quarterly*, 22 (1993), 184.

'between the editor and the artist' in Shakespearean editing. This is simply to beg the questions I have already raised, in relation to Gary Taylor's comment that editorial emendation is 'all too obviously an art', about the nature of scientific evidence and scientific knowledge, and about the possibility of valid knowledge in editorial decisions. Brown denies the possibility of any practical distinction 'between the editor and the artist', and he does so because he believes, like Taylor, that only strictly bibliographical textual problems are capable of 'scientific' solution, and that all other forms of editorial judgment are inescapably subjective. Now it is certainly true that such editorial judgments are no more *verifiable* than other kinds of judgment, including 'scientific' judgments, about complex data, but (as I have already argued) editing may nonetheless aim, by reference to appropriate criteria of interpretative validity, to reconstruct some credible approximation to the author's intended meaning. Such interpretative editorial judgments may be eclectic or conjectural, or both, but they are nonetheless different in kind from decisions made on the basis of subjective aesthetic criteria. Pope of course does not set out to test this possibility. His chief criterion remained, primarily, aesthetic. His editorial work makes no thoroughgoing attempt either to explain or reconstruct authorial meaning.

What is most striking about Pope's successors is not the lingering tendency to an aesthetic approach, but the extent of the movement towards explanation and emendation based, for the most part, on the assumption that there is an authorial text to be recovered and interpreted. Pope's contemporaries and successors understood very well that Pope's was the aesthetic editorial orientation of a poet, rather than the authorial orientation of a scholar. As the writer of *Some Remarks on the Tragedy of Hamlet* (1736) put it, in a remark that indicates how much views about editing had changed in the decade following Pope's Shakespeare, 'the Province of an Editor and a Commentator is quite foreign to that of a Poet. The former endeavours to give us an Author as he is; the latter, by the Correctness and Excellency of his own Genius, is often tempted to give us an Author as he thinks he ought to be.'[64] The significant change, however, had already been effected, in the work of the man who was without any doubt the first modern editor of Shakespeare, Lewis Theobald. The Preface to his 1733 edition contains this explicit statement of editorial purposes: 'The Science of Criticism, as far as it affects an Editor, seems to be reduced to these three Classes; the Emendation of corrupt Passages; the Explanation of obscure and difficult ones; and an Inquiry into the Beauties and Defects of Composition. This Work is principally confin'd to the two former Parts.'[65]

[64] Vickers, III. 41–2.

[65] *Works of Shakespeare*, I. xl–xli. This is one of a number of passages which Warburton claimed to have written for Theobald's Preface. See Peter Seary's argument that 'Theobald may be safely

This threefold division of the science of editing was a familiar one. It is striking and significant however that Theobald makes so clear and so emphatic his commitment to the restoration and interpretation of the text.

Theobald is of course most famous as the hero of the first *Dunciad*, though recent scholarship has been able to paint a fairer and fuller picture.[66] *Shakespeare Restored*, in which Theobald carried out a devastating attack on Pope's editorial methods, is an extraordinary piece of detailed and strenuous critical analysis which already reflects Theobald's qualifications for the task of Shakespearean editing: his practical knowledge of the theatre, his wide reading, his knowledge of secretary hand gained in the course of his training and employment as a lawyer,[67] his extensive familiarity with and recall of Shakespeare's plays themselves, and a striking critical intelligence. The greater part of *Shakespeare Restored* responds to Pope's treatment of *Hamlet*, with a great many of Theobald's own textual proposals and explanations. An Appendix deals with Pope's editorial comments on most of the rest of Shakespeare's plays, with a few further notes on *Hamlet*. After the publication of *Shakespeare Restored* Theobald prepared his own edition of Shakespeare's plays, eventually published in eight volumes in 1733. In the intervening years he appreciably extended his reading, and his knowledge of the literature of Shakespeare's period in particular, and engaged in a long and frequent correspondence with the then little-known cleric William Warburton, in which the two men discussed particular readings and interpretations in Shakespeare.[68]

It is difficult to overstate the innovative importance of Theobald's work on Shakespeare. He was conscious that his edition of Shakespeare was 'the *first Essay* of *literal Criticism* upon any Author in the ENGLISH Tongue', given that Bentley's edition of *Paradise Lost* just one year earlier had been, as Theobald himself put it, 'a Performance of another Species', designed to correct rather than to restore Milton's writing.[69] In his classical editing Bentley had worked in relation to an established traditional body of variorum annotation in the classics. Hume's *Annotations* on *Paradise Lost* are the only other precedent for extensive explanatory commentary on an

credited with the statements of editorial principle found in his Preface' (*Lewis Theobald*, pp. 221–30).

66 The important studies are Seary, *Lewis Theobald*, and Richard Foster Jones, *Lewis Theobald* (New York: Columbia University Press, 1919). A significant earlier defence is John Churton Collins, 'The Porson of Shakspearian criticism', *Quarterly Review*, 175 (1892), 102–31. See also Geoffrey Bullough, 'Theobald on Shakespeare's sources', in *Mirror up to Shakespeare*, ed. J. C. Gray (Toronto: University of Toronto Press, 1984), pp. 15–33.

67 On Theobald's knowledge of secretary hand see Seary, *Lewis Theobald*, *passim*, and especially pp. 213–14.

68 The correspondence is discussed by Seary, *Lewis Theobald*, pp. 102–30.

69 *Shakespeare Restored*, p. 193; Preface to *Works of Shakespeare*, I. xxxix. The comment on Bentley's *Paradise Lost* in the Preface was claimed by Warburton but is probably by Theobald: see note 65 above.

HAMLET, *Prince of* Denmark. 259

As are companions noted and moſt known
To youth and liberty.
Rey. As gaming, my lord——
Pol. Ay, or drinking, fencing, ſwearing,
Quarrelling, drabbing——You may go ſo far.
Rey. My lord, that would diſhonour him.
Pol. Faith, no, as you may ſeaſon it in the Charge;
You muſt not put another ſcandal on him, (23)
That he is open to incontinency,
That's not my meaning; but breathe his faults ſo quaint-
ly,
That they may ſeem the taints of liberty;
The flaſh and out-break of a fiery mind,
A ſavageneſs in unreclaimed blood
Of general aſſault.
Rey. But, my good lord——
Pol. Wherefore ſhould you do this?
Rey. Ay, my lord, I would know that.
Pol. Marry, Sir, here's my drift;

(23) *You muſt not put* another *Scandal on him.*] I once ſuſpected, and attempted to correct, this Paſſage. The old Gentleman, 'tis plain, is of Opinion, that to charge his Son with *Wenching* would not *diſhonour* him; conſequently, would be no Scandal to him. Why then ſhould he caution *Reynoldo* from putting *another* Scandal on him? There can be no *Second* Scandal ſuppos'd, without a firſt implied. On this kind of Reaſoning, I propos'd to correct;

You muſt not put an utter *Scandal on him.* Mr. *Pope,* I obſerve, ſeems to admit the Emendation, but I retract it as an idle, unweigh'd Conjecture. The Reaſoning, on which it is built, is fallacious; and our Author's licentious Manner of expreſſing himſelf elſewhere, convinces me that any Change is altogether unneceſſary. So in King *Richard* II.

Tend'ring the precious Safety of my Prince,
And free from other *misbegotten Hate,*
Come I Appellant to this princely Preſence.

Now, ſtrictly ſpeaking, here, *tendring his Prince's Safety* is his *firſt* miſbegotten *Hate*; which Nobody will ever believe was the Poet's Intention. And ſo, in *Macbeth*;

————— All theſe are portable,
With other *Graces weigh'd.*

Malcolm had been enumerating the ſecret *Enormities* he was guilty of; no *Graces* are mention'd or ſuppos'd; ſo that in grammatical ſtrictneſs, theſe Enormities ſtand in the Place of *firſt* Graces; tho' the Poet means no more than this, that *Malcolm*'s *Vices* would be ſupportable, if his *Graces* on the *other* hand were to be weigh'd againſt them.

R 2 And

Figures 5 and 6 *The Works of Shakespeare* (1733), edited by Lewis Theobald, VII. 259, 313.

Would ſtep from this to this? Senſe, ſure, you have, (50)
Elſe could you not have motion: but, ſure, that ſenſe
Is apoplex'd: for madneſs would not err;
Nor ſenſe to extaſy was ne'er ſo thrall'd,
But it reſerv'd ſome quantity of choice
To ſerve in ſuch a diff'rence.——What devil was't,
That thus hath cozen'd you at hoodman blind?
Eyes without feeling, feeling without ſight,
Ears without hands or eyes, ſmelling *ſans* all,
Or but a ſickly part of one true ſenſe
Could not ſo mope.——
O ſhame! where is thy bluſh? rebellious hell,
If thou canſt mutiny in a matron's bones,
To flaming youth let virtue be as wax,
And melt in her own fire. Proclaim no ſhame, (51)
When the compulſive ardour gives the charge;
Since froſt it ſelf as actively doth burn,

(50) ——*Senſe, ſure, you have,* &c.] Mr. *Pope* has left out the Quantity of about eight Verſes here, which I have taken care to replace. They are not, indeed, to be found in the two elder *Folio's*, but they carry the Style, Expreſſion, and Caſt of Thought, peculiar to our Author; and that they were not an Interpolation from another Hand needs no better Proof, than that they are in all the oldeſt *Quarto's*. The firſt Motive of their being left out, I am perſwaded, was to ſhorten *Hamlet*'s Speech, and conſult the Eaſe of the Actor: and the Reaſon, why they find no Place in the *Folio* Impreſſions, is, that they were printed from the *Play-houſe* caſtrated Copies. But, ſurely, this can be no Authority for a modern Editor to conſpire in mutilating his Author: Such *Omiſſions*, rather, muſt betray a Want of *Diligence*, in *Collating*; or a Want of *Juſtice*, in the *voluntary Stifling*.

(51) ——*Proclaim no ſhame,*
When the compulſive Ardour gives the Charge;
Since Froſt itſelf as actively does burn,
And Reaſon pardons *Will.*] This is, indeed, the Reading of ſome of the elder Copies; and Mr. *Pope* has a ſtrange Fatality, whenever there is a various Reading, of eſpouſing the wrong one. The whole Tenour of the Context demands the Word *degraded* by that judicious Editor;
And Reaſon panders *Will.*
This is the Reflexion which *Hamlet* is making, "Let us not call it "Shame, when Heat of Blood compells young People to indulge their "Appetites; ſince Froſt too can burn, and Age, at that Seaſon when "Judgment ſhould predominate, yet feels the Stings of Inclination, and "ſuffers Reaſon to be the Bawd to Appetite."

And

English classic. I have already remarked on the thinness of annotation in Pope's Shakespeare. In Theobald the sheer bulk of textual and explanatory notes, an obvious first indication of the difference in their purposes, is enormously and strikingly higher. Though perhaps half the pages of Theobald's text bear no commentary, many pages have notes of several lines, and some notes run to a quarter or a half or even three-quarters of a page. This is not yet the proportion found in the later eighteenth-century variorum editions by Johnson, or by Johnson and Steevens (variorums of course tend to grow incrementally), but here clearly is the foundation of that tradition.

For Theobald it is because Shakespeare 'stands, or at least ought to stand, in the Nature of a Classic Writer' that he is the proper subject for commentary, and anyone who has the talent to make comments and corrections 'does not only do a Service to the Poet, but to his Country and its Language'.[70] The national poet is seen as worthy of the care and scholarship which had in the past been lavished on the Greek and Roman writers. Theobald's editorial methods are in important respects based on those which had been employed in the editing of classical literature, and more especially those used by Richard Bentley. Theobald's positioning of a substantial commentary at the foot of the text page, unlike Hume or Pope, is explicitly Bentleian: 'I mean to follow the form of Bentley's Amsterdam *Horace* in subjoining the notes to the place controverted.'[71] More fundamentally, Theobald considered that the textual situation in Shakespeare was analogous to that of the classics, because no 'authentic Manuscript' survived and the textual tradition was radically insecure. Hence, text-editorial method might properly be similar: 'for near a Century, his Works were republish'd from the faulty Copies without the assistance of any intelligent Editor; which has been the Case likewise of many a *Classic* Writer . . . *Shakespeare*'s Case has in a great Measure resembled That of a corrupt *Classic*; and, consequently, the Method of Cure was likewise to bear a Resemblance' (Preface, *Works of Shakespeare*, I. xxxix). The 'Method of Cure' that Theobald had in mind was clearly that exemplified in Richard Bentley's classical editing: the diagnosis of a faulty passage, the proposal and then the substantiation of a conjectural emendation.[72]

Disciple of Bentley that he was, Theobald certainly was more generally inclined to conjectural emendation than a modern editor of Shakespeare would be. It is also true, however, that his work displays a striking contrast with the extensive revision of the original found in Pope's Shakespeare, or

[70] *Shakespeare Restored*, p. v.

[71] Letter to Warburton, 18 November 1731. Nichols, *Illustrations of the Literary History of the Eighteenth Century*, II (1817), p. 621.

[72] For an important and convincing demonstration of how Theobald followed Bentley in his procedures and even in his rhetoric, see Jones, *Lewis Theobald*, *passim*, especially pp. 61–99.

the numerous aesthetically based improvements of Bentley's Milton. His willingness to conjecture grew strikingly less between *Shakespeare Restored* and the edition of 1733. Theobald thought of editorial emendation as an interpretative process – a 'critical' process – designed to recover (to use two of Theobald's common formulations) 'the Meaning of our Author', 'the Poet's Intention'.[73] He insists on the distinction between such a process and 'arbitrary, fantastical, or wanton' conjecture. Certainly 'we should shew very little Honesty, or Wisdom, to play the Tyrants with any Author's Text; to raze, alter, innovate, and overturn, at all Adventures, and to the utter Detriment of his Sense and Meaning'; but it is the editor's responsibility, where no surviving text provides an intelligible meaning, to restore intended authorial sense. He who sets out to edit a book

> at the same time commences *Critick* upon his *Author*; and . . . wherever he finds the Reading suspected, manifestly corrupted, deficient in Sense, and unintelligible, he ought to exert every Power . . . to give Light and restore Sense to the Passage, and, by a reasonable Emendation, to make that satisfactory and consistent with the Context, which before was so absurd, unintelligible, and intricate. (*Shakespeare Restored*, pp. iv-v)

One of Theobald's most insistent themes is his belief that conjecture can be conducted according to principles of rational argument, that interpretative processes, in fact, could be subject to a process of validation. In *Shakespeare Restored* he asserts that 'The Want of *Originals* reduces us to a Necessity of *guessing* in order to amend him; but these Guesses change into Something of a more *substantial* Nature, when they are tolerably supported by *Reason* or *Authorities*' (p. 133). In a letter of 29 January 1730 he reminded the more speculatively inclined Warburton that 'that conjecture has the best chance to be espoused, which is backed with the best shew of reason, or probability'.[74] In the Preface to his edition of 1733 he made the claim that 'my Emendations are so far from being arbitrary or capricious, that They are establish'd with a very high Degree of moral Certainty', and assured his readers that 'where-ever I have ventur'd at an Emendation, a *Note* is constantly subjoin'd to justify and assert the Reason of it' (I. xlii, xliii). Furthermore, conjecture is by no means Theobald's only or indeed his primary resource. His pursuit of the critical process regularly enables him to construe and defend the reading of one of the existing texts, and he generally preferred to do so rather than to amend. This part of his policy is summed up in advice he offered to Warburton, underlined in Theobald's original letter with red ink: 'I ever labour to make the smallest deviations that I can possibly from the text; never to alter at all where I can by any means explain a passage into sense.'[75] Certainly Theobald was prepared to

[73] *Shakespeare Restored*, pp. 133–4, 146. [74] Nichols, *Illustrations*, II. 452–3.

[75] Letter to Warburton, 8 April 1729 (Nichols, *Illustrations*, II. 209–10). For a similar statement, see *Shakespeare Restored*, p. 165.

amend 'against all the Copies', and it is clear that his acquaintance with and use of the early editions, and his understanding of their relative authority, was by modern standards patchy.[76] Theobald nonetheless generally treats the surviving textual witnesses so far as they were known to him with some respect. In the Preface to his edition he claimed, at any point where corruption might be suspected, to have 'thought it my Duty, in the first place, by a diligent and laborious Collation to take in the Assistances of all the older Copies' (I. xlii), though his collation was no doubt much less thorough than that of such eighteenth-century successors as Capell and Jennens. Apparent authorial inaccuracies are not to be corrected against the authority of the copies: 'where the Authority of all the Books makes the Poet commit a Blunder, (whose general Character it is, not to be very exact;) 'tis the Duty of an Editor to shew him as he is' (IV. 112). Theobald justifies his restoration of the passages 'degraded' in Pope's edition by a similar appeal to the authority of the surviving witnesses: 'as we have no Authority to call them in Question for not being genuine I confess, as an Editor, I thought I had no Authority to displace them' (II. 109). The notes to Theobald's edition regularly appeal to the readings of 'the old Copies', the 'oldest Quartos', the 'genuine Copies'.

Whether in attempting to make sense of some obscure reading in an existing witness, or in putting forward a new reading, Theobald put into practice with something like consistency a recognizable set of interpretative criteria. A proposed reading should take into account the evidence provided by the surviving witnesses, and the logical, figurative, and dramatic context and coherence of the passage. Readings should be supported, as appropriate, by parallels from Shakespeare himself, or from other writers of his time, by historical knowledge, and by lexicographical or quasi-lexicographical information. And paraphrase should be used as an explicatory tool.

One of Theobald's most regularly applied procedures of interpretative validation has to do with the process of textual transmission. Where he proposes conjectural emendation he commonly considers 'the traces of the letters', that is, he bears in mind what mistakes might credibly have been made by the printer in construing the author's manuscript. Understanding

[76] F2, F4, and the fifth Quarto (1637) of *Hamlet* are the editions regularly mentioned in the body of *Shakespeare Restored*. By 1733 he had also been able to make use of F1 and the second and third Quartos of *Hamlet* (1605 and 1611); a note in his edition (VII. 321) makes clear they were not available to him in 1726. Printer's copy for Theobald's 1733 edition, no doubt for copyright rather than editorial reasons, was a marked-up copy of Pope's 1728 second edition, now British Library C.45.b.11. In his 'Table of the several Editions of Shakespeare's Plays, Collected by the Editor' (VII. [495–503]) Theobald lists F1 and F2 and a number of Quartos as 'Editions of Authority', F3 and some later Quartos as 'Editions of Middle Authority', and the editions of Pope and Rowe as 'of no Authority'. For a fuller discussion, see Seary, *Lewis Theobald*, especially pp. 132–5.

of the practical possibilities of errors in transcription allows the editor to infer, from the evidence provided by a corrupt printed text, what the author originally wrote. At *Julius Caesar* 2. 1. 40, where the first Folio reads 'first of March', Theobald insists that the logic of the passage requires 'Ides of March', but at once asks how the mistake could have happened:

> how could *Ides*, . . . be corrupted into *first*? What Similitude in the Traces of the Letters? This Difficulty may very easily be solv'd, by only supposing that the Word *Ides* in the Manuscript Copy happen'd to be wrote contractedly thus, j^{s}: The Players knew the Word well enough in the Contraction; but when the MSS came to the *Press*, the Compositors were not so well informed in it: They knew, that jst stood frequently for *first*, and blunderingly thought that j^{s}: was meant to do so too: and thence was deriv'd the corruption of the Text. (VI. 143)

The *ductus litterarum* is frequently appealed to as part at least of his arguments for conjectural emendations. One of his most famous and generally accepted emendations is of *Romeo and Juliet* 1. 1. 148–50, which in early Quarto and Folio texts[77] reads:

> As is the bud bit with an envious worm
> Ere he can spread his sweet leaves to the air
> Or dedicate his beauty to the same.

'The *same*' strikes Theobald, in *Shakespeare Restored*, as a mere expletive, and, beginning his argument with an appeal to figurative logic, he points out that 'there is some Power else besides *balmy Air*, that . . . makes the tender Buds spread themselves', and suggests 'dedicate his beauty to the *sun*'. He is aware, however, of the need to explain how such an error in the transmission of manuscript to print could occur, and improves the emendation with this note: 'or *Sunne*, according to the old Spelling, which brings it nearer to the Traces of the corrupted Text'.[78]

Theobald is often prepared to provide conjectural emendations which restore coherence lost in the corruption of the author's original text, or to use the argument from the coherence of the verbal or dramatic context to defend a choice amongst variants. Sir Toby tells Andrew Aguecheek in *Twelfth Night* that, had he followed the arts, he might have had 'an excellent head of hair', since, as the Folio has it, 'it will not *cool my* nature' (I. 3. 92–8). This is, as Theobald points out, an 'Absurdity': he suggests the emendation *curl by*, pointing out that 'the Context is an unexceptionable Confirmation' ('it hangs like flax on a distaff').[79] At *Hamlet* 3. 2. 160

[77] Qq. 2, 3, 4, and the Folios. The passage is not in Q1.

[78] *Shakespeare Restored*, pp. 190–1. For two further examples, see *Shakespeare Restored*, p. 171; and his note on *Timon of Athens*, 4. 3. 9 (*Works of Shakespeare*, V. 272–3).

[79] *Works of Shakespeare*, II. 465–6. Compare Theobald's similarly persuasive emendation of the Folio's 'Bank and *School* of Time', at *Macbeth* 1. 7. 6, to *shoal* (*Works of Shakespeare*, V. 405). The Oxford editors note that 'Theobald's reading "shoal", strictly a modernization, has the force of an emendation' (Wells and Taylor, *Textual Companion*, p. 544).

Theobald defends his choice of 'as my love is *siz'd*', based on Q2 *ciz'd*, as against Pope and Rowe's *fix'd*, which derives from F3 and F4, on the grounds that 'the whole Tenour of the Context demands this Reading. For the Lady evidently is talking here of the Quantity and Proportion of her Love and Fear, not of their Continuance.'[80] At *Hamlet* 5. 2. 219 Theobald reasons for the Folio reading, 'And in the cup an *union* shall he throw', against Q2 *onixe*, partly because he knows that a 'union' was 'a fine Sort of *Pearles*', but, more importantly, from the logic of the dramatic action. Fifteen lines later Claudius performs his promise by giving Hamlet a 'pearl' to drink in the cup: 'Now if an *Union* be a Species of *Pearl* . . . the King saying that *Hamlet* has earn'd the Pearl, I think, amounts to a Demonstration, that it was an *Union-pearl* he meant to throw into the Cup.' Here as ever Theobald is happy 'to expound the Author by himself; which is the surest Means of coming at the Truth of his Text'.[81]

Many of Theobald's text-critical decisions appeal to some aspect of the larger literary and historical context of Shakespeare's plays, a necessary factor for Theobald as for modern intentionalists in the valid construction of his author's willed meaning. He is entirely explicit about this. He offers a significant summary statement of his policy of contextualizing as a basis for interpretative judgment in the Preface to his edition:

Some Remarks are spent in explaining Passages, where the Wit or Satire depends on an obscure Point of History; Others, where Allusions are to Divinity, Philosophy, or other Branches of Science. Some are added to shew, where there is a Suspicion of our Author having borrow'd from the Antients: Others, to shew where he is rallying his Contemporaries; or where He himself is rallied by them. And some are necessarily thrown in, to explain an obscure and obsolete *Term*, *Phrase*, or *Idea*. (I. xliv)

In order to illustrate the historically specific elements in Shakespeare's characters, we are told, an editor should be 'well vers'd in the History and Manners of his Author's Age' (I. xlv–xlvi). Elsewhere in the Preface Theobald provides an account of the course of study he undertook to prepare himself for his editorial task:

to clear up several Errors in the Historical Plays, I purposely read over *Hall* and *Holingshead*'s Chronicles in the Reigns concern'd; all the Novels in *Italian*, from which our Author had borrow'd any of his Plots; such Parts of *Plutarch*, from which he had deriv'd any Parts of his *Greek* or *Roman* Story: *Chaucer* and *Spenser*'s Works; all the Plays of *B. Jonson*, *Beaumont* and *Fletcher*, and above 800 old *English* Plays, to ascertain the obsolete and uncommon Phrases in him. (I. lxvii–lxviii)

'800 old *English* Plays' may be an exaggeration, but *The Catalogue of the*

[80] *Works of Shakespeare*, VII. 297. Compare Theobald's argument for 'Reason *panders* will' at *Hamlet* 3. 4. 80 (*Works of Shakespeare*, VII. 313).
[81] *Shakespeare Restored*, pp. 127–9.

Library of Lewis Theobald, Deceas'd (1744) contains some hundreds of such items, including a lot of 'One hundred ninety-five old English Plays in Quarto, . . . *to many of which are Manuscript Notes and Remarks of Mr Theobald's*', in addition to works by Marston, Massinger, Lyly, and Beaumont and Fletcher, as well as Theobald's copies of early texts of Shakespeare himself.[82] Theobald's reading extended well beyond the works he listed. He had a wide acquaintance with the Greek and Latin classics. Like Patrick Hume and not many other contemporaries he had some knowledge of Old and Middle English literature. He had read in Caxton and Lydgate, in the antiquaries Stow and Camden, in Hakluyt's voyages, in such sixteenth-century poets as Wyatt, Surrey, Daniel, and Lodge, and in the records of the State Trials. And, to the considerable contempt of Pope, but to the considerable advantage of himself as an editor, Theobald was acquainted with a good deal of the ephemeral writing of his author's period.

Theobald's remarkably extensive knowledge of literature of all kinds from Shakespeare's time – what Pope dismissively called 'all such reading as was never read' – regularly allows him to support his textual judgment with validating historical contextualizations, or to illustrate and explain Shakespearean obscurities. Hamlet speaks (5. 1. 88) of playing at *loggats* with my Lady Worm's skull: Pope following Rowe amends to *loggers*, but Theobald, on the basis of a passage in Ben Jonson's *Tale of a Tub* ('Now are they tossing of his Legs and Arms / Like Loggats at a Pear-tree') and of Statute 33 Henry VIII, ch. 9, §16, knows that loggats was a game, and feels authorized to restore the Folio reading (VII. 347). He was the first to note that Edgar's mad speech at *Lear* 3. 4. 48ff. is not merely 'the Coinage of the Poet's Brain', but in part contemporary allusion, deriving from Samuel Harsnett's *A Declaration of Egregious Popish Impostures* (1603). Theobald understood the possible use of sources and allusions for interpretative purposes, writing in his Preface that 'in his *Historical Plays*, whenever our *English* Chronicles, and in his Tragedies when any *Greek* or *Roman* Story, could give any light; no Pains have been omitted to set Passages right by comparing my Author with his Originals'.[83] At *A Midsummer Night's Dream* 2. 1. 78, where Quarto and Folio read *Perigenia*, and Pope has *Peregenia*, he notes that this is a reference to 'a famous Lady, by whom *Theseus* had his Son *Melanippus*', and therefore corrects the place, 'from the Authority of the *Greek* Writers', to *Perigune* (*Shakespeare Restored*, pp. 159–60). Theobald at

[82] On Theobald's library, see Seary, *Lewis Theobald*, pp. 231–6; Lounsbury, *The First Editors of Shakespeare*, pp. 551–3; Churton Collins, 'The Porson of Shakspearian criticism', pp. 110–11. Theobald in fact contributed, with Seward and Sympson, to an edition of Beaumont and Fletcher, published in ten volumes in 1750, ten years after Theobald's death.

[83] *Works of Shakespeare*, I. xlii. On Theobald's scholarship in and use of Shakespearean sources, see Bullough, 'Theobald on Shakespeare's sources'.

least as frequently uses the identification of sources and allusions to explain as to amend. He is able to make sense of 'the dreadful Sagittary' of *Troilus and Cressida* (5. 5. 14) by reference to 'the Three Destructions of Troy, printed by Caxton in 1471, and Wynkyn de Werde in 1503',[84] which tells of 'a mervayllouse beste called *Sagittarye*, that *made the Grekes sore afrede*'.

Perhaps the best-known of Theobald's many persuasive conjectural emendations comes at *Henry V* 2. 3. 16, where the Folio has the Hostess report of the dying Falstaff that 'His nose was as sharp as a pen, and a table of green fields'. Pope, thinking not unreasonably that no sense could be made of this and that a conjectural emendation was therefore absolutely necessary, had surmised that 'a table of *green fields*' must have been a marginal instruction to a property man of that name. In his response in *Shakespeare Restored* to Pope's treatment of the passage, Theobald insists that emendation must be based not on guesswork but on appropriate knowledge, in this case, of Shakespeare's theatre: 'Something more than *Ingenuity* is wanting, to make [Pope's] Conjectures pass current; and That is a *competent Knowledge* of the *Stage* and its *Customs*.' Theobald demolishes Pope's guess with an account distinguishing the roles of prompter, property man, and scene-keeper, briefly proposes an alternative solution based like Pope's on a misplaced 'Direction to the *Scene-Keepers*', and then goes on to proffer instead the brilliant suggestion, 'a' babled of green fields'. This conjecture is supported by Theobald from the coherent sense it makes in its context, its closeness to the 'Traces of the Letters', and, tellingly, its human credibility: 'To *bable* . . . is to mutter, or speak indiscriminately, like Children that cannot yet talk, or dying Persons when they are losing the Use of Speech.'[85]

Time and again Theobald's arguments for retention of witnessed readings, or for the necessity of a conjectural emendation, are supported by parallel passages from elsewhere in Shakespeare. This is of course the principle of conference of places, which had long been established as a key principle of validation in classical and biblical criticism, and which was central to the Anglican argument for validity in scriptural interpretation. Theobald states this explicitly as a principle of interpretative validation in *Shakespeare Restored*: 'As every Author is best expounded and explain'd in *One* Place, by his own Usage and Manner of Expression in *Others*; wherever our Poet receives an Alteration in his Text from any of my *Corrections* or *Conjectures*, I have throughout endeavour'd to support what I offer by *parallel*

[84] Theobald's letter to *Mist's Journal*, 16 March 1728; reprinted by Nichols, *Illustrations*, II. 203–4.
[85] *Shakespeare Restored*, pp. 137–8. This, perhaps Theobald's most famous conjectural emendation, has been accepted by most subsequent editors, including Gary Taylor and Stanley Wells. For attempts to make sense of the Folio reading, see Zachary Grey, *Critical, Historical, and Explanatory Notes on Shakespeare. With Emendations of the Text and Metre* (2 vols., London, 1754), I. 381–2; and the list of modern defences given by John H. Walter in his Arden edition of *Henry V* (London: Methuen, 1965), p. [174]. For other instances of Theobald's use of his knowledge of stage-practice, see *Shakespeare Restored*, pp. 158, 159.

Passages, and *Authorities* from himself.'[86] In both *Shakespeare Restored* and his edition Theobald applies this method quite as frequently, and as consistently, as he claims. Another of Theobald's well-known conjectural emendations is of Polonius's warning to Ophelia about the honesty of Hamlet's intentions:

> Do not believe his vows; for they are brokers,
> . . .
> Breathing like sanctified and pious bonds.
>
> (1. 3. 130)

Thus Q2 and F1; thus, as Theobald puts it in *Shakespeare Restored*, 'all the Impressions, which have ever come in my Way'. But Theobald at once suspects the sense: 'What Ideas can we form to our selves of a *breathing bond*, or of its being *sanctified* and *pious*?' Because it makes no sense the reading 'is certainly corrupt', and Theobald therefore conjectures that the poet wrote: 'Breathing like sanctified and pious *bawds*', which has been accepted by most subsequent editors. The justification of the change is that 'it is usual with our Poet . . . to give those infamous Creatures the Style and Title of *Brokers*'. In *Shakespeare Restored* the usage is established with parallel passages from *The Two Gentlemen of Verona* and *All's Well*, concluding with an appositional phrase from *King John* which serves virtually to define the Shakespearean usage: 'This BAWD, this BROKER' (2. 1. 583).[87] As he very often does, Theobald here also provides evidence from other principles of validation; his change is 'a Continuation of the plain and natural Sense', consistent with the 'Chain of the . . . *Metaphors*'. In another place, Theobald's increasing familiarity with Shakespeare and other dramatists allows him to withdraw his own conjectural emendation and defend the existing reading. In the body of *Shakespeare Restored* he amends the Folio reading of *Hamlet* 4. 7. 114, 'a sword unbaited', to *imbaited*. By the time he wrote the Appendix, however, he had begun to suspect that *unbaited* means unblunted, 'not robb'd of its point'; and by the time he prepared his edition he was able to provide corroborating examples of this from *Measure for Measure*, *Love's Labour's Lost*, and the second part of *Henry IV*, as well as from Ben Jonson's *Sad Shepherd*:

> As far as her proud scorning him could bate
> Or blunt the edge of my Lover's Temper.[88]

Parallels are regularly found in non-Shakespearean writing. Where Hamlet's threat to 'drink up esill' (5.1.266, Qq; F *esile*) had baffled previous editors, Theobald was able to show, by citing parallels in Chaucer, More,

[86] *Shakespeare Restored*, p. viii. The point is emphatically reiterated, in very similar words, in the Preface to the *Works of Shakespeare* (1. xliii).

[87] *Shakespeare Restored*, pp. 26–8.

[88] *Shakespeare Restored*, pp. 119ff., 191–2; *Works of Shakespeare*, VII. 364.

and Shakespeare himself, that this is an old word for vinegar. He alters the spelling to *eisel*, the form he had found in Chaucer's *Romaunt of the Rose*, in *A Lover's Complaint*, and this demonstrative example from Sir Thomas More: 'How Christ for thee fasted with Eisel and Gall'.[89]

I have argued in chapter 2 that periphrastic explanation had been a feature of scriptural as well as classical commentary. As Hume and his successors had done in the editing of Milton, Theobald introduced periphrasis into his edition of Shakespeare as a key weapon in his interpretative armoury. One of many possible examples appears in *Hamlet*. In lines which Samuel Johnson would describe as 'obscure and affected', Laertes offers this poignant comment on Ophelia's loss of her wits following her loss of her father (and her loss of Hamlet):

> Nature is fine in love, and where 'tis fine
> It sends some precious instance of itself
> After the thing it loves.
>
> (4. 5. 163–4)

A puzzled Pope had conjectured that Shakespeare had meant to put into Laertes's mouth the words 'Nature is *fire* in love . . . *incense* of itself'. Theobald, however, always prepared to put more effort than his predecessor into explanation of the surviving texts, justifies the Folio reading. In the note on this passage in his edition he begins by offering this cogent paraphrase, conventionally identified as such by the double quotation marks, which modern editors have substantially followed:[90]

I conceive, that this might be the Poet's Meaning, "In the Passion of Love, Nature becomes more exquisite of Sensation, is more delicate and refin'd; *that is*, Natural Affection, rais'd and sublim'd into a Love-Passion, becomes more inflamed and intense than usual; and where it is so, as People in Love generally send what they have of most valuable after their Lovers; so poor *Ophelia* has sent her most precious Senses after the Object of her inflamed Affections." (VII. 733–4)

This credible explanation is, as so often, supported by parallel passages, expressing similar sentiments, in *As You Like it*, *Troilus*, and *Othello*.[91]

89 *Works of Shakespeare*, VII. 352–3.

90 See, for example, Harold Jenkins's note on this line in *The Arden Shakespeare: Hamlet* (London: Methuen, 1982). George Hibbard in the Oxford edition prefers to accept Samuel Johnson's more alchemical gloss: 'Love . . . is the passion by which [human] nature is most exalted and refined; and as substances, refined and subtilised, easily obey any impulse, or follow any attraction, some part of nature, so purified and refined, flies off after the attracting object, after the thing it loves.'

91 Theobald had put the substance of this note to Warburton in a letter of 4 December 1731. See Jones, *Lewis Theobald*, pp. 288–9. For other instances of Theobald's use of paraphrase, see, for example, his notes on *Hamlet* 3. 4. 80 (*Works of Shakespeare*, VII. 313: here he explains and defends the Folio reading 'and reason *panders* will'), and 3. 4. 144 (*Works of Shakespeare*, VII. 316–17) where he explains and defends the F and Q2 reading 'rank corruption, *mining* all within' against Rowe and Pope's adoption of F3 and F4 *running*.

A pervasive and persuasive feature of Theobald's editorial judgment is its constant reference to the question of what reading, and what meaning, is the most probable in the light of Shakespeare's *usus scribendi*: his figurative habits, his tendency to anachronism, his idiolect, his metrics. The implications of Theobald's correcting Shakespeare 'from himself' go further than particular readings. His knowledge of larger issues of Shakespearean poetic practice make him on the whole less willing than some of his contemporaries and successors to make editorial emendations on the basis of his own, rather than his author's, taste. This is already true of many of his judgments in *Shakespeare Restored* in 1726. The Folio reading of a line in *The Merchant of Venice* – 'Not on thy Sole, but on thy soul, harsh Jew' – struck Theobald, as it had struck Pope, as 'a sort of Conceit, and Jingle upon two Words'. Pope avoids this Shakespearean barbarity by amending to 'Not on thy SOUL'. Theobald however restores the Folio reading, partly by his familiar use of parallels, and partly because of his sense of the proper function of the editor. However infelicitous the jingle may seem to eighteenth-century sensibilities, it is nonetheless probably Shakespeare's own: 'I dare affirm, This is the very *Antithesis* of our Author; and I am the more confident, because it was so usual with him to play on Words in this manner.' The point is made by a particularly appropriate parallel from *Romeo and Juliet*:

> You have dancing Shoes
> With nimble soles, I have a soul of lead.
>
> (1. 4. 14–15)

If the words are those of the author, it is not the business of his editor to attempt aesthetic improvement: 'if I restore his Meaning, and his Words, he himself is accountable to the Judges for writing them'.[92] Similarly, amongst many such examples of acceptance of Shakespeare's figurative writing, Theobald accepts 'sea of troubles', 'considering the great liberties that this Poet is observed to take, elsewhere, in his *Diction*, and *Connexion* of *Metaphors*' (*Shakespeare Restored*, p. 82). One of Theobald's most important statements on Shakespearean anachronisms follows from his detection of Pope in an unacknowledged alteration of one of Hector's speeches from *Troilus and Cressida*:

> not much
> Unlike Young Men, whom *Aristotle* thought
> Unfit to hear moral Philosophy.
>
> (2. 2. 164–6)

[92] *Shakespeare Restored*, pp. 168–9. The point is a common one in the notes in Theobald's edition. Compare his remark on *Love's Labour's Lost* 5. 1. 51: 'Tho' my Correction restores but a poor *Conundrum*, yet if it restores the Poet's Meaning, it is the Duty of an Editor to trace him in his lowest Conceits' (*Works of Shakespeare*, II. 149).

Pope in his Preface had spoken of this as one of 'the many blunders and illiteracies of the first publishers of his works', and in his text adopted Rowe's emendation to 'whom *graver sages* thought'. Theobald writes a long note, which begins with derision (the concept of philosophy itself was no more contemporaneous with Hector than was Aristotle himself), and continues with a long and in some ways subtle discussion of Shakespeare's flexible dealings with time.[93] Such things were common in Shakespeare: Theobald provides several further instances from *Troilus*, and several from other plays, including the 'curfew' in *Lear* and the 'cannon' in *King John*, and then goes on to provide more both from the English drama and from the classics. There is a nice sense that in the case of a play on the stage considerations other than strict historical accuracy might apply: the audience might not have been 'so exactly inform'd in Chronology'; when Pandarus concludes *Troilus* with a reference to 'some galled goose of Winchester' he is addressing the audience directly, 'and then there may be . . . greater Latitude for going out of Character'; and in *Lear*, when the Fool promises that 'this prophecy Merlin shall make; for I do live before his time', Theobald is aware that Shakespeare is indulging himself in self-conscious irony ('our Author . . . may be presum'd to sneer at his own Licentiousness in these Points'). So Theobald is able to demonstrate that 'all these Transgressions in Time . . . are Liberties taken knowingly by the Poet', not necessarily blunders of his own or the first printers; and he is able to mount, against an editor proceeding on aesthetic lines, a defence of the reading of the surviving copies. There is a similar defence of Shakespearean practice against modern editorial emendation in the areas of Shakespearean syntax and metrics. In Claudius's speech at *Hamlet* 1. 2. 36–7, Pope's edition follows Rowe in a reading which first appeared in the 1676 Quarto:

> Giving to you no further personal power
> *Of Treaty* with the King.

'This is a Reading adopted', Theobald replies in *Shakespeare Restored*, 'and of a modern Stamp . . .; either from Want of Understanding the Poet's genuine Words, or on a Supposition of their being too stiff and obsolete', and he re-asserts the Folio reading, '*To business* with the King', justifying 'to business' as a typically Shakespearean coinage of a verbal usage from a substantive, and illustrating the point with no fewer than eighteen examples.[94] Theobald also resists modern attempts to smooth out the irregularities of Shakespeare's metres. At *Henry VIII* 3. 2. 47 he prefers to retain the

93 *Shakespeare Restored*, pp. 134–5.
94 *Shakespeare Restored*, pp. 7–11. Hibbard follows E. A. Abbott's *Shakespearean Grammar* (3rd edn, London: Macmillan, 1870; rptd New York: Dover, 1966), §186, in construing 'To business' as 'with regard to', 'for'.

reading of 'all the Old Copies' ('Marry, this is *yet* but young'). The 'modern Editors have expung'd this harmless Monosyllable, *yet*'; in this, insists Theobald, they 'advance a *false Nicety* of Ear against the *Licence* of SHAKESPEARE's *Numbers*: nay, indeed, against the Licence of all *English* Versification'.[95]

One of the most significant problems facing Theobald and the other pioneering editors of vernacular classics in general, and of Shakespeare in particular, was making sense of obscure, uncommon, or obsolete vocabulary. One of the modern editor's most regularly used interpretative aids has been the historical dictionary, especially the *Oxford English Dictionary*, and will be the electronic text database. No adequate historical dictionary was available to eighteenth-century editors before Johnson's *Dictionary*, a work heavily drawn on by Johnson himself in his work on Shakespeare. Theobald had to rely on much less satisfactory lexicographical resources, and on his own wide knowledge, and detailed recall, of writing of Shakespeare's time. He apparently intended to add to his edition 'a complete and copious glossary', which would have anticipated the Shakespeare glossaries of such later editors as Capell; it was not published, but may well have been prepared for publication.[96] In *Shakespeare Restored* and his edition Theobald regularly draws on such lexicographical aids as he could, and most frequently on Stephen Skinner's *Etymologicon Linguae Anglicanae* (1671), as validation of his interpretations and emendations. Where Pope had glossed 'unaneled' at *Hamlet* 1. 5. 77 ('Unhouseled, dis-appointed, unaneled') as 'no bell rung', Theobald appealed to Skinner to gloss the word correctly as '*Not being anointed*, or, *not having the extream Unction*'.[97] At *Hamlet*, A.xv.1, Theobald defends the Q5 (1637) reading, 'The *scrimers* of their nation', against the emendation *fencers* in the 1676 'Players' Quarto', 'which is but a Gloss of the more obsolete Word'. In his discussion of the passage in *Shakespeare Restored* Theobald cites from Skinner an elaborate etymology which might put us in mind of Patrick Hume's annotations on Milton.[98] On some occasions it is because the lexicographical information available to him was inadequate that Theobald feels the necessity of conjectural emendation in order to find his author's sense behind the faulty text. At *Macbeth* 3. 2. 15 all the early editions read 'We have *scorch'd* the snake, not killed it.' Theobald acutely realizes that 'scorched', in the modern sense, cannot be right, and proposes 'scotched', noting that 'To *scotch*, however the Generality of our *Dictionaries* happen to omit the Word, signifies to *notch*, *slash*, *cut* . . . *&c.* and so SHAKESPEARE more than once has used it in his

95 *Works of Shakespeare*, v. 57.

96 Preface, *Works of Shakespeare*, 1. xliv. See Seary, *Lewis Theobald*, p. 177n.

97 *Shakespeare Restored*, p. 53.

98 *Shakespeare Restored*, pp. 117–18 and n.; *Works of Shakespeare*, VII. 340.

Works.'[99] Here Theobald has penetrated to the likely meaning, but the emendation is nonetheless unnecessary: 'scorch' in the sixteenth and seventeenth centuries could, after all, mean to slash with a knife (OED, *scorch*, v.3, citing, together with earlier and later examples, this line from *Macbeth*). There are many such cases where Theobald amends, not wilfully, but because the information available to him made it otherwise difficult or impossible for him to find an interpretation. At *Hamlet* 3. 3. 88 Rowe and Pope's editions read 'Up sword, and know thou a more horrid *time*'. Theobald remarks in his edition that this 'is a sophisticated Reading, warranted by none of the Copies of any Authority' (it derives in fact from the 1676 Quarto), and that Q2 and Q3, and F1 and F2, all read *hent*. That must be a corruption, however, as 'there is no such *English* Substantive'. In a letter to Warburton he therefore concludes that 'we must either restore *bent* or *hint*'.[100] In his edition he chooses the former: 'with the Change of a single Letter, our Author's genuine Word was, *Bent*; i.e. *Drift, Scope, Inclination, Purpose*, &c.', a word commonly used by Shakespeare (VII. 309). Theobald was proud enough of this credible and reasoned emendation to claim that he had made it before seeing F4, where it is anticipated. Modern editors, with access to better lexicographical information, may choose to retain *hent*, meaning 'grasp' (Philip Edwards, in the Cambridge edition), or modernize to *hint*, for which *hent* was a possible seventeenth-century spelling (Hibbard, Wells, and Taylor, in their Oxford editions).[101]

It is of course true of the history of eighteenth-century editing that, as knowledge of all kinds increased, it became more possible to explain apparent difficulties in the terms of the text, its language, and its culture, rather than to seek conjectural correction in terms of the editor's own subjective criteria. It is possible to show an analogous process of development in Theobald's own editing. A key issue here is the notion of what is 'English' and what is not. A regular stratagem of subjective conjecture, especially in Warburton, was to complain that a reading of the early texts was not 'English', and to amend, accommodating the text to eighteenth-century standards of correctness of expression. A tendency to require Shakespeare to write a clear and logical English is one of the few subjective elements of Theobald's early method in *Shakespeare Restored*: if '*Grammar* and the *Idiom* of the Tongue' make against a surviving reading 'we have sufficient Warrant to make him *now*, at least, speak true *English*' (p. 41). He describes the 'dram of eale' passage in the Q2 text of the first act of *Hamlet* (A.ii.20) as 'more intricate and deprav'd in the Text, of less meaning to outward appearance' (p. 35) than any other he knows, and complains that it

[99] *Shakespeare Restored*, pp. 185–6.
[100] Nichols, *Illustrations*, II. 572.
[101] For analogous cases, see Theobald's notes on *Hamlet*, I. 2. 141 and 3. 2. 261 (*Works of Shakespeare*, VII. 236–7, 301–2).

has 'neither *Sense*, *Grammar*, nor *English* as it now stands'; in his edition he repeats the note, but drops the comment about the failure of 'English' (VII. 248). In *Shakespeare Restored* (pp. 60–1) Theobald feels the need to amend Polonius's instruction to Reynaldo, 'You must not put another scandal on him' (*Hamlet*, 2. 1. 29) to make it conform to the logic of an English that he would understand, suggesting 'You must not put *an utter* scandal on him', as usual explaining the reasons for the change by paraphrase. By 1733 he has changed his mind: 'our Author's licentious Manner of expressing himself elsewhere, convinces me that any Change is altogether unnecessary'. In the place of his earlier conjecture he offers, as he so often does, a sophisticated explanation with validating parallels, in this case from *Richard II* and *Macbeth*.

Some editors in Theobald's own time and in ours have felt able to indulge themselves in feelings of superiority, on account of some deficiencies in his work evident enough by hindsight: a readiness to entertain conjectural possibilities that became less fashionable as the eighteenth century passed, a tendency in some of his work to a Bentleian rhetorical tone, and a very imperfect understanding of the early Shakespearean textual situation. Theobald however opened up some of the key areas which were exploited and developed by later editors, and indeed set much of the agenda for their work. He brought to his editing a keen interpretative intelligence, and a specialized knowledge of Shakespeare and of the literature of Shakespeare's time that would be approached by very few other scholars before Edward Capell. Early though he may come in the process, Theobald's work reveals much about how rational criteria may be used in editing and interpretation, and especially about the validating uses of linguistic, literary, and historical knowledge.

Warburton and his antagonists: Upton, Edwards, Johnson

While he was working on his edition of Shakespeare (and for some period thereafter) Theobald conducted a lengthy correspondence with William Warburton, in which the two men discussed numerous particular problems in Shakespeare.[102] By the mid-1730s, however, the two men had fallen out, chiefly because of Warburton's sense that the suggestions he had made towards the annotation of Shakespeare had not been adequately used in Theobald's edition, and that neither these, nor his contributions to Theobald's Preface, had been adequately acknowledged.[103] In 1738 the

[102] Most of Warburton's letters are lost. Theobald's side of the correspondence may be found in John Nichols, *Illustrations*, II. 189–656; additional letters are printed by R. F. Jones (*Lewis Theobald*, pp. 258–346). Seary provides a reasoned discussion of the correspondence (*Lewis Theobald*, pp. 102–30).

[103] See Seary, *Lewis Theobald*, p. 130, and n. 93; Jones, *Lewis Theobald*, pp. 343–4. The personal rights and wrongs of the argument have usually been assessed in Theobald's favour: see

ambitious Warburton hitched his wagon to an altogether brighter star, with his defence in the *History of the Works of the Learned*[104] of Pope's *Essay on Man* against the strictures of Crousaz. Warburton became the closest ally of the great poet in his last years, and, after Pope's death in 1744, his literary executor. In 1747 Warburton's own eight-volume edition of Shakespeare was published as the product of Pope as well as himself, with a title which made clear his exceptions against Theobald and the 'Oxford' editor, Thomas Hanmer: *The Works of Shakespear . . . Restored from the Blunders of the First Editors, and the Interpolations of the Two Last.*

Warburton's edition is of little value in itself, but as it looks back to and reacts against Theobald, and as later scholars and editors would in their turn formulate their reactions against Warburton, it may be seen as a key moment of theoretical negotiation in Shakespearean editing in the eighteenth century, in rather the same way as Richard Bentley's 1732 edition of *Paradise Lost* had been for Miltonic editing. Warburton's statements and practices in his edition raise important theoretical questions about the use, basis, and validation of conjectural procedure, and about the assessment of authorial and documentary authority.

If Warburton were to be accepted at his own valuation he might appear to be a responsible and qualified humanist editor, believing in the vital cultural importance of the editorial endeavour, and concerned in particular to rescue Shakespeare from the ravages of the past. In his Preface to his edition Warburton argues that 'Nature and true Wisdom' have thought one's mother tongue best served by editing, or commenting on, its literary writings (I. xxiv). He notes with approval the imminent appearance of editions of Fletcher and Milton,[105] and concludes with a defence of the 'deathless labours' of Scaliger, Casaubon, Bentley, and others, without which 'the western World, at the revival of Letters, had soon faln back again into a state of ignorance and barbarity' (I. xxiv–xxviii). Shakespeare's plays in particular require the humanist editor's assistance, having come to light 'so disguised and travested, that no classic Author, after having run ten secular Stages thro' the blind Cloisters of Monks and Canons, ever came out in half so maimed and mangled a Condition' (I. vii). Warburton

Churton Collins, 'The Porson of Shakspearian Criticism', pp. 105–7; Lounsbury, *The First Editors of Shakespeare*, p. 521; Leslie Stephen, biography of Warburton in *Dictionary of National Biography*; R. F. Jones, *Lewis Theobald*, especially pp. 166–8; Seary, *Lewis Theobald*, pp. 102–30 *passim.* For judgments more favourable to Warburton, see A. W. Evans, *Warburton and the Warburtonians* (London: Oxford University Press, 1932), pp. 143–7; David Nichol Smith, *Eighteenth-Century Essays on Shakespeare* (2nd edn, Oxford: Oxford University Press, 1963), pp. xlv–l.

[104] Collected and published as *A Vindication of Mr Pope's Essay on Man* (1739).

[105] Presumably he had in mind Thomas Newton's edition of Milton, and *The Works of Beaumont and Fletcher, with Notes critical and explanatory by Messrs Theobald, Seward and Sympson* (10 vols., 1750). Theobald was responsible for vol. I and parts of II and III.

gives promises that he will explain Shakespeare in the light of Shakespeare's own linguistic and cultural usage and context. Shakespeare's 'genuine Text' can be established only by recognizing and showing 'the peculiar Sense of the Terms', by clarifying his 'hard and unnatural Construction', by explaining his 'far-fetched and quaint Allusions' (I. xvi, xvii). As Warburton undertakes the bringing to bear of relevant contextual knowledges in his explanatory notes, so he promises a considered and supported use of conjecture, in those places only where 'the Poet's genuine Text' was apparently inextricably obscured: 'how much soever I may have given Scope to critical Conjecture, where the old Copies failed me, I have indulged nothing to Fancy or Imagination; but have religiously observ'd the severe Canons of literal Criticism; as may be seen from the Reasons accompanying every Alteration of the common Text' (I. xiv). In its statement of first resort to the surviving early witnesses, its eschewing of the fanciful and subjective in conjecture, and its assertion that there are principles of procedure for textual criticism, this is a formulation broadly consistent with Theobald's position, and not obviously criminal, except in its reference to the 'common Text' or *textus receptus*, even by more modern theoretical standards.

In Warburton's edition itself, however, these promises of principled procedure in explication and emendation were notoriously contradicted. Warburton's massive reading and learning was mostly in his own professional fields of law, theology, and church history, whose bearing on the understanding of Shakespeare's text is only from time to time to the purpose.[106] Warburton did not have Theobald's familiarity with the literature, more particularly the dramatic literature, of Shakespeare's age. Furthermore, and characteristically, despite his protestations in the Preface, Warburton was the clearest instance amongst Shakespeare editors, as Bentley was the clearest instance amongst Miltonic editors, of the use of fanciful, insubstantiable, and unnecessary conjecture. Though the loss of Warburton's own letters to Theobald makes assessment difficult, Peter Seary, in his recent book on Theobald, has convincingly represented the correspondence of the two men as a ghastly dance in which Warburton dreamt up, and sent almost with every post, a series of improbable conjectural emendations; to each of which Theobald would, often by return, send a reply explaining, as courteously as he could, his reservations (the traffic was by no means wholly one way; in this private correspondence

[106] Often such knowledge leads in Warburton to length as well as light, for example in his notes on *Hamlet*, I. 5. 30, where he takes 'meditation' in the sense used by religious mystics; *The Tragedy of King Lear*, I. 2. 116, where he inveighs against the prevalence of 'judicial astrology' in Shakespeare's time (*Works of Shakespear*, VI. 16); or *The Tragedy of King Lear*, I.4.17, where he expatiates on the refusal to eat fish as 'this disgraceful badge of popery' in the reign of Elizabeth (*Works of Shakespear*, VI. 28).

Theobald too was capable of speculation). Seary suggests, in fact, that Theobald tried to educate his collaborator into method and restraint. Warburton however made not only an unapt but a resentful pupil. His resentment surfaced, very clearly associated with an explicit difference of theoretical principle, in his edition. Having in his Preface accused Theobald, as well as Hanmer, of conjectural licence, Warburton in his notes repeatedly attacks Theobald for a pedantic concern with literal accuracy and a misguided trust in the surviving printed texts. His note on *eisel* (*Hamlet* 5.1.266) tells us, in a formulation Warburton used with an insulting regularity, that the word is 'spelt right by Mr Theobald' (*Works of Shakespear*, VIII. 250). The implication is that Theobald can at least spell if he can do no more, though in truth Theobald had not merely corrected the orthography of this line but, probably, recovered the sense. Warburton's derisive words are closely related to Pope's dismissive lines on Theobald in the *Epistle to Dr Arbuthnot*:

> Each wight who reads not, and but scans and spells,
> Each word-catcher that lives on syllables.
>
> (165–6)

In the Preface to his edition, Warburton denies Theobald any abilities or achievement as what Theobald himself would have called an 'intelligent editor'. He had, in Warburton's view, neither sufficient knowledge of Shakespeare's language to understand his words, sufficient critical discrimination to identify a false reading, nor sufficient 'sagacity' to put one right once found:

> By a punctilious collation of the old Books, he corrected what was manifestly wrong in the *latter* Editions by what was manifestly right in the *earlier*. And this is his real Merit; and the whole of it. For where the Phrase was very obsolete or licentious in the *common* Books, or only slightly corrupted in the *other*, he wanted sufficient Knowledge of the Progress and various Stages of the *English* Tongue, as well as Acquaintance with the Peculiarity of *Shakespear*'s language to understand what was right; nor had he either common Judgment to see, or critical Sagacity to amend, what was manifestly faulty. (*Works of Shakespear*, I. xi)

A brief note by Warburton on *Hamlet* cuttingly expresses his contempt for what he took to be Theobald's excessively documentary orientation, his blinkered regard for the evidence of the surviving early texts. In Pope's edition, Claudius's avuncular advice to Hamlet on the pointlessness of grief is phrased (without editorial comment) thus:

> – your father lost a father;
> That father his.
>
> (I. 2. 89–90)

Theobald, however, accurately notes that 'this supposed refinement is from

Mr Pope, but all the editions else, that I have met with, old and modern, read, "That Father *lost*, *lost* his"'. Warburton, having failed to understand the sense of this reading of Q2, F1, and subsequent editions, provides a paraphrasing explanation which represents it as sheer nonsense ('That father after he had lost himself, lost his father'), and concludes with this sardonic remark on the naïve foundations of Theobald's critical judgment: 'But the reading is *ex fide Codicis*, and that is enough'.[107] Samuel Johnson's reply was a withering note in his 1765 edition, retaining the reading of 'the old copies', and suggesting that 'The nonsense imputed to them is only in the mind of the critick.'[108] This three-way conversation between Theobald, Warburton, and Johnson is one of the more significant moments in the history of changing attitudes to the original texts.

Warburton was capable of impressively acute editorial conjecture. His '*fanned* and winnowed opinions' (*Hamlet* 5. 2. 154) is generally accepted, and his 'if the sun breed maggots in a dead dog, being a *god*, kissing carrion' (*Hamlet* 2. 2. 182; *good*, Q2, F) has had some supporters.[109] These however are exceptions. The regular pattern is that, in a manner recognizably derived from Bentley's Milton, Warburton objects, often unnecessarily, to the logic and sense of the witnessed reading, and then supplies what he imagines to be a better reading of his own, frequently without warrant in any surviving witness, and often without reasoned justification. So, in *Hamlet*, the Prince contemplates taking arms against *assail* of troubles; Ophelia's 'virgin *crants*' (Q2) become *chants*; the ground on which Hamlet and Laertes struggle is invited to singe 'his pate against the burning *sun*'.[110] These are decisions made essentially on the basis of taste. Warburton was concerned to retain in his editing that evaluative function which Pope had claimed and which Theobald had substantially put aside. He does not, unlike Pope, 'degrade' exceptionable passages, but he retains Pope's marking, by single inverted commas, of beautiful passages, and adds extensive selections of his own, marked by double inverted commas. In Warburton's edition, however, an aesthetic orientation is given a mask of an authorial orientation. As Bentley had constructed a fiction of an incompetent editor of *Paradise Lost* who could be blamed for all the passages that Bentley considered incoherent, so Warburton (by no means uniquely in his century) presumed to recover the 'genuine text' of Shakespeare from the damages wrought by the incompetence of earlier editors. Consistently

[107] Theobald, *Works of Shakespeare*, VII. 234; Warburton, *Works of Shakespear*, VIII. 127.

[108] The note was cancelled: see *Johnson on Shakespeare*, VIII. 962.

[109] See *Hamlet*, ed. H. H. Furness (New York: Dover, 1963), I. 146–50, and, more recently, C. J. Sisson's edition of the *Complete Works* (London: Odhams, 1954). The conjectures at 2. 2. 182 and 5. 2. 154 both appeared in Hanmer's Oxford edition of 1746, but probably at Warburton's suggestion.

[110] *Hamlet*, 3. 1. 160, 5. 1. 222, 5. 1. 272; Warburton, *Works of Shakespear*, VIII. 182, 248, 250.

his editorial discourse maintains the fiction that his conjectures are not personal inventions, but restorations of the authorial original: 'I believe Shakespeare wrote', 'much nearer Shakespeare's words', 'I conclude Shakespeare wrote'.

These protestations of authenticity were no more credible than Bentley's similar claim in his edition of *Paradise Lost.* Frequently Warburton writes extended comments attacking, by eighteenth-century or Warburtonian standards of syntactical logic, the readings of the early printed texts. He demonstrates that 'a seal'd compact / Well ratified by law and heraldry' means no more than '*An act of law well ratified by law*, which is absurd', and amends to 'law *of* heraldry'. The tortured constructions of Claudius's guilty self-questionings are 'nonsense', and their logic is questioned at enormous length. Warburton's editorial decisions are often based on his own taste in language rather than a knowledge of Shakespeare's usage. In Hamlet's teasing words to Osric about the weather, for example, Warburton rejects the Folio reading '*For* my complexion,' because 'this is not *English*', preferring 'it is very sultry, and hot, *or* my complexion', the Q2 reading which most modern editors think a misprint. Warburton does provide an explanation of its sense: '[Hamlet] was going on to say, *Or* my complexion deceives me; but the over-complaisance of the other interrupted him.'[111] This argument has not convinced modern editors (though Johnson follows Warburton here), and Warburton's choice between the Quarto and Folio readings remains primarily aesthetic in its motive, rather than authorial.

Warburton's approach and methods were already out of date when his edition was published, and they were not well received. By the late 1740s the Bentleian 'rage of emendation' was essentially past, and Warburton seemed to many a text-critical dinosaur. In much of the angry response to Warburton's edition, however, may be seen not merely evidence of changing fashion, or an instinctive urge to protect the national poet, but more or less developed examinations of the text-theoretical issues which Warburton's edition with all its eccentricities had raised, and a concern for rational and knowledge-based method in the editing and explication of Shakespeare.

Amongst the many who replied to Warburton directly, or engage with Warburton as their main antagonist,[112] I would like to concentrate on three writers whose work demonstrates particularly clearly and fully the

[111] *Hamlet*, 1. 1. 87, 5. 2. 99; Warburton, *Works of Shakespear*, VIII. 119, 203–4.

[112] Amongst the other significant responses are Zachary Grey, *Remarks upon a Late Edition of Shakespeare with a Defence of Sir Thomas Hanmer* (1747) and *An Answer to Certain Passages in Mr W[arburton]'s Preface to his edition of Shakespeare, together with some Remarks on the many Errors and False Criticisms in the Work itself* (1748); Benjamin Heath, *A Revisal of Shakespeare's Text, wherein the Alterations Introduced into it by the More Modern Editors and Critics are Particularly Considered* (London, 1765).

nature of the theoretical, as well as the practical, debate in Shakespearean editing: John Upton, Thomas Edwards, and Samuel Johnson.

John Upton, whose main claim to fame was to be his edition of *The Faerie Queene* (1758), published his *Critical Observations on Shakespeare* in 1746. For the second edition, which appeared in 1748, Upton wrote a lengthy Preface which was substantially a response to Warburton and the orientations and methods of his edition. Opinions differ concerning the value of Upton's detailed discussions of critical and text-editorial and exegetical matters. Samuel Johnson, perhaps partly because of an inclination to defend Warburton the eminent Churchman, thought Upton lacking in 'vigour of genius or nicety of taste', and alleged that, though Upton 'professed to oppose the licentious confidence of editors,' he was nonetheless 'unable to restrain the rage of emendation' in his own writing.[113] Yet Upton is a remarkable instance of the clear, self-conscious formulation in this period of essential theoretical positions on textual editing and interpretation. His book is a polemic, whose main features are a recognizably and strikingly humanist regard for the integrity of the printed book, an overriding assumption that the end of editing is the 'genuine text' produced by an author's intention, an insistence on the necessity of historical knowledge to reliable textual explication, and the considered rejection of evaluative and interpretative judgment founded merely on an unsubstantiated subjectivism.

Upton's 1748 Preface begins by asking a necessary question: can literary value judgments which appeal merely to a standard of taste be thought to be adequately grounded: 'while I perceived critics so numerous, (for who more or less does not criticize?) and found every one appealing to a standard and a tast, where could be the absurdity of enquiring, whether, or no, there really is in nature any foundation for the thing itself; or whether the whole does not depend on meer whim, caprice, or fashion?' (*Critical Observations*, Preface, sig. a3^r). In my Introduction I outlined E. D. Hirsch's argument that '[evaluative] judgments that are accurately made upon explicit criteria furnish the grounds of their own validation and therefore qualify as knowledge' (*Aims of Interpretation*, p. 108). The question Upton asks, effectively, is whether the sorts of essentially evaluative editorial judgment made by such editors as Warburton are founded upon explicit and credible criteria. If not, in Upton's view as in Hirsch's, they cannot qualify as knowledge. A keynote of Upton's book is that real knowledge of literature must be founded not on the fashion of our own moment, but on a genuine understanding of the literary object in its historical particularity. Upton makes the point most clearly in a ringing and insistently humanist

[113] *Johnson on Shakespeare*, VII. 101.

assertion of the distinctiveness of past writing, and our duty to understand it in its distinctiveness:

it is to be remember'd, that things are not as we judge of them, but as they exist in their own natures, independent of whim and caprice. So that I except against all such judges, as talk only from common vogue and fashion; 'why, really 'tis just as people like – we have different tastes now, and things must be accommodated to them'. They who are advanced to this pitch of barbarism, have much to unlearn, before they can have ears to hear. (*Critical Observations*, p. 385)

There is no necessary opposition for Upton between literary humanism and scholarship. A thoroughgoing knowledge of the cultural and linguistic past is necessary to understand Shakespeare in Shakespeare's own terms. The essence of Warburton's 'barbarism' is precisely that he lacks, or at least does not invoke, such knowledge, preferring resort to his own taste. In the procedures adopted by Warburton and others like him, authority is taken from the author and appropriated by the commentator. 'Scarcely any one', complains Upton, 'pays a regard to what Shakespeare *does* write, but they are always guessing at what he *should* write' (p. 8). Upton uses an imagery of usurpation, of the commentator forgetting the bounds of his own area of authority, invading the author's territory, and imposing upon the author conformity to inappropriately personal and modern aesthetic criteria: 'the commentator . . . has forgot his province, and the author himself has been arbitrarily altered, and reduced to such a fancied plan of perfection, as the corrector, within himself, has thought proper to establish' (Preface, p. vi). This is of course a literary version, and application, of an imagery associated with the humanist, and Protestant, regard for the primacy of text over gloss. For Upton, as for others, the author's text (for which Upton regularly uses the word 'context'[114]) is a protected and sacred area into which only profane editors would intrude their own imaginings. Correcting Shakespeare's 'heterogeneous metaphors' for instance is no business of the editor's: 'The poet is to take his share of the faults, and the critic is to keep his hands from the context' (p. 398). If emendations are to be proposed, they should make their appearance in the commentary, not in the text. Too many modern critics, amongst them Warburton:

set up for correctors and successors of Aristarchus, . . . intruding their own guesses and reveries into the context, which, first meeting the reader's eye, naturally prepossess his judgment: mean while the author's words are either removed entirely out of the way, or permitted a place in some remote note, loaden with misrepresentations and abuse, according to the great goodness of the most gracious critic. (*Critical Observations*, pp. 2, 3)

[114] See my note '*Context* in eighteenth-century usage', *Notes and Queries*, n.s. 40 (1993), 308–10.

Upton represents Aristarchus, the greatest Homeric editor of antiquity, and his modern follower Bentley, as the main sponsors of the shift from author to commentator in modern textual editing. (The genealogy had been familiar enough after Pope's immortalization of Bentley as the modern Aristarchus in the fourth book of the *Dunciad*.) Aristarchus and Bentley both 'altered passages, for no other reason, oftentimes, than because they disliked them' (Preface, p. lix); worse, both of these critics took an aesthetic view of the text, remaking it according to their own tastes. Upton quotes both Cicero's remark of Aristarchus, that 'whatever displeased him he would by no means believe was Homer's' (pp. 132–3), and Bentley's notorious assertion in his edition of *Paradise Lost* that 'I have such an esteem for our poet, that which of the two words is the better, *that I say* was dictated by Milton' (p. 1). Upton acknowledges the critical greatness of Aristarchus and Bentley, but insists such editorial policies are of bad tendency, striking at the possibility of truth and honesty in print.

The blame however for the destabilizing of Shakespeare, for the almost sacrilegious offence against the integrity of the genuine text, is not to be laid only at the door of presumptuous scholarly commentators. Upton identifies the poets too as culprits: 'Our poets write to the humour of the age; and when their own little stock is spent, they set themselves to work on new-modelling Shakespeare's plays, and adapting them to the tast of their audience; by stripping off their antique and proper tragic dress' (*Critical Observations*, p. 7). Here no doubt there is a by-blow at Pope, whose edition, with all its large aesthetic changes, had been praised in Warburton's Preface specifically as an example of the editorial achievement of a great poet. Primarily however Upton seems to refer in this quotation to the eighteenth-century adapters of Shakespeare for the theatre. In their hands Shakespeare becomes a victim of 'improvement', 'look'd on . . . as one by no means proper company for lords and ladies, maids of honour and court-pages, 'till some poet or other, who knows the world better, takes him in hand, and introduces him in this modern dress to *good company*' (p. 8). Here as elsewhere in fact Upton is a defender of the literary Shakespeare, the Shakespeare of the printed book, rather than the stage.

Print itself of course has its problems, though Upton like Erasmus certainly believed it at least potentially capable of the reliable transmission of meaning. The coming of the printed book brought to an end the radical instability of manuscript culture, and for Upton that has editorial consequences. Editors of pre-Gutenberg authors must be free to correct the accumulated and disparate errors, the palimpsests and lacunae, of manuscript transmission, but the restorers of authors whose works were printed while they lived must be bound by a stricter discipline:

Who is there but will allow greater liberty for altering authors, who wrote before the invention of printing, than since? Blunders upon blunders of transcribers – interpolations – glosses – omissions – various readings – and what not? But to try these experiments, without great caution, on Milton or Shakespeare, though it may be sport to you, . . . 'tis death and destruction to the little tast remaining among us. (*Critical Observations*, sig. B2r)

Upton is prepared to accept the eighteenth-century orthodoxy that the 'copies' of Shakespeare, the first printed texts, contain more errors than 'any one book, published since the invention of printing' (p. 174), but he does so in the light of a general understanding of the nature of authorial manuscripts, of which Shakespeare's manuscripts were an extreme case, and the consequent need for editorial interpretation:

Authors are not careful enough of their copies, when they give them into the printer's hand; which, often being blotted or ill written, must be help'd out by meer guess-work. Printers are not the best calculated for this critical work, I think, since the times of Aldus and the Stephens's. What wonder therefore if in such a case we meet, now and then, with strange and monstrous words, or highly improper expressions, and often contradictory to the author's design and meaning? (*Critical Observations*, p. 242)

This is a humanist's view of the history of the transmission of the book. The great renaissance printers who were themselves scholars and humanists, Aldus and the Estiennes for example, were capable of the task of the 'intelligent editor', which is to find the authorially intended text, 'the author's design and meaning'. Their successors have not been. Shakespeare's authorial manuscripts were already in an imperfect state as they were delivered to the print shop, and could not expect competent editorial handling from the printers themselves.

This argument might seem to lead to an impasse. If the 'meer correctors of printing presses' (Preface, p. vi) who were closest to Shakespeare failed to exercise critical judgment, and if to put editing into the hands of such commentators as Warburton can only lead to a situation where 'even the credit of all books must sink in proportion to the number of critical, as well as uncritical hands, thro' which they pass' (p. 133), what can possibly be done?

At a number of points in his book Upton gives an account of the necessary procedures and methods for an adequate edition of Shakespeare, essentially consistent with Theobald's stated principles and practice though with some emphases of Upton's own. If the 'genuine text' is to be 'discovered and retrieved' the 'various copies of authority' must be fully consulted and collated, the readings for which they provide witness must be 'exhibited before the reader's eyes' and 'the best of these . . . should be chosen, and placed in the text'. In order to discover where a corruption has arisen consideration must be given to 'the various ways that books generally become corrupted'.[115] In a key passage Upton makes clear that critical choices between readings are interpretations, grounded not on modern taste and conjectural 'divination', but on knowledge of the author himself. The 'careful and critical reader':

> would consider that originals have a manner always peculiar to themselves; and not only a manner, but a language: . . . would compare one passage with another; for such authors are the best interpreters of their own meaning . . . I omit the previous knowledge in ancient custom and manners, in grammar and construction; the knowledge of these is presupposed; to be caught tripping here is an ominous stumble at the very threshold and entrance upon criticism; 'tis ignorance, which no guess-work, no divining faculty . . . can atone and commute for. (*Critical Observations*, pp. 137–8)

The advocacy here of the use of parallel passages to explain and validate readings in the original copies recalls Theobald as well as the methods of biblical exegesis. The insistence that 'authors are the best interpreters of their own meaning' – that is, that particular passages are best explained by comparison with other passages of that author's writings – should no doubt put us in mind of the Anglican stress on 'Scripture its own interpreter'. Above all, such writers as Shakespeare are to be interpreted in the light of the culture and language of their own time.

Upton's application of these principles may be readily illustrated from many passages in which he discusses detailed questions of interpretation in Shakespeare, whether explicating a difficult sense or defending a reading of the early texts against conjectural criticism. Hamlet's expression 'dearest foe' is illustrated with parallels from Douglas's translation of the *Aeneid*, and by comparison with Anglo-Saxon *derian*; here Upton makes explicit the point that 'instances of our poet's using words contrary to the modern acceptation of them are numberless'. In his discussion of 'Unhouseled, disappointed, unaneled' Upton provides glosses of all three words, careful etymologies, and parallels from Chaucer's 'Parson's Tale', Spenser (*Faerie Queene* I. 12. 37), and Holinshed's *Life of King John*, as well as from Shakespeare himself ('appointment', *Measure for Measure*, 3. 1. 57), concluding that 'I cannot here but admire the ignorance as well as boldness of those editors, who have changed this undoubtedly genuine reading'.[116]

Upton however goes far beyond a consideration of particular cases to give, in Book III of his *Critical Observations*, an extended account of the 'rules' governing Shakespeare's expression. Here he focusses on those features of Shakespearean syntax which would seem 'peculiar' by the standards of the

115 *Critical Observations*, pp. lx–lxi, 386.

116 *Hamlet*, 1. 2. 182, 1. 5. 77; Upton, *Critical Observations*, pp. 327–8, 179–81. The parallel with *Measure for Measure* had already been made by Theobald, in *Shakespeare Restored*, p. 55.

eighteenth-century reader. Upton's Rule 4 for example tells us that Shakespeare often 'uses one part of speech for another', Rule 8 that he 'frequently omits the auxiliary verb', Rule 9 that 'he uses But, for *otherwise than*' (pp. 330, 345, 347). Upton's description of Shakespeare's language, together with a brief explanation of his versification, is one of the earliest of a number of important contributions by eighteenth-century editors and commentators to the reference library of knowledges – grammars, glossaries, indexes, metrics – which he thought essential to the interpretation of Shakespeare; he was followed in this project, as we shall see, by Richard Warner and Edward Capell, amongst others.

Upton's use of the word 'rules' may suggest that his approach to Shakespeare was at least partly shaped by familiar eighteenth-century arguments for prescriptive standards of correctness. Certainly he writes in Book III of the need in his time for a good grammar and dictionary to regulate the 'Proteus' of usage, according to a 'standard in nature' rather than 'whim, caprice or arbitrary will' (p. 295). In illustrating the 'rules' of Shakespearean grammar he frequently finds parallels in classical Latin, and occasionally in classical Greek. This is an apparent accommodation of the greatest writer of English secular scripture to classical literary standards which might recall, for example, Anthony Blackwall's more thoroughgoing illustration and justification of the language of the Holy Scriptures by reference to the writers of classical antiquity, in his *Sacred Classics Defended* (1725). Yet though Upton had a concept of a natural standard in the language, he makes clear at many points in his book that the 'rules' by which Shakespeare's writing may be judged can only be derived from a study of Shakespeare's own writing, and that what 'may lead the way to a right reading of our author' is not an abstract or generalized standard, but Shakespeare's particular set of usages, his idiolect: 'Concerning the strict propriety of all these rules, as being exactly suitable to the genius of our language, I am not at all concerned: 'tis sufficient for my purpose if they are Shakespeare's rules' (*Critical Observations*, pp. 364–5). Upton's establishment and application of the 'rules' is in practice descriptive rather than normative, and in this it represents a considerable change from the criterion of correct 'Englishness' in Pope or Warburton, or even in Theobald's earlier work. Furthermore, Upton repeatedly insists that an understanding of Shakespeare's language in its distinctiveness is basic to principled editing. Shakespeare's language may be 'peculiar', but when we understand that peculiarity 'we shall be less liable to give a loose to fancy, in indulging the licentious spirit of criticism; nor shall we then so much presume to judge what Shakespeare *ought to* have written, as endeavour to discover and retrieve what he *did* write' (*Critical Observations*, p. 296). Sadly, editors before Upton have lacked that knowledge, and have therefore exercised an unacceptable conjectural licence: 'there has not been one editor of our poet, but has erred against every one of these rules' (pp. lxi–lxii). One example amongst many is Warburton's emendation of 'law and heraldry' noted above. Upton knows that Shakespeare 'sometimes expresses one thing by two substantives', and validates the reading of this line in *Hamlet* by implied comparison with parallel passages in Shakespeare and Virgil.[117]

Despite Johnson's withering assessment, Upton's stated principles, and many at least of the particular critical judgments made in his commentary, tend towards the historical authentication of Shakespeare's witnessed expression, rather than giving encouragement to conjecture. Like all eighteenth-century commentators, and like most modern textual theorists, Upton understood that conjecture cannot be entirely avoided, especially in the case of such a problematic transmission history as that of the writings of Shakespeare. Conjecture must be seen however as an interpretative act, taking a restricted role within a coherent editorial method. Upton comments that conjectural emendation:

> seems one of the easiest parts of criticism; and what English reader thinks himself not master of so trifling a science? When he receives a letter from his friend, errors of this kind are no impediment to his reading: and the reason is, because he generally knows his friend's drift and design, and accompanies him in his thoughts and expressions. And could we thus accompany the diviner poets and philosophers, we should commence criticks of course. (*Critical Observations*, p. 177)

Upton here describes the process or series of interpretative guesses that we make when we construe any text.[118] Some texts are easy for us to decipher, Upton argues, even when obscured by error, because the horizon of meaning is one with which we are very well acquainted; literary texts, however, distanced as they are from us by time, not to say by the divine gifts of their authors, have a meaning horizon inevitably much more foreign to us. Conjecture is a natural and essential part of the reading process with anything but a flawless text; it becomes problematic when the conditions for interpretation are themselves problematic. The more knowledge we have, the less problematic the conditions for interpretation become, and the more circumscribed is the permissible playing field for emendation.

Perhaps Upton's most sustained piece of contextualization is his discussion in the Appendix of his book of Shakespeare's uses of the vice figure, in *Twelfth Night*, 1 and 2 *Henry IV*, *Richard III* and *Hamlet* 3. 4. 90. References to Jonson's *The Devil is an Ass*, *Staple of News*, and *Alchemist* establish Upton's

[117] *Antony and Cleopatra*, 4. 2. 42.ff.; *Georgics*, 2. 192. *Critical Observations*, p. 336, n. 8.

[118] There are striking similarities between Upton's interpretative principles here and E. D. Hirsch's account of the role of the concept of intrinsic genre in textual interpretation; see *Validity in Interpretation*, pp. 78–89.

contention that 'THE INIQUITY was often the VICE in our old Moralities', and allow him to reject, as 'out of all rule of criticism', emendations by previous editors of 'the formal Vice, Iniquity' (*Richard III*, 3. 1. 82) to 'the formal wise Antiquity'. Upton goes on to argue that Hamlet's words to his father's ghost, 'Ah ha boy, sayst thou so? Art thou there, truepenny?' (*Hamlet*, 1. 5. 157), are words of a kind commonly addressed to the devil by the Vice in the old drama, suggesting both Hamlet's suspicion of the diabolic nature of the ghost, and that 'good humour is the best weapon to deal with the devil'. In this unusually developed commentary, contextual knowledge is used to support an editorial judgment, and to provide a remarkably rich and suggestive interpretation of an important, and problematic, dramatic moment.[119]

While Upton brought to his task considerable scholarship and theoretical sophistication, the second of my three answerers of Warburton, Thomas Edwards, brought a penetrating understanding of the issues and a telling wit. Edwards's 'Supplement' to Warburton's edition was published in 1748, and in its much-enlarged third edition of 1750 was given its familiar title, *The Canons of Criticism, and Glossary, Being a Supplement to Mr Warburton's Edition of Shakespear, Collected from the Notes in that Celebrated Work.*[120] This title of course is ironic. Warburton's Preface reveals that 'he had once intended to have given the reader *a body of canons* for literal criticism, drawn out in form, and a general alphabetic *Glossary*'. What Warburton had hinted at, Edwards now provided, not, indeed, as Warburton would have written them, but as Edwards thought most accurately reflected the implicit principles, and the detailed practice, of Warburton's work.

Warburton's failures of verbal comprehension, and the absurdities of explication and conjecture they led him into, are displayed in remorseless and cumulative detail in Edwards's *Glossary*, which constructs out of Warburton's notes a little dictionary of words he had 'introduced to Shakespeare's acquaintance', or wrongly interpreted, or entirely invented, in his forcing and subjective explications. Edwards represents Warburton in fact as that bogey of the Anglican interpretative theorist, a wrester of meanings. The *Glossary* makes it appear that Warburton had abandoned any notion of shared verbal usage as a standard in interpretation: words are made malleable. 'Cap' is made by Warburton to mean 'property' or 'bubble'; 'gust' is glossed as 'aggravation'; 'incorrect' as 'untutor'd'; 'question' as 'force' or 'virtue'; and so on. Some of Warburton's mistakes are due to ignorance, rather than mere perversity. 'Carbonado'd', for

[119] *Critical Observations*, pp. 393–7. Modern editors have not taken up Upton's suggestion in respect of *Hamlet*, 1. 5. 157.

[120] Edwards's book was one of the most successful contributions to the Shakespearean debate, reaching its seventh edition (from which all quotations here are taken) in the year of Johnson's edition, 1765.

example, he reads as 'mark'd with wounds made with a carabine', rather than, correctly, 'scotch'd', 'slit'. Where the word in the surviving copy cannot be understood according to his own purposes, however, Warburton changes it for another, unwitnessed, word, or invents an entirely new one: 'conseal'd', 'fraine', 'pouled', 'geap', 'to gaude' ('"rejoice." from the Fr. Gaudir . . . a word of Mr W's coining').

In the *Glossary* Edwards represents Warburton's verbal perversities in concentrated form, but not wholly unfairly. Edwards had much additional material of the same kind to hand which he could have employed had he wished. The *Glossary* exposes the chaotic consequences of using an interpretative and conjectural model insufficiently grounded in any coherent principle of knowledge or meaning.

At the centre of Edwards's work are the twenty-five 'Canons' which he derives from Warburton's practice, and the extensive examples of each which he provides. Some of the canons are concerned with Warburton's incivilities: the dishonesty, vanity, scurrility, inconsistency, and triviality of his notes. The 'Canons' however deal too with what Edwards understood as problematic areas in Warburton's theoretical assumptions and methodological practices.

Most importantly Edwards alleges that Warburton makes unnecessary emendations, 'without reason and against the Copies' (Canon 25), superseding documentary authority by his own. Warburton is convicted, for example, of altering a line in *Macbeth*, 'Ere humane statute purg'd the gentle weal' to '*general* weal' (3. 4. 75), 'without any reasonable care, and *confessedly* against the concurrent testimony of all the Editions, thrust into the Text by his own Authority' (*Canons of Criticism*, p. 229). Further, alleges Edwards, Warburton claims the right 'to alter any passage, which He does not understand' (Canon 2), proceeding to emendation without adequate attempt at explication. 'What language is this?' Warburton had asked, of 'flights *singing*' (*Hamlet*, 5. 2. 313). 'We should certainly read, ". . . *wing* thee to thy rest"'. '*What language is this?*' replies Edwards: 'why English, certainly, if he understood it. A *flight* is a flock, and is a very common expression . . . and why a *flight* of angels may not *sing*, as well as a *flight* of larks, rests upon Mr Warburton to shew' (p. 49). Once Warburton is embarked upon a conjecture, he makes (unlike Theobald) no adequate attempt to provide reason or evidence for the chosen reading or his interpretation of the passage: 'He may prove a reading, or support an explanation, by any sort of reasons; no matter whether good or bad' (Canon 8). Hamlet's 'let the devil wear black, for I'll have a suit of sables' (3. 2. 120–1) certainly invites explanation. The context seems to require the sense: '(if my mother can look cheerful two months after my father's death) then the devil can as usual wear black, but I do not need to wear such shows of mourning'. But sables are sometimes thought of as black.

Warburton proceeds at once to emendation of what he takes to be the 'nonsensical blunder' of the '*senseless* editors': 'let the Devil wear black, '*fore* I'll have a suit of sable'. Edwards responds by pointing out the consequences of such licence: 'if every passage, which our professed Critic does not understand, must be thus altered; we shall have, indeed, a complete edition of Shakespear' (that is, a complete *new* edition of Shakespeare), and goes on to find sense in the reading of the first editions. 'Sables' are furs, 'and every body knows, that they are worn by way of finery in that country'. (Johnson would later dismiss Warburton's resistance to the original reading with the more brusquely dismissive, 'I suppose it is well enough known that the fur of sable is not black.')[121]

One of Edwards's major and explicit complaints is that Warburton's emendations and interpretations pay all too little regard to authorially intended meaning. The 'Professed Critic may interpret his Author so; as to make him mean directly contrary to what he says' (Canon 9), even to the extent of finding out 'puns' and 'quaintnesses', and 'bawdy' and 'immoral' meanings, 'where, perhaps, the Author never thought of them' (Canons 12, 14). One of Edwards's instances is Warburton's treatment of Gertrude's horrified lines in response to Hamlet's accusation in the closet scene:

> —— Ay me! what act
> That roars so loud and thunders in the index?
>
> (3. 4. 53)

Edwards's own explanation of the line is typical of contemporary authorially orientated editing. The word 'index' is glossed by the usage of Shakespeare's time: 'I think it is plain, that Shakespear has used *index*, for *title*, or *prologue* . . . the Index used formerly to be placed at the beginning of a book'. As often in his work, Edwards further supports the usage by adducing parallel usages, in this case from *Richard III* and *Othello*. Warburtcn however assigns the second line, with Q2, to Hamlet, and failing to comprehend 'index', amends the line to read '*it* thunders *to* the *Indies*'. Beyond the resort to a textually unsupported conjecture, this suffers, as Edwards points out, a difficulty with respect to the logic of the dramatic context, representing 'an act as . . . *making a noise all over the world* . . . which was probably known only to the murderer himself, and to Hamlet'.[122]

Instead of authorial meaning, Edwards alleges, the criterion of judgment has become, in Warburton's edition, the critic's understanding, and the

121 Edwards, *Canons of Criticism*, pp. 132–4. Edwards's and Johnson's understanding of the passage differs from that offered in the Arden and Oxford editions, but may not be inferior.

122 *Canons of Criticism*, pp. 156 and n., 157. Edwards's parallels are with *Richard III*, 4. 4. 85 and 2. 2. 149, and *Othello*, 2. 1. 52–3. Compare *Canons of Criticism*, pp. 32–3, where he adds Ps. 58:8, Eccles. 12:6, and Acts 23:15 to the parallel passages Upton had provided in defence of the wording of the fool's prophecy in *Lear*.

critic's taste. The function of editorial annotation 'is not so much to explane the Author's meaning, as to display the Critic's knowledge' (Canon 20). Such imperialism gives the Warburtonian critic 'a right to declare, that his Author *wrote* whatever he thinks he *ought* to have written' (Canon 1), and Edwards cites many examples of Warburton's introductions of his licentious changes with such characteristic phrases as 'Shakespear wrote', 'Shakespear *must have wrote*', 'we should read' (pp. 39–45). This is a rhetoric which recognizably derives from Bentley's implementation of a similar aesthetic method in his edition of *Paradise Lost*. Like Bentley, Warburton finds fault with the unfamiliar, and 'incorrect', idiolect of his author, and uses the imputed incompetence of the early editors as his pretext for tampering: 'where he does not like an expression, and yet cannot mend it: He may abuse his Author for it . . . or He may condemn it, as a foolish interpolation' (Canons 4, 5).

Such methods, riding rough-shod over documentary authority, and rejecting any reasoned process by which an authorial original behind the surviving witnesses might be approximated, must result, Edwards argues, in a radical destabilization of the text, in which 'any word or phrase', whether it apparently needs amendment or not, can be replaced by some fanciful emendation, which the critic 'imagines *will do better*' (Canon 6).

Edwards's *Canons* would be dismissed by Samuel Johnson, in his Preface, as a mere squib, attacking Warburton's errors 'with airy petulance, suitable enough to the levity of the controversy',[123] but this judgment may again be coloured by Johnson's prejudice in favour of the great Churchman. To this writer Edwards's *Canons* seem a telling and exemplary summary statement of Warburton's methods, and their failures.

The enormous critical power and range of Samuel Johnson's own edition of Shakespeare continues to be revealed in modern discussions. Here I wish to confine myself to those elements of Johnson's editorial work which bear immediately on my discussion of eighteenth-century editing: his consideration of the grounds and procedures of interpretation and conjectural emendation.[124]

Johnson's edition of 1765 is in some ways closest to that of Warburton, his immediate predecessor. Though Johnson's eye examined every line and took little on trust, his text is, like that of previous editions, traditionary, deriving from Warburton's and Theobald's texts.[125] Johnson's edition was

[123] *Johnson on Shakespeare*, VII. 100.

[124] Johnson's position on the issue of conjecture has been especially considered by C. S. Lim, 'Emendation of Shakespeare in the eighteenth century: the case of Johnson', *Cahiers Elisabéthains*, 33 (1988), 23–30; Thomas Reinert, 'Johnson and conjecture', *Studies in English Literature, 1500–1900*, 28 (1988), 483–96.

[125] On Johnson's use of Warburton and Theobald, see A. Cuming, 'A copy of Shakespeare's Works which formerly belonged to Dr Johnson', *Review of English Studies*, 3 (1927), 208–12; G. Blakemore Evans, 'The text of Johnson's *Shakespeare* (1765)', *Philological Quarterly*, 28 (1949),

PRINCE OF DENMARK. 141

But now, my coufin *Hamlet*, and my fon——

Ham. [8] A little more than kin, and lefs than kind.
[*Afide.*

King. How is it, that the clouds ftill hang on you?

Ham. Not fo, my lord, I am [9] too much i' th' Sun.

Queen. Good *Hamlet*, caft thy nighted colour off,
And let thine eye look like a friend on *Denmark.*
Do not, for ever, with thy veiled lids,
Seek for thy noble father in the duft;
Thou know'ft, 'tis common: all, that live, muft die;
Paffing through nature to eternity.

Ham. Ay, Madam, it is common.

" go, *Laertes*; make the faireft " ufe you pleafe of your time, " and fpend it at your will with " the faireft graces you are maf- " ter of." THEOBALD.

I rather think this line is in want of emendation. I read,

——*Time is thine,*
And my *beft graces; fpend it at thy will.*

[8] Ham. *A little more than kin, and lefs than kind.*] The *King* had called him, *coufin* Hamlet, therefore *Hamlet* replies,

A little more than kin,——

i. e. A little more than coufin; becaufe, by marrying his mother, he was become the King's fon-in-law: So far is eafy. But what means the latter part,

——*and lefs than kind?*

The King, in the prefent reading, gives no occafion for this reflection, which is fufficient to fhew it to be faulty, and that we fhould read and point the firft line thus,

But now, my coufin Hamlet.—
KIND *my fon*——

i. e. But now let us turn to you, coufin *Hamlet. Kind my fon*, (or, as we now fay, Good my fon) lay afide this clouded look. For thus he was going to expoftulate gently with him for his melancholy, when *Hamlet* cut him fhort by reflecting on the titles he gave him;

A little more than kin, *and lefs than* kind.

which we now fee is a pertinent reply. WARBURTON.

A little more than kin, and lefs than kind.] It is not unreafonable to fuppofe that this was a proverbial expreffion, known in former times for a relation fo confufed and blended, that it was hard to define it. HANMER.

Kind is the Teutonick word for *Child. Hamlet* therefore anfwers with propriety, to the titles of *coufin* and *fon*, which the King had given him, that he was fomewhat more than *coufin*, and lefs than *fon*.

[9] ——*too much i' th' Sun.*] He perhaps alludes to the proverb, *Out of heaven's bleffing into the warm fun.*

VOL. VIII. K 7 *Queen.*

Figures 7 and 8 *The Plays of William Shakespeare* (1765), edited by Samuel Johnson, VIII. 141, 148.

148 HAMLET,

Within his truncheon's length; whilſt they, diſtill'd
Almoſt to jelly [8] with the act of fear,
Stand dumb, and ſpeak not to him. This to me
In dreadful ſecreſy impart they did,
And I with them the third night kept the watch;
Where, as they had deliver'd, both in time,
Form of the thing, each word made true and good,
The Apparition comes. I knew your father:
Theſe hands are not more like.

Ham. But where was this?

Mar. My lord, upon the Platform where we watcht.

Ham. Did you not ſpeak to it?

Hor. My lord, I did;
But anſwer made it none; yet once, methought,
It lifted up its head, and did addreſs
Itſelf to motion, like as it would ſpeak;
But even then the morning cock crew loud;
And at the ſound it ſhrunk in haſte away,
And vaniſh'd from our ſight.

Ham. 'Tis very ſtrange.

Hor. As I do live, my honour'd lord, 'tis true;
And we did think it writ down in our duty
To let you know of it.

[8] *—with the* ACT *of fear,*] *Shakeſpear* could never write ſo improperly as to call the *paſſion of fear*, the *act of fear*. Without doubt the true reading is,

——*with* TH' EFFECT *of fear.*

WARBURTON.

Here is an affectation of ſubtilty without accuracy. *Fear* is every day conſidered as an *agent*. *Fear laid hold on him*; *fear drove him away*. If it were proper to be rigorous in examining trifles, it might be replied, that *Shakeſpeare* would write more erroneouſly, if he wrote by the direction of this critick; they were not *diſtilled*, whatever the word may mean, *by the effect of fear*; for that *diſtillation* was itſelf *the effect*; *fear* was the cauſe, the active cauſe, that *diſtilled* them by that force of operation which we ſtrictly call *act* in voluntary, and *power* in involuntary agents, but popularly call *act* in both. But of this too much.

Ham. In-

already a variorum, and would become more obviously so in the revisions of 1773 and 1778, with alterations and additions by Johnson and, mostly, George Steevens.[126] Amongst the notes of previous commentators in these editions, none is more fully represented than Warburton, with whose comments Johnson enters into a dialogue which threatens at times to take over the page.[127] Johnson's editorial method, and the theoretical foundations on which his method was built, underwent a fascinating process of exploration and development, to some extent in relation to, and increasingly in opposition to, those of Warburton. That development may be traced from the *Miscellaneous Observations on the Tragedy of Macbeth* (1745), the *Proposals* (1756) for Johnson's edition, and the edition itself.

In the early *Observations on Macbeth* there is already an attempt to address issues of historical and cultural context, in the opening note on witchcraft, for instance, or in the resort to sources such as Camden's *Britannia* and *The Destruction of Troy*.[128] There are many acute explanatory and critical Notes, a number of which survived, in altered forms, into the 1765 edition. Many of the Notes however offer conjectural emendations, always reasoned and occasionally convincing,[129] but often with limited regard for the language of Shakespeare's time and his own idiom,[130] and only the most occasional explicit invocation of the readings of the early editions. What is perhaps most striking is the presence in the *Observations on Macbeth* of some familiar rhetorical habits of conjectural emendation, echoes of Theobald especially in *Shakespeare Restored*, and of Bentley in his *Paradise Lost*, and anticipations of Warburton. So, at *Macbeth*, I. 5. 45, where the Folio reads *keep peace*,

> it cannot be doubted that Shakespeare wrote differently, perhaps thus.
>
> '[. . .] nor *keep pace* between
> Th'effect and it'.

Similarly, at I. 2. 47 Lenox 'undoubtedly said "[. . .] *teems* to speak things strange"' (Folio *seems*). In some of these conjectures the aesthetic element of the judgment is explicit: so at I. 3. 146 Johnson supposes that 'every reader is disgusted at the tautology in this passage, "Time and the hour,"

425–8; Arthur M. Eastman, 'The texts from which Johnson printed his Shakespeare', *Journal of English and Germanic Philology*, 49 (1950), 182–91.

126 See Arthur Sherbo, *Samuel Johnson, Editor of Shakespeare* (Urbana: University of Illinois Press, 1956), pp. 102–13; Sherbo, '1773: the year of revision', *Eighteenth-Century Studies*, 7 (1973), 18–39; *Johnson on Shakespeare*, VII. xxxix.

127 A representative instance is the disagreement over the phrase 'hearsed in death' (*Hamlet*, I. 4. 26), where Warburton's extended logic-chopping in justification of his conjectural 'hearsed in *earth*' is answered by an equally lengthy rebuttal.

128 *Johnson on Shakespeare*, VII. 3–6, 25, 35.

129 For example, '*pall* [Folio *pull*] in resolution' at *Macbeth*, 5. 5. 40 (*Johnson on Shakespeare*, VII. 42–3).

130 For example, the correction of *ow'd* to *own'd* (*Johnson on Shakespeare*, VII. 13).

and will therefore willingly believe that Shakespeare wrote it thus, "[. . .] *Time! on!* – the hour runs thro' the roughest day"'.[131]

By the time he came to write his *Proposals for Printing, by Subscription, the Dramatick Works of William Shakespeare*, Johnson's emphases had shifted towards explanation and contextualization. In the *Proposals* he makes a promise which needs to be quoted at length:

The editor will endeavour to read the books which the authour read, to trace his knowledge to its source, and compare his copies with their originals . . . by comparing the works of Shakespeare with those of writers who lived at the same time, immediately preceded, or immediately followed him, he shall be able to ascertain his ambiguities, disentangle his intricacies, and recover the meaning of words now lost in the darkness of antiquity.

When therefore any obscurity arises from an allusion to some other book, the passage will be quoted. When the diction is entangled, it will be cleared by a paraphrase or interpretation. When the sense is broken by the suppression of part of the sentiment in pleasantry or passion, the connection will be supplied. When any forgotten custom is hinted, care will be taken to retrieve and explain it. The meaning supplied to doubtful words will be supported by the authorities of other writers, or by parallel passages of Shakespeare himself.[132]

This is one of the more impressive statements in the eighteenth century of the editor's duty to locate Shakespeare in his original cultural environment, to 'illustrate' (to use Johnson's own word) Shakespearean meaning by the writings of his contemporaries, to explain obscurity by paraphrase, and to validate the interpretation of ambiguities by the citation of parallel passages within and beyond the works of the playwright himself. Johnson's mind was of course superbly prepared for this task, particularly by his reading in connection with the Harleian Library catalogue, and, more especially, the *Dictionary*, which was not only the most important preliminary work for the edition, but is itself, in its many thousands of citations and glosses of Shakespearean usages, a major work of Shakespearean exegetical scholarship. Johnson claimed in the *Proposals* that 'with regard to obsolete or peculiar diction, the editor may perhaps claim some degree of confidence, having had more motives to consider the whole extent of our language than any other man from its first formation'.[133] He was well acquainted with the 'pure sources of genuine diction', those authors from Sidney to the Restoration who were a predominant source for the *Dictionary*, though he was no doubt less familiar than Theobald with the dramatic writings of Shakespeare's age.

In his exemplary statement of methodological intentions, however, and in the way in which Johnson carried through his edition, there are perhaps echoes of the large programme, and lesser practice, of the *Dictionary*.

[131] *Johnson on Shakespeare*, VII. 8, 12, 16.
[132] *Johnson on Shakespeare*, VII. 56–7.
[133] *Johnson on Shakespeare*, VII. 56.

Johnson the humanist scholar was doomed to awake a professional editor, pressurized by subscribers, booksellers, and the vastness of the task itself. Already in the *Proposals* Johnson is to be found acknowledging the difficulties of the contextualizing explication of an author distanced from us by time, culture, and linguistic usage: 'When a writer outlives his contemporaries . . . he is necessarily obscure. Every age has its modes of speech, and its cast of thought; which, though easily explained when there are many books to be compared with each other, become sometimes unintelligible, and always difficult, when there are no parallel passages that may conduce to their illustration.'[134] The colloquial speech, the proverbs, the common allusions, and the idioms of an age are inevitably transient, likely to be recorded in print, if at all, only in the great lumber room of 'all such reading as was never read'. They are the 'fugitive cant' which Johnson's *Dictionary* does not include. Shakespeare's usage of words or expressions that have now passed out of the language can be clarified and supported by parallel passages; but where, as often, such confirming knowledge is missing, the editor may be led (as Warburton regularly was) to reject a peculiar expression known only in one Shakespearean crux or even be tempted to concoct a *hapax legomenon* where an apparently more normal usage seems beyond explanation.

In the Preface to his 1765 edition Johnson states another kind of difficulty for the editor striving to find meaning in a text embedded in the historical and cultural past:

> The compleat explanation of an authour not systematick and consequential, but desultory and vagrant, abounding in casual allusions and light hints, is not to be expected from any single scholiast. All personal reflections, when names are suppressed, must be in a few years irrecoverably obliterated; and customs, too minute to attract the notice of law . . . are so fugitive and unsubstantial, that they are not easily retained or recovered. What can be known, will be collected by chance, from the recesses of obscure and obsolete papers . . . Of this knowledge every man has some, and none has much.[135]

This is an argument, of course, for the variorum edition, where the disparate kinds of explanatory knowledge which are the property of many different scholars may be brought together, and where obscurities left by one may be resolved by the 'happier industry, or future information' of another. It describes the process by which, comprehensively or partially, and with or without acknowledgment, Pope (in his second edition) and Warburton had drawn on Theobald, Johnson himself drew on all these predecessors as well as on such later commentators as Heath and Upton, and Steevens would draw on Capell.

There is also a specifically textual source of interpretative difficulty. As

[134] *Johnson on Shakespeare*, VII. 52. [135] *Johnson on Shakespeare*, VII. 103.

we have seen, Johnson believed, with other eighteenth-century editors, that the surviving Shakespearean texts were 'corrupt in many places, and in many doubtful'. The necessary editorial restoration of corrupted passages must be attempted either 'by collation of copies or sagacity of conjecture'.[136] Though he did not approach the textual thoroughness of his successors Capell and Jennens, Johnson at least claimed that collation came first. In the 1756 *Proposals* he had promised that 'the corruptions of the text will be corrected by a careful collation', and 'all the observable varieties of all the copies' would be made available to the reader. There are problems, however, which, because 'all the books are evidently vitiated', and (as he would phrase it in the Preface) 'the greater part of the plays are extant only in one copy', cannot be solved by the comparison of texts. At this point collation of copies, and critical discrimination between the readings they supply, must inevitably give way to 'critical sagacity', the proposal of unwitnessed amended readings.[137]

Johnson's view of this editorial question does not differ from the stated theory of many of his contemporaries, but he was, as ever, particularly aware of, and perceptive about, the issues involved. What special authority have the readings witnessed by the surviving early copies? At what point of the enquiry does the editor seek to go beyond the documents? On what bases may an unwitnessed reading be proposed, and by what criteria should it be validated?

In some ways Johnson seems to remain in his edition surprisingly hospitable to conjecture as an act of creation or fancy. All eighteenth-century editors made adjustments in matters of punctuation, Theobald often with detailed discussion, others more or less silently, and all indulged to a greater or lesser degree in substantive emendation. There are certainly still some elements of an eighteenth-century aesthetic orientation in Johnson's edition, the accommodation, if only in restrained ways, of the text to the taste of the editor and his readers. Johnson's edition includes a great many conjectural emendations to pointing and to 'particular or other words of slight effect'. In a few cases Johnson alters substantial readings on his own account.[138] And at some points in his commentary Johnson responds to Warburton's emendations with a warm appreciation of the older man's conjectural creativity. Warburton's conjecture 'if the sun breed maggots in a dead dog, being a *god*, kissing carrion' (2. 2. 182), for instance, is praised by Johnson as 'a noble emendation, which almost sets the critick on a level with the authour'.

Johnson's edition, however, is for much the greater part based on a

[136] *Johnson on Shakespeare*, VII. 104–5. [137] *Johnson on Shakespeare*, VII. 55, 105.

[138] At *Hamlet*, I. 2. 65, for instance, Johnson fails to elicit sense from Claudius's 'Take thy fair hour, Laertes; time be thine, / And thy best graces spend it at thy will', and makes without reasoned support the conjecture '*my* best graces'.

cautious attitude to the employment of conjectural 'sagacity'. In the *Proposals* he had already promised that conjecture would not be 'wantonly or unnecessarily indulged', and as his work progressed he became more and more conscious of its dangers. 'As I practised conjecture more, I learned to trust it less', he wrote in the Preface: 'and after I had printed a few plays, resolved to insert none of my own readings in the text.' For Johnson as for Upton, the text has become a sacred place. Conjecture, which is an act of 'imagination', that 'fugitive and vagrant faculty', must be 'confined to the margin' if indulged at all. The exercise of conjecture is a presumption, in which the critic tries, impossibly, to do what no mortal can:

> he must have before him all possibilities of meaning, with all possibilities of expression. Such must be his comprehension of thought, and such his copiousness of language. Out of many readings possible, he must be able to select that which best suits with the state, opinions, and modes of language prevailing in every age, and with his authour's particular cast of thought, and turn of expression. Such must be his knowledge, and such his taste. Conjectural criticism demands more than humanity possesses.[139]

Johnson's modification of his approach in the course of his work on the edition was certainly a response to his growing sense of uncertainty in his own guesses: 'every day increases my doubt of my emendations'. It was also, as the Preface makes explicit, a result of consideration of two important theoretical issues: the authority of the first copies, and the degree of determination an editor must employ in explicating a difficulty before resorting to conjectural correction. If Shakespeare had published his own works, if we had direct access to the unmediated authorial word, 'we should have sat quietly down to disentangle his intricacies, and clear his obscurities'. We know, however, that the surviving witnesses suffered error in transmission, and underwent non-authorial change: 'his works were transcribed for the players by those who may be supposed to have seldom understood them; they were transmitted by copiers equally unskilful, who still multiplied errours; they were perhaps sometimes mutilated by the actors, for the sake of shortening the speeches; and were at last printed without correction of the press'.[140] Nonetheless, we must resist the temptation to 'tear what we cannot loose, and eject what we happen not to understand'.[141] However careless the player-editors may have been, they had the essential advantage that they had in front of them the ultimate source of authority, Shakespeare's manuscript:

> It has been my settled principle, that the reading of the ancient books is probably true, and therefore is not to be disturbed for the sake of elegance, perspicuity, or

139 *Johnson on Shakespeare*, VII. 55, 108, 95.
140 *Johnson on Shakespeare*, VII. 92, 93.
141 *Johnson on Shakespeare*, VII. 92.

mere improvement of the sense. For though much credit is not due to the fidelity, nor any to the judgment of the first publishers, yet they who had the copy before their eyes were more likely to read it right, than we who read it only by imagination.[142]

The old books are 'true' because they give us most immediate access to what the author himself wrote. The first 'editors' had (like the Church Fathers in respect of Holy Scripture) the interpretative privilege conferred by nearness in spirit and time. For Johnson therefore the balance must shift from a free exercise in conjecture, which will inevitably tend to the aesthetic, towards the use of all possible means to make sense of the early textual authorities as we have them: 'where any passage appeared inextricably perplexed, [I] have endeavoured to discover how it may be recalled to sense, with least violence. But my first labour is, always to turn the old text on every side, and try if there be any interstice, through which light can find its way.'[143] Few moments in Johnson's editorial writings are more resonant than this figure of his struggle with the original copies in search of meaning.

As might be expected, the consequences of Johnson's engagement with this issue frequently appear in his notes, at those points especially where he confronts Warburton. This is a line from Claudius's conversation with Laertes in the fourth act of *Hamlet*, included in the Quartos, though omitted from F1:

And then this *should* is like a spendthrift sigh
That hurts by easing.

(A. xvi. 9)

To Warburton, this is 'nonsense', and should read *spend-thrift's sign*: '*i.e.* tho' a spendthrift's entering into bonds or mortgages gives him a present relief from his straits, yet it ends in much greater distresses' (*Works of Shakespear*, VIII. 238). Johnson's reply is noteworthy, both for its statement of admiration of Warburton's conjectural ingenuity, and for the principle which it embodies:

This conjecture is so ingenious, that it can hardly be opposed, but with the same reluctance as the bow is drawn against a hero whose virtues the archer holds in veneration . . . Yet this emendation, however specious, is mistaken. The original reading is, not a *spendthrift's* sigh, but a *spendthrift* sigh; a *sigh* that makes an unnecessary waste of the vital flame. It is a notion very prevalent that *sighs* . . . wear out the animal powers.

Attracted though he is to the emendation, Johnson rejects it, on the two grounds we might expect: that the reading *spendthrift sigh* is present in early copies and that it is capable of explanation.[144]

142 *Johnson on Shakespeare*, VII. 106. 143 *Johnson on Shakespeare*, VII. 106.

144 *Johnson on Shakespeare*, VIII. 1000. Warburton's *sign* is his own conjecture. Warburton's *spendthrift's* derives from Pope's conjecture *spendthrift's*. *Spendthrift* is the reading of Q5, presumably a

Elsewhere Johnson is less equivocal. Time and again he questions the necessity of emendation, and the validity of whatever new reading Warburton proposed, and finds an interstice for meaning. Warburton makes, for instance, little attempt to understand Hamlet's lines at 5. 2. 42–3:

As peace should still her wheaten garland wear
And stand a comma 'tween their amities.

and conjectures, with a rather misplaced certainty,

The poet without doubt wrote:

And stand a *commere* 'tween our amities.

The term is taken from a traficker in love, who brings people together, a procuress. (*Works of Shakespear*, VIII. 253)

Johnson objects on two grounds: first, that the proposed correction is an alien word, whose credentials as an English, still less as a Shakespearean, usage cannot be demonstrated; and, second, that the original reading, difficult and mannered though it is, offers a sense, which is consistent with its author's usage and style and may with some editorial effort be explained esssentially by paraphrase:

I am again inclined to vindicate the old reading. That the word *commere* is French, will not be denied; but when or where was it English?

The expression of our authour is, like many of his phrases, sufficiently constrained and affected, but it is not incapable of explanation. The *comma* is the note of *connection* and continuity of sentences; the *period* is the note of *abruption* and disjunction . . . This is not an easy stile; but is it not the stile of Shakespeare?[145]

Such a use of paraphrase to explain the original reading, where Warburton had resorted to emendation, is a regular feature of Johnson's edition. Warburton's amendments to words uttered by Claudius in his attempt to pray, 'May one be pardon'd and retain th'offence?', are demolished thus: 'I see no difficulty in the present reading. He that does not amend what can be amended, *retains* his *offence*. The king kept the crown from the right heir.'[146]

As with Theobald, there is in Johnson a regular and determined rejection of aesthetic editorial choices in favour of readings which may be believed authorial. Particularly strikingly, despite his own profound

correction of the readings of Q2 (*spend thirfts*) and Q3 (*spend-thrifts*). Modern editors read *spendthrift*, and, turning the text on the same side as Johnson, find essentially the same meaning.

145 *Johnson on Shakespeare*, VIII. 1005. Johnson included the word *commere* in the first edition of his *Dictionary* (London, 1755), where the word is glossed 'a common mother', and the example is this line from *Hamlet*. In the fourth edition of the *Dictionary* (London, 1773) the word has been dropped.

146 *Hamlet*, 3. 3. 56 (*Johnson on Shakespeare*, VIII. 989); Warburton had altered *offence* to *effects*. For Johnson's use of periphrastic explanation, compare, for example, his note on *Hamlet*, 5. 2. 30–2 (*Johnson on Shakespeare*, VIII. 1004).

distrust of metaphoric expression, Johnson refuses to visit his own taste in figurative expression on Shakespeare. Johnson dismisses both Pope's proposal of '*siege* of troubles' and Warburton's '*assail* of troubles' (for '*sea* of troubles', *Hamlet*, 3. 1. 60) with a brusque reference to Shakespearean figurative usage: 'I know not why there should be so much solicitude about this metaphor. Shakespeare breaks his metaphors often.' Similarly, despite his own view that 'words too familiar or too remote defeat the purposes of the poet', Johnson refrains from reducing Shakespeare's language to his own standards of correctness, preferring for example, 'In *hugger-mugger* to inter him' (*Hamlet*, 4. 5. 80), the F and Q reading, to *private*, the emendation in Warburton's, and other editions: 'That the words now replac'd are better, I do not undertake to prove; it is sufficient that they are Shakespeare's.'[147]

In such representative passages of Johnson's edition of Shakespeare we see a powerful mind wrestling with central issues of editorial explication and emendation, and closely engaged in the contemporary discussion. Though willing at first to entertain and instigate conjecture, over a period of twenty years he became increasingly determined to ascertain and preserve authorial words, to illustrate authorial meanings, and to apply his knowledge of the writings, culture, and language of Shakespeare and his contemporaries to interpretative purposes. The aesthetic tendencies implicit in Warburton's conjectural method had long been unfashionable. The substantially different methods of Johnson's edition, and its considerable prestige, served to move Shakespearean editing further, and more decisively, towards an authorial orientation.

Edward Capell

My attempt to outline some of the theoretical tendencies of eighteenth-century Shakespeare editing might appropriately conclude with discussion of a work which represents a substantial, in some respects a radical, development in textual procedure, and in the forms and methods of editorial commentary. In 1749 Edward Capell began the remarkable fair transcript of Shakespeare's dramatic works, now in the Library of Trinity College, Cambridge, which would be a central part of his scholarly labour for the next seventeen years, and would be the printer's copy for his ten-volume *Mr William Shakespeare his Comedies, Histories, and Tragedies* (1768).[148]

[147] *Johnson on Shakespeare*, VIII. 981, 996.

[148] Capell was born in 1713. After attending Bury St Edmunds Grammar School he went on to St Catharine's Hall, Cambridge, and then to the Middle Temple. He was appointed Deputy Inspector of Plays in 1737, and Groom of the Privy Chamber in 1745. The income of these public positions, and his inheritance of the manors of Troston (his mother's home) and Stanton (which came to him through his father) gave him the financial independence to dedicate much

Capell's edition departs from the main textual tradition of eighteenth-century literary editing of Shakespeare, and, with the extensive associated editorial matter which made its way into print over the next fifteen years, constitutes a major step forward both in Shakespearean textual editing, and in the interpretative uses of scholarship.

Clearly the edition of Shakespeare is Capell's major achievement, but there are two significant editorial projects which he published or completed before 1768. The title of the first of these already states Capell's beliefs in scholarly honesty, and the pursuit of authenticity: *Prolusions; or, Select Pieces of Antient Poetry, – Compil'd with Great Care from their Several Originals, and Offer'd to the Publick as Specimens of the Integrity that should be Found in the Editions of Worthy Authors* (1760). The Dedication reiterates his intention to offer 'an Example of Care and Fidelity to Persons who take upon them the Publication of our best Authors' (sig. A4[r]). The book is made up of editions of *The Nutbrown Maid*, Sackvile's *Induction*, Sir Thomas Overbury's *A Wife, Now a Widowe*, *Edward the Third*, and Sir John Davies's *Nosce Teipsum*. Capell's Preface offers only a very brief account of these works, chiefly on such matters as dating. The interest in this edition lies not in any commentary, but in its choice of subjects, relatively minor writings of the sixteenth and early seventeenth centuries, and, especially, in its formulations of bibliographical and text-editorial method. The Preface already contains what is, I think, the first, and startling, statement of what we would recognize as the essential outline of a modern methodology of literary text-editing:

> When a poem was to be proceeded upon, the editions that belong to it were first collated; . . . In the course of this collation it well appear'd, that some one edition was to be prefer'd to the others: that edition therefore was made the ground-work of what is now publish'd; . . . and it is never departed from, but in places where some other edition had a reading most apparently better; or in such other places as were very plainly corrupt, but, assistance of books failing, were to be amended by conjecture. (p. i)

I will return to the implications of this statement when I examine Capell's *Shakespeare*. For the moment it will be enough to point to Capell's account of the process of gathering, distinguishing, and describing the early texts; the choice of one such text by detailed collation as the 'ground work' for the edition; the use of critical intelligence in choosing between the substantives of that base text and the other textual witnesses; and the resort, where the sense requires, beyond a superstitious reverence for surviving documents to properly grounded conjecture. If there is no false

of his adult life to the pursuit of literary scholarship, and, in particular, to his edition of Shakespeare. Capell's manuscript text of *The Merry Wives of Windsor* is dated 25 November 1749 to 18 January 1750, that of *The Taming of the Shrew* is dated 4 July to 1 August 1766.

idolatry of the worldly text, there is in Capell's *Prolusions* already a conception of rigour, openness, and honesty in the duty of the editor that amounts to another kind of piety. Each of the poems is followed by a list of editions consulted, with the 'best' editions identified, and all described with a careful bibliographical accuracy. Title pages are transcribed meticulously. A brief list of Conjectural Readings is provided for *The Nutbrown Maid*, and lists of Various Readings, including variants between different impressions of a given edition, are given for the other pieces. The reader is offered, Capell claims, a record of 'every departure' from the 'establish'd text'.

Capell's second non-Shakespearean editorial project was a good deal more ambitious than the *Prolusions*, and was completed but never published. In the Library of Trinity College, Cambridge, with the other books he donated to the College, is Capell's manuscript edition of *Paradise Lost*.[149] This holograph is clearly intended as printer's copy. There is scarcely a correction anywhere, and every detail of format, down to a full manuscript title page lacking only a printer's name, is provided. There are no explanatory annotations, either with the text or following it. There is no Preface, but the work is dedicated to the Bishop of Rochester, that is, to Zachary Pearce, whose answer to Richard Bentley's conjecturally licentious and subjective edition of 1732 had been applauded by many before Capell as one of the century's key defences, and exemplifications, of the application of scholarship to textual criticism and exegesis: 'the pattern of critique that you have given us', writes Capell in the Dedication (dated 23 June 1767), 'will be a means . . . of securing not Milton only, but all our other Authors . . . from the depredation of the confident, the unskilful, and the necessitous, – under one or other of which denominations most criticks will generally come'. As in the *Prolusions*, Capell went back to the original texts: there is no question of taking the text of a previous modern editor and working from that, nor is there any question of the indulgence of wholesale and undisciplined conjecture. Capell personally possessed copies of the first, ten-book edition of *Paradise Lost* (1667–9) bearing a total of four of the five variant title pages.[150] He also owned a copy of the twelve-book second edition of 1674. The text of the poem in Capell's manuscript edition is followed by a list of Editions Consulted, and some five pages of Various Readings. The list of editions provides transcripts of the five variant title pages of the first edition, which are in fact more scrupulously exact even than Walter Greg's transcripts in his catalogue of the Capell Collection at

[149] Capell Collection, MSS. B.17. Notes in Capell's hand, placed before Milton's Advertisement to the poem, and at the end of Book 12, record the starting (23 July 1759) and finishing (18 December 1760) dates of his transcript.

[150] See R. G. Moyles, *The Text of Paradise Lost* (Toronto: University of Toronto Press, 1985), pp. 4–14.

Trinity.[151] Capell takes the twelve-book second edition as his base text, but he clearly collated it throughout with all the different copies available to him of the first edition, and in the case of substantive variations he makes, as modern editors continue to make, eclectic critical decisions on the basis of the merits of each particular case. There are a very small number of conjectures. The list of textual variants aims at, and achieves with only the most isolated exceptions, completeness.[152]

The manuscript edition of *Paradise Lost* and the *Prolusions* set some part of the agenda for Capell's textual policy in his edition of Shakespeare. Though Capell was little appreciated in his own time, partly for methodological reasons which will become clear, his status as the first eighteenth-century Shakespearean editor to establish coherent principles of procedure, and to undertake a thoroughgoing and fully documented collation, is now well known, and has been described by Alice Walker and Brian Vickers amongst others.[153] I would like briefly to set out the situation Capell found himself in and the solutions he proposed and put into effect, and to explore some of their implications. Shakespeare, of course, presents textual problems very different from those of *Paradise Lost.* Most eighteenth-century Miltonic scholar-editors, including Zachary Pearce, Thomas Newton, and Capell himself, though not Richard Bentley, had been able to agree that the early editions of Milton's epic were relatively reliable. Before Capell, some Shakespearean editors, including Pope, had begun to understand the independent value of the Quartos, and some, including Johnson, had seen that the first Folio had an authority superior to the second, third, and fourth. Nonetheless, the 'common text' of early eighteenth-century Shakespeare did not make a clean start from the best early witnesses but was traditionary. Rowe mainly followed F4; Pope followed Rowe, though he understood something of the Quartos; Theobald sent to the printers his annotated copy of Pope's 1728 second edition,[154] though he made extensive use of the early texts; Warburton followed Pope and Theobald and his own fancy; Johnson followed Warburton and Theobald. Capell, however, as in his *Prolusions* and his edition of Milton, went back to the originals and bypassed traditionary textual corruption. He gives, in the Preface to his

[151] W. W. Greg, *Catalogue of the Books Presented by Edward Capell to the Library of Trinity College in Cambridge* (Cambridge: printed for Trinity College at the University Press, 1903).

[152] Capell's manuscript edition is discussed in R. G. Moyles, 'Edward Capell (1713–1781) as editor of *Paradise Lost*', *Transactions of the Cambridge Bibliographical Society*, 6 (1975), 252–61.

[153] See Alice Walker, 'Edward Capell and his edition of *Shakespeare*', *Proceedings of the British Academy*, 46 (1960), 131–45; Vickers, v and vi *passim.*

[154] Theobald wrote fair copy of his annotations and notes on the text, including considerable additions to the stage directions, in an interleaved copy of Pope's second edition which had been sent to him by Tonson. Of this copy, nine plays are in Winchester College Library, and *Antony and Cleopatra* is British Library C.45.b.11. See Richard Corballis, 'Copy-text for Theobald's "Shakespeare"', *Library*, 6th ser., 8 (1986), 156–9.

1768 edition of Shakespeare, a highly significant account of his procedures. He began by collecting all the editions, not only those of the 'moderns', the eighteenth-century editors, but virtually all the Folios and Quartos (his collection was deposited, with the remainder of his Shakespearean collection, at Trinity College). He then proceeded to 'collation, which is the first step in works of this nature . . . first of moderns with moderns, then of moderns with ancients, and afterwards of ancients with others more ancient'. So far so familiar, though Capell's collations were carried out with a thoroughness which would not be matched by any other editor before Charles Jennens. At this point on the road to the editorial Damascus, however, he received, as he recounts in his Introduction, an almost Pauline revelation:

> at the last, a ray of light broke forth upon him, by which he hop'd to find his way through the wilderness of these editions into that fair country the Poet's real habitation. He had not proceeded far in his collation, before he saw cause to come to this resolution; – to stick invariably to the old editions, (that is, the best of them) which hold now the place of manuscripts, no scrap of the Author's writing having the luck to come down to us; and never to depart from them, but in cases where reason, and the uniform practice of men of the greatest note in this art, tell him – they may be quitted; nor yet in those, without notice.[155]

Broadly speaking, this key statement of method is in line with his stated principles and practice in the *Prolusions* and *Paradise Lost.* His text is to be built directly on the early printed editions, not on the false foundation of the modern editors. Where previous editors submitted to the printer a marked-up copy of a predecessor's work, Capell provided a complete fair copy, every word and every letter written in his own hand.[156] By careful

[155] *Mr William Shakespeare his Comedies, Histories, and Tragedies* (10 vols., London, 1768), I. 20. Hereafter *WSCHT.* Jarvis (*Scholars and Gentlemen*, pp. 184–5) warns against taking this as a radical statement of a new paradigm in textual science, pointing out that Capell's collation began with moderns (but this was Capell's procedure *before* the light on the Damascus road); and that his acknowledgment of the authority of 'the uniform practice of men of the greatest note in this art' is an evidence of persistent '*receptus*-thinking' (this may be a more significant reservation about Capell's statement of principle, if not about his practice).

[156] It needs to be noted, however, that Capell seems to have used a copy of the first edition of Pope's *Works of Shakespear*, now in Trinity College Library (Capell Collection, E. 6, E. 8), as an initial working text in his preparation of part at least of his fair copy. The text of *The Tempest, Much Ado, Merry Wives*, and *A Midsummer Night's Dream* in volume I of this copy of Pope's edition, and of *Lear* in volume III, are annotated throughout in Capell's hand (there are no annotations in volumes II, IV, V, and VI). On a number of pages Capell writes his characteristic single line of textual footnotes; at many points he enters in the margin, as in his fair draft of the 1768 edition, the initial letter of the name of a previous editor to indicate the provenance of a reading; Pope's own footnotes are deleted; and there is careful attention to typography, orthography, and stage directions. The textual decisions incorporated in these annotations are repeated with considerable though not total fidelity in the fair draft for *WSCHT.* Probably Capell produced his holograph fair draft with the annotated Pope in front of him. A copy of the Lintot edition of Shakespeare's *Poems* (1709), similarly annotated in Capell's hand, and preserved in the Library of Trinity College (Capell Collection, MS. 5), suggests that Capell

collation he would determine which, in the case of each play, is the best of those early texts, and in fact he generally found that 'the scale of goodness preponderated' on the side of 'the most ancient', that is, on the side of texts of independent authority (*WSCHT*, I. 21). That best text becomes, as in the *Prolusions*, his explicit base text. Where a satisfactory Quarto is available, in the case of eleven of the plays, Capell follows that; otherwise he follows the first Folio. His base text for *Hamlet* predictably is the 'good' Quarto, Q2. A 'Table of his Editions' following the Introduction to Capell's edition provides an impressively accurate bibliographical account of the early printed texts, both Quarto and Folio. In the separately published *Notes and Various Readings*, Capell would give, as he promised in the Introduction to his edition, a full list of Various Readings for every play which includes 'all discarded readings, . . . all additions . . . and variations of every kind' and specifies 'the editions . . . to which they severally belong' (*WSCHT*, I. 22).

However, Capell's approach to editing does not privilege the document itself; he is not a historical but a literary editor. No eighteenth-century editor of secular vernacular literary texts practised anything like facsimile or diplomatic editing, and Capell is no exception; for him authority lies not in the document, but in the author's intention. 'That fair country the Poet's real habitation' is to be found not in any specific textual witness, but through the careful examination of the printed texts which, in the case of Shakespeare's writings, 'hold now the place of manuscripts'. Those printed texts, even those which are earliest and closest to the manuscripts which most immediately embody the author's intentions, are inevitably from this point of view imperfect. This leads the editor to an eclectic process of collation of the chosen base text with other early witnesses: 'it . . . became proper and necessary to look into the other old editions, and to select from thence whatever improves the Author, or contributes to his advancement in perfectness' (*WSCHT*, I. 21). Further than this, the derivativeness of the early printed texts leads the editor into conjecture. As modern theorists regularly argue, the editor who seeks to reproduce 'what the author wrote' may very well need to propose readings which are instanced in no surviving witness. For Capell this is, in the Shakespearean textual situation, inevitable:

> But, when these [i.e. collational] helps were administer'd, there was yet behind a very great number of passages, labouring under various defects and those of various degree, that had their cure to seek from some other sources, that of copies affording it no more: for these he had recourse in the first place to the assistance of modern copies: and, where that was incompetent, or else absolutely deficient, . . . there he sought the remedy in himself, using judgment and conjecture; which . . .

adopted a similar working method for his projected edition of the poems. This copy contains, on a folio tipped in after the title page, the text of a Preface for this unpublished edition, written in Capell's hand, and dated 1766.

he will not be found to have exercis'd wantonly, but to follow the establish'd rules of critique with soberness and temperance. (*WSCHT*, I. 22–3)

It is often asserted that the editorial pursuit of authorial intention rather than documentary authenticity leads to conjectural licence, and in the cases of Bentley's edition of *Paradise Lost* and Warburton's Shakespeare it clearly did so. Capell however, like Theobald, is prepared to argue that conjectural criticism can be a principled and disciplined process. The authority of the early texts may be overridden where 'reason' and 'the establish'd rules of critique' allow. I shall illustrate later how Capell understood these two things.

One of Capell's near contemporaries practised collation with equal precision. Charles Jennens produced, in the years between the appearance of Capell's text of the plays, and his *Notes and Various Readings*, editions of five of Shakespeare's plays 'collated with the old and modern editions': *Lear* (1770), *Hamlet*, *Macbeth*, and *Othello* (1773), and *Julius Caesar* (1774).[157] Each of these offered the reader 'one play of Shakespeare faithfully collated, line by line, with the old as well as modern editions; the different readings whereof are given with notes at the bottom of the page'.[158] This was a promise that had been made by many editors; Jennens, unusually, fulfilled it. For *Hamlet*, for instance, he collated the editions we now know as Q2, Q3, and Q5, and F1, F2, F3, and F4. He also collated all the 'modern' editions, up to and including Capell, and was aware of changes to the text incorporated into the traditionary text in the eighteenth century, sometimes silently and sometimes without the authority of any textual witness. At *Hamlet*, I. 3. 63, for instance, Jennens reads 'hoops of steel', and remarks that 'all the editions before P[ope]. read *hoops*, who alters it to *hooks*, and is followed by the succeeding editors'. There are limitations however in Jennens's method which show by contrast how remarkable Capell's textual achievement was. Jennens does little more than to collate, and to list the results of his collation. There is little understanding of the relative authority of different editions. There is no principled choice of base text, and at very few points does Jennens offer a rationale for preferring one reading over another. Typically, Jennens prints the Q2 reading 'a *moth* it is to trouble the mind's eye' (*Hamlet*, A. i. 5); he knows of, but does not adopt, the correction *mote* which appeared in Q4 and subsequently. At *Hamlet*, I. 2. 132, Jennens similarly prints 'His *cannon* 'gainst self-slaughter', without any attempt to

[157] Charles Jennens (1700–73) was one of several wealthy eighteenth-century amateur editors or commentators of Shakespeare. He was distinct both in the scale of his wealth and in his eccentricity. His edition of *Lear*, published anonymously, is dedicated by Jennens to himself: 'under whose Patronage, by access to whose Library, and from whose hints and remarks, the editor hath been enabled to attempt an Edition of Shakespeare'. See Gordon Crosse, 'Charles Jennens as editor of Shakespeare', *Library*, 4th ser., 16 (1935), 236–40.

[158] Charles Jennens, ed., Preface to *Lear* (London, 1770), p. x.

engage in the interpretative debate on the outcome of which must hang the editorial choice between *cannon* and *canon*. Jennens's method is an unreasoned eclecticism. He provides all the data, and he is extremely conservative in his attitude to conjectural emendation, arguing that no 'fair dealing' editor 'has a right to impose upon every body his own favourite reading, or to give his own conjectural interpolation, without producing the readings of the several editions'.[159] This modesty however amounts to a failure to establish grounds of editorial judgment, to settle on either a faithfully documentary or a critically authorial orientation. For all his completeness and honesty Jennens is not, unlike Capell, an 'intelligent editor', attempting to establish a genuine text by making judgments on an explicitly interpretative basis.

In terms of the evolution of Shakespearean editing in the eighteenth century, Capell's textual openness and thoroughness, his return to the first printed texts, and his consistently critical method, amounted to a revolution. All this, however, was not enough, and seems still not to be enough, to have made Capell's edition seem either startlingly new in its scholarship, or especially accessible and usable, and there is no doubt that this is at least partly due to the format and chronology of the publication of Capell's Shakespearean researches. Capell published his ten-volume edition of Shakespeare's plays in 1768. It is a clean, beautifully designed and printed octavo. The text of the plays is preceded by the Introduction, which has more to say on text-editorial than on critical matters, and by the 'Table of Editions'. There are, however, no explanatory notes on the plays. Each page, in stark visual as well as methodological contrast to the encumbered variorum editions of Johnson and Steevens, carries no more than a single line of notes of textual variants, keyed to the text by line numbers (but the text itself, resembling in this other instances of humanist printing, has no line numbers). The first volume of Capell's *Notes and Various Readings to Shakespeare* did not appear until 1774, and the work was not published in its complete three-volume form until after Capell's death, from 1779 to 1783. The casual reader could not, and notoriously did not, benefit from the quality of Capell's text editing and explanatory annotation. Gerald Graff has recently remarked that a coherent and sympathetic understanding of past writings is not likely to be achieved by the average modern student through 'bare unmediated contact with the work itself'.[160] Eighteenth-century readers equally stood in need of linguistic, syntactical, historical, literary-historical, and textual aid. Capell's edition, because of its format, apparently withholds that.

In some respects the curious make-up of Capell's edition of Shakespeare

[159] Preface to *Lear*, p. ix.
[160] *Professing Literature* (Chicago: University of Chicago Press, 1987), pp. 254–5.

continues to make its distinctive achievements hard to recognize. Margreta de Grazia denies to Capell the sort of concern for authenticity which she identifies and describes in Malone, arguing that Capell's presentation of the text essentially 'clean' – his preference, as she puts it, of 'aesthetic appearance to scholarly lemma' – is in conflict with the demands of authenticity, part of his appeal to 'universal taste rather than textual recension'.[161] Capell indeed speaks in his Introduction of the 'advancement' or improvement of his author.[162] He certainly means by that, however, not the imposition on Shakespeare's text of uncontrolled editorial aesthetic preferences, but progress by acts of critical discrimination towards a text which more accurately represents the author's original intentions. As I shall hope to show, Capell's procedure was in its essentials similar to that eclectic procedure which is normal in most modern literary editing. Capell's objection to what he called the 'paginary intermixture of text and comment'[163] should be seen not as an assertion of editorial taste, but as privileging the authorial text over any form of editorial gloss. His manuscript of the 1768 edition, still in Trinity College Library, does include marginal initials identifying the provenance of readings derived from other moderns, but they are dropped in the text as published, not only because they are 'unsightly', but because 'his only object has been, to do service to his great Author';[164] in other words, he does not wish to dilute the special authority of the Shakespearean text with even the briefest allusion to modern, non-authoritative sources. Capell's strategy may be represented as a dramatic privileging of the true word, the restored scripture of the author over the intrusions of the editor's secondary

[161] *Shakespeare Verbatim* (Oxford: Oxford University Press, 1991). De Grazia's judgment is in agreement however with that of Charles Jennens: 'that man must be greatly mistaken in his ideas of beauty, who prefers the handsome appearance of a page in black and white, to the quick and easy information of his readers in matters necessary to be known for their becoming proper judges of the sense of the author, and the goodness of the edition' (Jennens, ed., *Lear*, p. viii). For suggestive remarks on unadulterated gentlemanly, or amateurs', or humanist editions of the mid eighteenth and early nineteenth centuries, see E. J. Kenney, *The Classical Text* (Los Angeles and London: University of California Press, 1974), p. 154.

[162] Capell's argument as we have seen is that, because the early texts were neither printed carefully, nor remained uncorrupted after their first printing, it is therefore necessary to select from 'the other old editions . . . whatever improves the Author, or contributes to his advancement in perfectness . . . That they do improve him, was with the editor an argument in their favour' (*WSCHT*, I. 21). From this De Grazia concludes that Capell believed in 'improvement as sufficient authorization for emendation' (*Shakespeare Verbatim*, p. 54, n. 16). Improvement for Capell is, however, 'an argument', not 'sufficient authorization'. De Grazia's understanding of Capell's use of the word in an aesthetic, rather than a textual and interpretative, sense does not seem to me to be borne out in Capell's practice.

[163] *WSCHT*, I. 30.

[164] Introduction, *WSCHT*, I. 24 n. These marginalia appear in the manuscript fair copy in these forms: 'R.' (Rowe), 'P.' (Pope), 'T.' (Theobald), 'P.$^{\text{w.}}$' (Pope and Warburton), 'T.$^{\text{w.}}$' (Theobald and Warburton), 'O.' (Oxford, that is, Sir Thomas Hanmer), 'T.$^{\text{o.}}$' (Theobald and Hanmer), 'P.$^{\text{o.w.}}$' (Pope, Hanmer, Warburton).

authority. Certainly it stands in remarkable contrast to the variorum editions of Warburton, Johnson, and Steevens, where the primary text increasingly struggles to maintain its hold on the page against a steadily accreting traditionary and secondary commentary. Capell's 'regard to the beauty of his page' (*Prolusions*, p. iii) is a *visually* but not an *editorially* aesthetic concern. His respect for the antique, his care for its recovery and restoration, and his presentation of the text itself in the clearest, least adulterated, and visually purest possible form together make this edition characteristically a work of humanist scholarship. The appearance of Capell's page is not merely a matter of eighteenth-century 'taste', but an attempt to give his reader the original text of Shakespeare as he conceived it.

De Grazia's judgment of Capell however raises large issues which can only be resolved by a much fuller consideration of the individual components of Capell's edition, and of how Capell intended that they should interact. I would want to argue not only that the 1768 edition, taken together with all the materials of the *Notes and Various Readings*, constitutes a decisive step forward in textual method, but also that it is the most impressive eighteenth-century project of contextualization of Shakespeare's writings, at least before Malone. And I would want to argue that Capell's assembling of contextual material is not by any means merely an exercise in naïve aggregating pedantry, but a necessary condition of textual understanding. Those modern theorists who argue that written texts are capable of valid interpretation regularly appeal to a notion of validation through the linguistic and cultural norms within which the text was composed.[165] In Capell's edition particular explanations of the meaning of the text, and the textual discriminations which regularly arise out of them, are acts of critical interpretation founded on a detailed and documented knowledge of the appropriate context.

The contextualizing components of Capell's edition are the Glossary, separate sections of Notes to the individual plays, and the *School of Shakespeare* with its Index.

Capell's Notes on individual plays take up most of volumes I and II of the *Notes and Various Readings*. These commentaries are tough-minded and extensive – there are 28 double-column pages on *Hamlet* for example – but they are at first sight strikingly, and surprisingly, short of explanations and supporting illustration. Their purpose is announced in the Advertisement to the *Notes and Various Readings* published in 1774: 'the sole intent of the "*Notes*", is – to *establish* the Author's text, and to *explain* it: matters not of that tendency are but rarely admitted' (sig. a3^{v}). These Notes however are preceded in the first volume of the *Notes and Various Readings* by a Glossary,

[165] See above, pp. 21–3.

which is clearly designed to be used in conjunction both with the text of the plays and with the Notes. Each of nearly 3,000 entries in the Glossary is keyed to a specific occurrence of a word (or, rarely, phrase) in a play or plays, which it explains, often in the absence of a note in the *Notes and Various Readings*, sometimes in conjunction with a note or notes. That such a connection was intended is made explicit by Capell in the 1774 Advertisement: 'the "*Notes*;" was hardly begun upon, before evident tokens appear'd of a necessity for it's present suspension, to make way for another work, which should facilitate the business of note-writing, abridge it, and make it's process more regular: . . . – a "*Glossary*", – which took up no little time, nor little labour' (Advertisement to *Notes and Various Readings*, sig. a3^r).

The third element of Capell's contextualizing materials, and much the most striking, is the remarkable corpus of illustrative passages from Elizabethan and Jacobean literature of every sort that makes up the third volume of the *Notes and Various Readings*: that is, *The School of Shakespeare: or, authentic Extracts from divers English Books, that were in Print in that Author's Time*. There are extracts in the *School* from hundreds of predecessors and contemporaries of Shakespeare, in every literary kind, based, in the words of Capell's promise of this work in the Introduction to his 1768 text, on consultation of 'every book . . . that it was possible to procure, with which it could be thought he was acquainted, or that seem'd likely to contribute anything towards his illustration'.[166] Included, as Capell notes in the Preface to the *School*, are passages 'conveying knowledge of plays unpublish'd, dates of publish'd ones, of players, of stages, points relating to Shakespeare, further and more particular knowledge of stories follow'd by him, his borrowings, and things borrow'd from him'.[167] The *School* draws heavily on the collection of books printed in Shakespeare's time which Capell brought together, and which he gave to Trinity College and to the newly founded library of the British Museum. Capell himself wrote a fair manuscript draft 'Catalogue of a Collection intitl'd Shakesperiana; comprehending All the several Editions of the Works of Shakespeare, old & new; divers rare old Editions of Writers, prose-men & verse-men; with a Variety of other Articles, chiefly such as tend to illustrate him; – made by his last Editor, E. C.'.[168] The Capell Collection at Trinity College contains some 245 books, including Capell's copies of plays by Shakespeare himself, and non-dramatic writings by Shakespeare's near contemporaries (most of the non-Shakespearean dramatic writings were given to

[166] *WSCHT*, I.31.

[167] The three pages of the Preface bear neither numbers nor signatures.

[168] The catalogue was printed from Capell's manuscript at the end of 1779 by Steevens. Bound into the British Library copy (82.e.21) is what purports to be a MS copy of part of a letter by Steevens, dated 4 January 1780: 'I am so plagued for Transcripts of *Capell's* Catalogue, that I have printed 30 Copies of it to give away.' W. W. Greg compiled a new *Catalogue* (see n. 151).

the Museum).[169] This is a working library remarkable in range and quality. Key sources include copies of Holinshed's *Chronicle* (1577), Hakluyt's *Voyages* (1598–1600), and North's *Plutarch* (1579, 1612). Milton and Spenser, as well as the early editions of Shakespeare, are areas of strength. Reference books include early dictionaries by Cooper (Latin and English, 1573), Florio (Italian and English, 1598), Minshew (Spanish and English, 1599), and Cotgrave (French and English, 1650); Skinner's English etymology (1671); Bullokar's *Orthography* (1580); and Butler's *English Grammar* (1633). There are foreign-language works by Homer, Virgil, Ovid, Ariosto, Montemayor, Tasso, and others, in English translation. Amongst other notable books are a folio Chaucer, *Piers Plowman*, Erasmus's *Encomium Moriae*, Lyly's *Euphues*, Sidney's *Apology for Poetry*, the *Mirror for Magistrates*, Florio's Montaigne, the poems of Skelton, Googe, Drayton, Donne, and Crashaw, and the jest-books of Scogins and Peele. There are unique copies of Belleforest's *Hystorie of Hamblet* (1608), Ulpian Fulwell's *Ars adulandi* (1576), Nicholas Breton's *Arbor of Amorous Deuices* (1597), and some half a dozen other works. A very few books bear annotations by Capell: in a copy of John Cotgrave's *English Treasury of Wit and Language, Collected out of . . . our English Drammatick Poems* (1655) he has marked the Shakespearean quotations with a marginal 'S.'.

The *School* is a selected and ordered printing of Capell's research materials, chosen out of this impressive personal library. It is, as it were, a very large set of file cards assembled into the form of a printed book (if Capell had been working today he would certainly have organized it as an electronic database). Each extract in the *School* has the specific purpose of shedding focussed light on some Shakespearean dark corner. The examples taken together provide general illustrations of language and custom, not always confined to the Shakespearean: 'when the books were before him,' wrote Capell in the Preface, he did not always 'consider whether the word, the phrase, or the passage, concern'd his Author immediately; but whether they were analogous, or might be useful to publishers of an author contemporary who shall be thought a fit object for them'. The *School* is not by any means however a vague construction of a background to Shakespeare and his contemporaries. Some of the texts from which the extracts are chosen are sources or analogues for Shakespeare: Holinshed, a translation of Plutarch, the 1608 *Hystorie of Hamblet*. Most of the passages of the *School* are chosen to present examples of, and to explain, some specific Shakespearean allusion or usage. Very occasionally a brief note printed amongst the examples makes explicit some Shakespearean connection: Capell observes for instance that an extract from the *Fair Maid of Bristol*

[169] Capell's catalogue lists 363 titles, many of which seem to have been removed from the collection before the donation to Trinity. Some may never have been in Capell's collection.

(*c*. 1605) 'has a good deal of resemblance with a Dialogue in *"As you like it"*, between the Clown and *Audrey*' (p. 113). Invariably, the word in the selected passage that is actually used by Shakespeare is enclosed in double quotation marks. There are no lengthy continuous passages, even from such works – the *Faerie Queene* for example – as are represented *in extenso*; rather, specific paragraphs or sentences, or (short) speeches, are chosen to provide instances of the usage of a *Shakespearean* word. The method that lies behind the construction of the *School* might be compared with Samuel Johnson's process of reading and annotation in a wide field of literature in order to find exemplary passages for his *Dictionary*. The difference is that Capell's examples are for much the greater part focussed around Shakespeare and Shakespeare's language.

The *School*, then, was partly intended as a source book, but its chief function, which had been tantalizingly promised in Capell's Introduction in 1768, was to provide 'almost innumerable examples . . . of words and modes of expression which many have thought peculiar to SHAKESPEARE', with the purpose not only of demonstrating how far Shakespeare's usages were more or less familiar in his own time, but also 'the true force and meaning of [these] unusual words and expressions; which can no way be better ascertain'd, than by a proper variety of well-chosen examples' (p. 32). The phrase 'true force and meaning' indicates that the *School* is intended as an act of authentication and explanation of Shakespeare's language and sense. Its materials are genuine in themselves (Capell asserts in his Preface 'the authenticity both of Extracts and Readings, and the truth in general of what is elsewhere advanc'd by him'). They constitute the essential basis for valid interpretation, as Capell insists: 'Acquaintance in some degree with the writers of Shakespeare's time and of times prior to him, their merits in point of matter, and the language they had to dress it in, is of the utmost necessity for a right comprehension of *his* language throughout, and right estimate of his merit' (Preface to the *School*).

The *School* was not designed to stand alone, but to form an integral part of the whole interconnected structure of the edition. The Glossary might be thought of as a historical dictionary, with word-definitions but without illustrative quotations within the body of the Glossary itself; the extracts provided in the *School*, as Capell makes explicit in its Preface, 'serve *now* for confirmance of glossary explanation'. Furthermore, in the third volume of the *Notes and Various Readings* is to be found an Index to the words and phrases which are highlighted in the passages in the *School*. This Index, which contains some 3,000 entries, serves the reader therefore as an essential finding list to the specific illustrations of Shakespearean usage that the *School* offers, a guide to the reader in locating both the contextual support for the Notes, and the illustrative examples for the

Glossary.[170] How valuable the Index is to Capell's commentary can be confirmed simply by listing some of the significant and difficult words and phrases from, for example, *Hamlet* appearing in it: 'cry havocke', 'hearse', 'quiddities', 'stythie', 'vice', 'miching', 'overcrowe', 'cautel', 'paddock', 'loggets', 'howsell', 'pollax', 'polack', 'beteeme', 'eisel'. Time after time, Capell's comments on textual and exegetical points – on 'this *vice* of kings', for instance, or the *unbated* foil, or *Unhouseled* – are corroborated by illustrative passages within the *School*, which may be traced through the Index.

More detailed consideration of a small number of examples from *Hamlet* might make clearer the way in which the disparate materials of Capell's edition were designed to work together in justifying textual choices and in explicating the text. The historical contextualization that the text required for its understanding in 1768, or requires now, is offered at a number of points in Capell's Notes on *Hamlet*; on the 'aerie of children, little eyases', for example (2. 2. 334), or on Hamlet's reference to the forgotten hobby-horse (3. 2. 125), about which Capell remarks: 'The "*hobby-horse*" was a constant part of the diversions of May-day, for several centuries; 'till the puritans set themselves against it, in the days of our Author, and brought about a suppression: the fall of it was lamented by a wit of that time, in a ballad or such-like poem, of which this is a line' (*Notes*, I. 136). Often, however, contextualization is to be found not in Capell's Notes, but in the Glossary and *School*. Hamlet jocularly welcomes one of the boy players: 'your ladyship is nearer heaven than when I saw you last by the altitude of a *chopine*' (2. 2. 419). Capell's Notes make no comment on this word, but it is explained, with a reference to this line of the play, in the Glossary: 'a Shoe with high Heels of Cork, us'd by Women in Spain' (*Notes*, I. 12). The Glossary as usual offers no examples, but the *School* gives several instances of usage of the word contemporary with Shakespeare, from John Marston's *Dutch Courtesan*, Lodowick Barrey's *Ram Alley*, and from Puttenham's *Arte of English Poesy*: '"These matters of great Princes were played upon lofty stages, and the actors thereof ware upon their legges buskins of leather called *Cothurni*, and other solemne habits, and for a speciall preheminence did walke upon those high corked shoes or pantofles, which now they call

[170] For reasons of principle or incapacity, or both, Capell refrained from including his Index, leaving it to the discretion of those who saw the three volumes of the *Notes and Various Readings* through the press. In the Preface to the *School* he asserts that Indexes 'are for the idle, and negligent'. John Collins, in his Dedication to Lord Dacre in *Notes and Various Readings*, notes that Capell's Index 'was nearly compleated when his papers came into my hands; and, it's object being glossary explanation, and that only, it was consider'd, – that such an addition might be acceptable and useful to many readers' (I. sig. a1^{r-v}). Capell's stated reservations should no doubt be read as a late Augustan's objection to readers who, unable to make a serious engagement with Shakespeare and his culture, contented themselves with mere index learning.

in Spaine & Italy 'Shoppini' ".'[171] This is an unusually extended quotation in the *School*, and it is clearly meant to provide not only an instance of the use of the word in question, but also an account of the use of the chopine in the theatre, and the type of drama to which it was appropriated. It is a particularly valuable explanatory contextualization because it refers to the state of knowledge in Shakespeare's own time.

Regularly, Capell's Notes on individual plays work together with the Glossary. His Note on the phrase 'vice of kings' (*Hamlet*, 3. 4. 90), for instance, points to the Glossary entry, which reads: 'Vice: . . . a very important Personage of the Drama in old Time, that sprung from the ancient Moralities, (in which particular Vices were personated, and sometimes Vices in general by the Name of – Iniquity) and was call'd in the Plays that succeeded them, – the Vice, *Vitium*; a buffoon Character, and Father of the modern Harlequin'. In his Note itself, Capell expands considerably. Vices:

> were of two sorts: both of them mixt characters; one, a villain with some spice of the fool; the other, a fool with a little dash of the knave; the first belong'd to ancient moralities, the latter to the plays that succeeded them, and these begot the Clowns of our Shakespeare. The '*Vice*' the king is compar'd to, is – the morality Vice: and 'tis no ways improbable, – that the feat attributed to him in [the next two lines] was taken from a piece of that sort to which the audience were no strangers: and if so, their relish of the lines above-mention'd might be greater than we can have for them now. (*Notes*, I. 140–1)

The *School* provides two examples, from *Wits, Fits, and Fancies* (1614), and from George Chapman's *Alphonsus, Emperor of Germany* (1654).[172]

Capell's struggle with the line 'Unhouseled, dis-appointed, unaneled' (*Hamlet*, 1. 5. 77), which had exercised commentators from the beginning, is a particularly clear example of his method. Capell's Note on the passage refers to his Glossary definition, which reads: '*unhousel'd, un-anointed, un-anneal'd* . . . *i.e.* without receiving the Sacrament, without extream Unction, or Absolution in *Articulo Mortis*, here call'd – annealing, a Process of the Artists on Metals in Order to harden them. "Housel" is an old English Word for the Sacrament, or Host receiv'd in it, which SKINNER derives from – *Hostiola, parva Hostia*' (*Notes*, I. 74). In the Notes Capell explains that he follows Pope, Theobald (in his 1733 edition, though not in *Shakespeare Restored*), and Warburton in reading *unanointed* in preference to the reading of all the old editions. The modern reading provides the *un-* prefix for all three terms, and the three original terms include no reference to extreme unction. These are arguments from aesthetics and sense. He rejects *disappointed* and *unappointed* on the grounds that '*appointing* is a general word, . . . whereas the passage requires a specific one'. Twentieth-century editors

[171] *School*, pp. 225, 230, 235. [172] *School*, pp. 461, 532.

Hamlet. 29

All my ſmooth body.
Thus was I, ſleeping, by a brother's hand,
Of life, of crown, of queen, at once diſpatch'd:
Cut off even in the bloſſoms of my ſin,
Unhouſel'd, unanointed, unanneal'd;
No reck'ning made, but ſent to my account
With all my imperfections on my head:
O horrible! o horrible! moſt horrible!
If thou haſt nature in thee, bear it not;
Let not the royal bed of *Denmark* be
A couch for luxury and damned inceſt.
But, howſoever thou purſu'ſt this act,
Taint not thy mind, nor let thy ſoul contrive
Againſt thy mother ought; leave her to heaven,
And to those thorns that in her bosom lodge,
To prick and ſting her. Fare thee well at once;
The glow-worm ſhews the matin to be near,
And 'gins to pale his uneffectual fire:
Adieu, adieu, adieu; remember me. [*Exit* Ghoſt.
HAM. O all you hoſt of heaven! o earth! What elſe?
And ſhall I couple hell?—Hold, hold, my heart;
And you, my ſinews, grow not inſtant old,
But bear me ſtiffly up!—Remember thee?
Ay, thou poor ghoſt, while memory holds a ſeat
In this diſtracted globe. Remember thee?
Yea, from the table of my memory
I'll wipe away all trivial fond records,
All ſaws of books, all forms, all preſſures paſt,
That youth and observation copy'd there;
And thy commandment all alone ſhall live
Within the book and volume of my brain,
Unmix'd with baſer matter: yes, by heaven.

5 diſappointed, 21 hell, ô fie, hold

Figure 9 *Mr William Shakespeare his Comedies, Histories, and Tragedies* (1768), x. 29.

Figures 9–12 Edward Capell's editorial examination of *Hamlet*, act 1, scene 5, line 77: 'Unhouseled, dis-appointed, unaneled'.

74 *Gloſſary.*

unhouſed (O. 10, 26.) unconfin'd.

unhouſel'd, un-anointed, un-aneal'd (H. 29, 5.) *i. e.* without receiving the Sacrament, without extream Unction, or Abſolution in *Articulo Mortis*, here call'd—annealing, a Proceſs of the Artiſts on Metals in Order to harden them. " Housel" is an old Engliſh Word for the Sacrament, or Hoſt receiv'd in it, which SKINNER derives from—*Hoſtiola, parva Hoſtia.*

un-intelligent (*w. t.* 3, 14.) giving no Intelligence.

Union (H. 131, 6 & 133, 14.) a Pearl. *Ital. Unione.*

to **unkennel** (H. 66, 16.) the Earth a Fox lodges in is call'd—his Kennel; and " to unkennel him," is—to drive him from that Earth.

to **unlooſe** (H. 5. 6, 6.) unlooſen.

unluſtrous (Cym. 26, 15.) void of Luſtre.

unman'd (R & J. 58, 11.) a Term proper to Falconry: a Hawk, that will not come to the Fiſt, and bear Company, is ſaid to be " unman'd;" and the bringing her to it is effected by a Number of Practices, known to Sportsmen, and chiefly—hooding.

un-owed (*k.* J. 71, 31.) unown'd, without Owner.

unplauſive (T & C. 63, 1.) unapplauſive, *i. e.* un-applauding.

unpolicy'd (A & C. 119, 22.) unfurniſh'd of Policy.

unprizable (Cym. 16, 14. *t. n.* 75, 14.) invaluable, not to be valu'd, as being above it: invaluable alſo, but as being beneath it; worthleſs.

unquality'd (A & C. 70, 24.) depriv'd of Qualities, or mental Endowments.

unqueſtionable (*a. y. l. i.* 53, 22.) endleſs in queſtioning.

unreconciliable (A & C. 106, 24.) not to be conciliated, *i. e.* accorded.

unrecuring (T. A. 41, 28.) not to be recur'd. *v.* to **recure.**

unreſpective (R. 3. 85, 17.) thoughtleſs, not regarding Reſpects or Conſiderations of this or that.

unreverend (*k.* J. 10, 28 & *k.* L. 42, 18.) unreverent, unrevering.

unrooſted (*w. t.* 35, 5.) driven from Rooſt, a Fowl's Perch or Reſting-place.

unrough (M. 72, 2.) unbearded.

to **unſeam** (M. 4, 25.) to open Seams or rip up.

unſeaſon'd (*a. w. t. e. w.* 5, 22. 2. H. 4. 53, 16.) that wants it's Seaſoning: alſo,—unſeaſonable.

unſecret (T & C. 58, 22.) deficient in Secreſy.

unſeminar'd (A & C. 20, 12.) gelded, rob'd of that which is Man's *Seminarium.*

to **unſex** (M. 15, 21.) to alter or take away the Sex, meaning—the Qualities proper to it.

to **unſhape** (*m. f. m.* 78, 5.) deſtroy a Thing's Form.

unſhifting (*m. f. m.* 67, 1.) unopening: a Door open'd ſhifts, *i. e.* changes its Position.

Figure 10 *Notes and Various Readings to Shakespeare* (1779–83), Glossary, I. 74.

Hamlet. 127

ſuch a weak'ning of the force of this line, that even the rigid critick may not be diſpleas'd to ſee it accented otherwise, and overlook the means that have help'd to effect it.

27, 2.

to faſt in fires,] *i. e.* to do penance in fires; a poetical application of what is only a part of penance, to penance in general: the word was probably chosen for the ſake of alliterating; a practice that is not without beauty when judiciouſly manag'd, as it is in this place, which it causes to move with greater ſolemnity. ☙ "*an end,*" l. 10, is made—*on end*, by the moderns: but ease is deſtroy'd by it; the expreſſion is frequent, and usage ſupplies an—*on* without ſeeing it. ☙ "*meditation,*" in l. 21, is—*divine* meditation; in the fervency of which, a mind, truly poſſeſſ'd of it, takes a flight of more rapidneſs than it ever uses upon any other occasion. ☙ The moderns have ſunk a great beauty, by following the folio's in the diſſolution of "*know't*" in l. 20: and ſome of them (the third, and the laſt) have loſt another by *not* following them in l. 25; for in "*roots*" is an idea of action that diminiſhes the compariſon's beauty, which conſiſts in *in*action.

29, 5.

Unhousel'd, &c.] The editor's ſenſe of these words may be ſeen in the "*Gloſſary*:" but a reason will perhaps be expected, why he puts this ſenſe upon one of them; and why a modern correction is follow'd, in preference to the uniform reading of all old editions. For the latter,—he is not aſham'd to own, in the firſt place, that his choice was not a little determin'd by ſimilarity of the word's composition,—"*un-anointed*:" in the next place, unleſs the word be adopted, *extreme unction* is wanting, (a capital preparation for death among the catholicks) for it is not contain'd in the laſt of these words, which the quarto's write—"*unanveld*," the folio's "*unanneld*," and the Oxford copy rightly ſpells—*unanneal'd*: and laſtly, "*diſappointed*," nor *unappointed* neither, cannot be approv'd of at any rate; for *appointing* is a general word, and includes all the preparations at once, whereas the paſſage requires a ſpecific one. Granting then that *unanointed* is neceſſary if not included in the word that comes after it, what ſhall we ſay is that word's meaning? Why, even that which is always put on it: only it is apply'd by a figure to the laſt of that church's paſſports,—abſolution *in articulo mortis*; by which the party provided with it was harden'd (*v.* SKINNER's "*Exp. Voc. For.*" *in V.* annealing) againſt the flames of their purgatory, and fortify'd by a ſort of *annealing*. And thus we have all the main articles of a catholick preparation for death, and that in their due order: the latter, the

Figure 11 *Notes and Various Readings to Shakespeare* (1779–83), Notes on *Hamlet*, I. 127.

Hey for Honeſty. Hoffman. *Shoemaker a Gentleman.* 163

Hey for Honeſty. c. RANDOLPH. Thomas 1651. 4°.

Why, the Whores of *Pict-hatch, Turnbull,* or the unmercifull Bawds of *Bloomsbury,* &c. B. 3.^{b}

Did not *Will Summers* break his wind for thee?
And *Shakeſpeare* therefore writ his Comedy?
All things acknowledge thy vaſt power divine,
(Great God of Money) ———— *D*°.

You ſwore I could not be above fifteen, when I tranſlated my "Stammel-Petticoat" into the maſculine gender, to make your Worſhip a paire of Scarlet-breeches. F. 2.^{b}

Venus may ſet up at "*Pict-hatch,*" or *Bloomsbury*; F. 4.^{b}

Hoffman. *t.* 1631. 4°. J. N. *for* Hugh Perry.

I ask't thee for a ſolitary plot,
And thou haſt brought me to the diſmal'ſt grove
That ever eye beheld, noe wood nimphes here
Seeke with their "agill" ſteps to outſtrip the Roe,
Nor doth the ſun ſucke from the "queachy" plot
The ranknes and the venom of the Earth
It ſeemes "frequentleſſe" for the uſe of man: I.^{b}
Thou in thy end wert rob'd of Funerall rites,
None ſung thy requiem, noe friend clos'd thine eyes,
Nor layd the hallowed earth upon thy lips,
Thou wert not "houſeled," neither did the bells ring
Bleſſed peales, nor towle thy funerall knell, I. 2.

Shoemaker a Gentleman. c. W. R. 1638. 4°. J. Okes, *ſold by* John Cowper.

Fantaſticke complement ſtalkes up and downe,
Trickt in out-landiſh Fethers, all his words,
His lookes, his oathes, are all ridiculous,

Y 2

Figure 12 *Notes and Various Readings to Shakespeare* (1779–83), vol. III: *School of Shakespeare*, 163.

no doubt rightly believe that there is no adequate reason for questioning the unequivocal reading of the Quarto and Folio texts. Hibbard, for example, argues that *dis-appointed* is specific, and he glosses the word 'unprepared (for death), not having made confession and received absolution', referring to the *Oxford English Dictionary* (ppl. a. 2). But the *Oxford English Dictionary* simply gives 'improperly appointed, equipped, or fitted out, unfurnished, unprepared. *Obs.*', with this example from *Hamlet*, and another from Cleveland (1659). It might reasonably be thought that Capell's emendation is an instance of a responsible eighteenth-century editor forced into emendation because of inadequate lexicographical resources. (It might also be argued, not much less reasonably, that the evidence the *Oxford English Dictionary* provides is not in fact enough to refute Capell's argument absolutely.) The other two terms of the triplet, which had been much less problematic once Theobald had demolished Pope's explanation of *unanealed* as 'no bell rung', are copiously exemplified in the *School*, *houseled* by passages from Henry Chettle's *Hoffman* (1631) and by two passages from the second volume of Holinshed's *Chronicle*, *aneyled* by three passages from Thomas More's *Works* (1557).[173]

Sometimes an extract or extracts in the *School* are intended as an independent source of light on a Shakespearean passage. Hamlet laments that 'a beast, that wants discourse of reason / Would have mourned longer' than his mother (I. 2. 150). Neither Capell's Glossary nor his Notes help, but there are two instances of the phrase 'discourse of reason' in the *School*, of which the second – from *Fearful Fancies of the Florentine Cooper* (translated by William Barker, 1599) – is especially to the point, discriminating between the rational capacities of humans and beasts: 'beasts have hate, but not envy, & that comes bicause not having the "discourse of reason", they cannot judge of the felicitie of other'.[174]

Capell regularly justifies his choices amongst variant readings on critical, that is on interpretative, grounds, and the information which provides the grounds for these choices may often be found not only in his Notes, but also in the Glossary and the *School*. Gertrude urges the beclouded Hamlet not to 'for ever with thy vailèd lids / Seek for thy noble father in the dust' (I. 2. 70). Capell follows his 'best' text, Q2, in reading *vailed*, rather than *veiled*, which is the reading of the Folio and the 'moderns' – the eighteenth-century editors inheriting the Folio tradition from Rowe. In the Notes Capell makes the argument from the logic of the verbal context: lids are not veiled, but veil other things (*Notes*, I. 123). The argument from the historical linguistic evidence is made in the Glossary, which explains *to vail* as meaning 'to abase or let down, to lower. *Fre. avaller*', and in the *School*,

[173] *School*, pp. 163, 298, 345, 379, 404, 431. [174] *School*, pp. 460–1.

which offers as a parallel the line from *Venus and Adonis* in which the stallion 'like a melancholly male-content, / . . . "vales" his taile'.[175]

The *School* stands as extraordinary evidence of Capell's scholarly method. Its exemplary passages are not loads of learned lumber, but an essential part of his project of editorial commentary, not only the main location of his exemplification and illustration of Shakespeare's larger historical and linguistic contexts, but also the chief source of validation of his particular textual and interpretative choices. It is clear that the *School*, together with the Glossary and Index, serves belatedly as a documentary guarantor of Capell's verbal readings, both in his 1768 text, and in his Notes. The function of the *School* and Glossary in providing evidence for editorial decisions might in part be compared to that of the *Oxford English Dictionary* for a modern Shakespearean editor, though they clearly served not only as a historical dictionary of Shakespearean usage, but as something approaching an interpreter's concordance.

If this is remarkable, it is nonetheless representative of a significant eighteenth-century change in the nature and function of glossaries and indexes in Shakespearean editing from an aesthetic and moral, towards an interpretative, orientation. The topic index as it is found in Pope's edition had aimed to point out poetic beauties and moral sentiments. By the middle of the century it is progressively replaced by indexes and glossaries which serve a lexicographical and a concordancing function, and thus assist in the illustration and explication of the language of Shakespeare's text. Clearly one of the most important Shakespeare glossaries before the *Oxford English Dictionary* is provided by Johnson's *Dictionary*. This does not of course focus exclusively on Shakespearean usage, and in the case of many particular words gives far less information of particular interpretative value than is offered by Capell, but more of the illustrative quotations in Johnson's first edition are taken from Shakespeare than from any other poet. It is possible to think of Johnson's work on Shakespeare as providing him with passages with which the verbal definitions in his *Dictionary* might be illustrated; it is also possible to think of some of the definitions in the *Dictionary* as glosses to key words in the exemplary passages chosen from Shakespeare. More specifically, it has been argued by David Fleeman that Johnson's third edition, of 1765, was published 'as a kind of supplement to Johnson's edition of Shakespeare to which it served as an enlarged glossary'.[176] The closest contemporary parallel for Capell's construction of

[175] *Venus and Adonis*, lines 313–14; *School*, p. 257. Twentieth-century editors note the more appropriate parallel at *Venus and Adonis*, 956: 'She vailed her eyelids.'

[176] See Anne McDermott and Marcus Walsh, 'Editing Johnson's *Dictionary*', in *The Theory and Practice of Text-Editing*, ed. Ian Small and Marcus Walsh (Cambridge: Cambridge University Press, 1991), p. 53; Anne McDermott, 'The defining language: Johnson's *Dictionary* and *Macbeth*', *Review of English Studies*, n.s. 44 (1993), 521–38.

a glossary may be found in Richard Warner's published *Specimen*, in his *Letter to David Garrick, Esq. Concerning a Glossary to the Plays of Shakespeare, on a More Extensive Plan than has Hitherto been Attempted* (1768).[177] This is a substantial and important piece of work, anticipating in a number of respects, on a smaller scale, the Glossary, Index, and *School* of Capell's edition. If glossaries have been published, Warner argues, on such classic authors as Hesiod, Homer, Aristophanes, Plautus, and Virgil, and on the Greek New Testament, surely 'our bard' merits the same, particularly as dictionaries so far published do not provide explanations of all the Shakespearean words that require it (pp. 78–9). Warner sets out to gloss not only obsolete and unfamiliar words, but also 'technical terms, local words, and common words us'd in an uncommon sense' (p. 21): all words in fact not readily understood by 'common readers'. Warner's method, combining the functions Capell fulfilled in his Glossary and *School*, is clear even from the twenty-five words that make up his published sample. Each word is followed by a brief definition, and by illustrative examples from Shakespeare and (unless the word is one of those peculiar to Shakespeare) from other writers and works mostly contemporary with him: Chaucer, the Authorized Version, Sidney, Beaumont and Fletcher, Massinger, Spenser, Drayton, Bacon, Jonson, Fairfax, Harrington. Warner's illustrative passages are of variable length, but always provide 'so much of the context as serves to make a complete sentence' (p. 6); as in Capell's *School*, in fact, always enough to perform an interpretative function, substantiating a given sense and usage. The citation of multiple illustrative passages serves in effect to evidence meaning and usage by conference of places: thus for 'affront' examples are provided from Drayton's *Polyolbion*, and from *Hamlet*, *Troilus*, *The Winter's Tale*, and *Cymbeline* (pp. 98–9). Warner makes quite explicit his intention that his *Glossary* should 'serve as an Index' to the published text of Shakespeare's plays (p. 65); to this end every illustrative citation is followed not only by the name of the play in which it occurs (which is all the reference Johnson's *Dictionary* provides), but also by act and scene number, and by the name of the speaker. In offering for each word both a definition and illustrative passages Warner's *Glossary* has the format of a dictionary. In focussing however on the work of Shakespeare, in choosing for illustration exemplary passages from Shakespeare's near contemporaries, and in setting out to make the *Glossary* usable as an index, facilitating resort to numerous parallel places, Warner is providing eighteenth-century readers with a sophisticated tool for the interpretation of writings which had become central to an English literary history.

[177] Warner's published *Specimen* covers only the letter 'A', but manuscripts of his materials for a complete alphabetical glossary, running to 51 quarto and 20 octavo volumes, are in the British Library.

Capell's Index and Glossary, and the detailed and extensive collection of analogues provided in his *School*, are not only of course fuller and richer than Warner's published sample, but also, as we have seen, closely interwoven with his text, textual apparatus, and Notes. The complex integration of the elements of Capell's edition, his conception of an interpretative project as an interrelating whole, significantly distinguishes his work from his predecessors and contemporaries. Many of the features of his edition nonetheless represent a further and no doubt substantial advance in editorial procedures which had already been established or at least broached, or which were being increasingly employed as eighteenth-century editors more and more firmly rejected the aesthetic orientation which had been dominant in Pope's edition, and more and more frequently turned to an authenticating scholarship, the exploration of Shakespeare's cultural and linguistic horizon as a means to textual judgment and explication. The intimate relationship of Capell's text with glossary explanation, and with exemplary passages from writings closely contemporary with Shakespeare, echoes, despite all differences of form, the close interdependence of the editorial and lexicographical which recent commentators have found in Samuel Johnson's Shakespearean work.[178] Some at least of what Capell provides on many of the key cruxes – the 'union' in Claudius's cup, for instance, the 'vice of kings', or 'Unhouseled, disappointed, unaneled' – draws on the work of Theobald, Upton, and other scholar-critics, exemplifying in practice Johnson's profound remark that the work of annotating broadly referential literary writings from the past must be the work of many scholars. Capell's work itself contributed to that cooperative endeavour. The provision of illustrative quotation from Shakespeare's contemporaries and near contemporaries which is George Steevens's impressive contribution to the 1773 and more especially the 1778 editions is in substantial part, and plagiaristically, indebted to Capell. Thus, though Capell had himself refused to provide *notae variorum*, as he had refused to provide another generation of the traditionary 'common' text, his work was nonetheless curiously incorporated into the eighteenth-century tradition of contextualizing interpretative commentary.[179]

[178] Notably Bertrand H. Bronson, Introduction to *Johnson on Shakespeare*, VII. xiv; Simon Jarvis, *Scholars and Gentlemen*, especially pp. 152–8; Robert de Maria, Jr, *The Life of Samuel Johnson* (Oxford: Blackwell, 1993), pp. 218–19.

[179] John Collins, in his dedication of Capell's *Notes and Various Readings* (1779) to Lord Dacre, finds in the Johnson and Steevens editions of 1773 and 1778 'a regular system of plagiarism, upon a settl'd plan': they steal from Capell 'many conjectural emendations adopted into the text, or propos'd in the Notes', the order in which the plays are arranged, scene and act divisions, and stage directions (I. sig. a2^{v}–a3^{r}). Collins had previously made the allegation in *A Letter to George Hardinge, Esq., on the subject of a Passage in Mr Steevens's Preface to his Impression of Shakespeare* (published in 1777; written in 1774).

Many histories of Shakespearean editing in the eighteenth century have stressed the particularities of personal disagreements, the restrictions of copyright, problems of publication, or arguments (between Warburton and Theobald, for example, or between John Collins and Steevens) about the ownership of intellectual property. Others have suggested that, before the end of the eighteenth century, and particularly before the great work of Edmond Malone, editorial scholarship was plural, personal, based on idiosyncratic taste rather than coherent method.[180] What might also be emphasized however is a developing consensus, at least after the aesthetically orientated editions of Pope and Warburton, about the need to determine and explain, with the aid of appropriate knowledge and interpretative discrimination, what Shakespeare intended to write and what Shakespeare intended to mean. If this is understood, despite all the differences amongst those involved, it becomes possible to see the eighteenth-century editors of Shakespeare as involved in a substantially common if not a communal pursuit, in which the least important motive was the aesthetic.

That pursuit presents itself as an extension of scholarly humanism to the world of vernacular literature. The embattled Alexander Pope could claim to be the protector of a more ancient rhetorical and ethical ideal of the *studia humanitatis* against the modern verbal criticks who dealt, not in the meal of the larger messages of Homer and Shakespeare, but in the fragments of particular sense. Theobald and Capell however were also humanists, though of a different kind, textual, historical, and philological scholars, restorers of original authorial meanings against modern reinterpretations.[181] The argument was made explicitly and eloquently by John Upton, as we have seen, but it is implicit in the work of other commentators and editors. If the past is to be recovered, it has to be explained, and explained in its own terms. In the work of some at least of the eighteenth-century editors of Shakespeare we see the development and use of rational procedures of interpretation, adapting and applying to a new field of writing techniques and approaches which had already been familiar in classical scholarship, and in biblical exegesis.

[180] Jerome McGann, *A Critique of Modern Textual Criticism* (Chicago: University of Chicago Press, 1983), pp. 3, 11; Margreta de Grazia, *Shakespeare Verbatim, passim.*

[181] The importance of the paradoxical relationship of these two aspects of humanism in eighteenth-century letters is fully and eloquently described in Joseph M. Levine's *The Battle of the Books.*

Conclusion

If I conclude my study by seeing eighteenth-century editors as participants in a humanist enterprise, I do so at a time when it seems increasingly possible to understand many phenomena of their culture as manifestations of a late, or belated, humanism. Two recent studies especially have informed and reinforced our sense of Samuel Johnson as an author who identified himself with a late Latin cultural heritage, and sought in his own career to emulate the great European humanist scholars, in bibliography, lexicography, translation, the history of letters, and, not least, in editing.[1] Growing up amongst the works of a Latin and Anglo-Latin culture, and aspiring to be another Poliziano or Scaliger, Johnson, however, found himself compelled to re-direct his labours and re-define his scholarly ideals in relation to vernacular English letters. The *Dictionary* in its ethical and encyclopaedic as well as its philological purposes is perhaps the most obviously humanist of Johnson's achievements, but his edition of *Shakespeare*, so closely related to the *Dictionary*, is itself as Robert de Maria puts it a 'brilliant compromise' with the scholarly methods of European editors of classical writings. Both works belong to a series of Johnsonian projects in the history of learning, running from early translations and proposed editions through the *Harleian Catalogue*, and culminating in the *Lives of the English Poets*.

Johnson's personal progress, from an ideal of European and Latin learning to the realized and different achievement of a dictionary of his native language and an edition of a dramatist of the age of Elizabeth and James I, mirrors a more general cultural process by which eighteenth-century literary scholarship turned to the vernacular, and especially to the editing of the great texts of an English literary tradition. Such central works of eighteenth-century scholarship as Theobald's or Capell's editions of Shakespeare, or Pearce's commentary on *Paradise Lost*, or Newton's variorum edition, together with Johnson's *Shakespeare* and *Dictionary*, participate in a common project of understanding the writings of past authors by

[1] Robert de Maria, Jr, *The Life of Samuel Johnson* (Oxford: Blackwell, 1993); J. C. D. Clark, *Samuel Johnson* (Cambridge: Cambridge University Press, 1994).

the exercise of historical and philological scholarship. Though the texts with which they were concerned were written, not in classical antiquity but in a recent past, not in the marble of Latin but in the less stable material of a modern language, that project has fundamental similarities with European humanism in its scholarly aspect. Anthony Grafton, in a thrilling recent book on the humanist 'defence of the text' from the fifteenth to the eighteenth centuries, has argued that the humanists of the Renaissance, in dealing with ancient literature,

> saw knowledge as being concerned above all with what earlier men had thought and written. But understanding of earlier thought must rest on textual exegesis . . . The humanists read [their texts] as clouded windows which proper treatment could restore to transparency, revealing the individuals who had written them . . . the serious effort to obtain that sort of knowledge became the first characteristically modern form of intellectual life.[2]

To the extent that the work of the eighteenth-century English scholar-editors is characterized by just such a turn to textual exegesis, to the recovery of authorial meanings, it is identifiably an enterprise of scholarly humanism. This is of course an understanding of the nature of writing and reading which belongs generally to post-Renaissance humanism, and to a print culture, and which has had a vital relation to methods of interpreting both books in general and the Book itself. It is an understanding which has been congenial to English humanist literary theorists from the Renaissance onwards, including Ben Jonson, Samuel Johnson, and William Wordsworth. Meyer Abrams provides this clear and compelling outline of what he identifies as the 'salient and persistent features of the traditional, or humanistic paradigm' of literary communication:

> The writer is conceived, in Wordsworth's terms, as 'a man speaking to men'. Literature, in other words, is a transaction between a human author and his human reader. By his command of linguistic and literary possibilities, the author actualizes and records in words what he undertakes to signify . . . about matters of human concern, addressing himself to those readers who are competent to understand what he has written. The reader sets himself to make out what the author has designed and signified, through putting into play a linguistic and literary expertise that he shares with the author. By approximating what the author undertook to signify the reader understands what the language of the work means . . . a competent reader of Milton, for example, develops an expertise in reading his sentences in adequate accordance both with Milton's linguistic usage and with the strategy of reading that Milton himself deployed, and assumed that his readers would deploy.[3]

[2] Anthony Grafton, *Defenders of the Text* (Cambridge, Mass.: Harvard University Press, 1991), p. 8.

[3] 'How to do things with texts', in *Doing Things with Texts* (New York and London: Norton, 1989), pp. 269–96 (pp. 269–70, 287). Compare 'The Deconstructive Angel' (*Doing Things with Texts*, p. 238).

In Abrams's account, the reading and writing of literature is a human transaction, a means by which men and women in the past speak to the present, and by which both authors and readers belong to an enduring community of understanding.[4] The author actualizes from the theoretically infinite range of linguistic possibility a controlled subset, a 'core of determinate meanings',[5] which the reader is able to construe. Though understanding is never final, it is sufficiently supported both by the linguistic skills and knowledges that we share with the author, or in principle can acquire, and by the evidence that the writings of an author, and other writings, more especially those of an author's contemporaries, can provide.

It is a recognizable version of this humanist model, I would argue, which lies behind the works of the eighteenth-century editors. In Theobald for instance, and in Pearce, Capell, Upton, and of course Samuel Johnson himself, there is a growing knowledge of and respect for the particularities and otherness of sixteenth- and seventeenth-century authors, and a growing sense of the need to learn and to make interpretative use of their languages and cultural horizons. Procedures of interpretation and explanation are developed, theoretical understandings are articulated, and an increasingly sophisticated, expansive, and pertinent scholarship underwrites the essential aim of ascertaining authorial sense. If my account is convincing, eighteenth-century editing needs to be seen not (or not only) as an accommodation of writings of the past to the values of a later culture, or their solipsistic appropriation to personal and subjective tastes, but as an informed, coherent, and self-conscious attempt at genuine understanding of the communications of the great authors of an English literary history.

[4] Abrams, 'A colloquy on recent critical theories', in *Doing Things with Texts*, pp. 333–63 (p. 353).
[5] Abrams, 'Rationality and imagination in cultural history', in *Doing Things with Texts*, pp. 113–34 (p. 126).

Select bibliography

Manuscript sources

Theobald, Lewis. Manuscript corrections in Alexander Pope, ed., *The Works of Shakespear* (2nd edition, 8 vols., London, 1728), VII. [3]–109. Bound separately as British Library C.45.b.11.

Stillingfleet, Benjamin. Manuscript annotations in Richard Bentley, ed., *Milton's Paradise Lost* (London, 1732). British Library C.134.h.1.

Capell, Edward. Holograph of his edition of the works of Shakespeare. Library of Trinity College, Cambridge, Capell Collection, B.1.

Holograph of his edition of *Paradise Lost.* Library of Trinity College, Cambridge, Capell Collection, B.17.

Manuscript corrections in Alexander Pope, ed., *The Works of Shakespear* (6 vols., London, 1723–5), volumes I and III. Library of Trinity College, Cambridge, Capell Collection, E. 6, E. 8.

Manuscript corrections in his edition of *Mr William Shakespeare his Comedies, Histories, and Tragedies* (10 vols., London, 1768). Library of Trinity College, Cambridge, Capell Collection, S40–9.

Holograph of 'Notes and Various Readings', and 'School of Shakespeare'. Library of Trinity College, Cambridge, Capell Collection, B.17.

'Catalogue of a Collection intitl'd Shakesperiana; comprehending All the several Editions of the Works of Shakespeare, old & new; divers rare old Editions of Writers, prose-men & verse-men; with a Variety of other Articles, chiefly such as tend to illustrate him; – made by his last Editor, E. C.; and by him deposited in the Library of Trinity College in Cambridge, this eleventh Day of Iune in the Year 1779'. Library of Trinity College, Cambridge, Capell Collection.

Printed sources

Seventeenth- and eighteenth-century editions of literary works are listed under the name of the editor. Later editions are listed under the name of the author.

Abrams, Meyer H. *Doing Things with Texts: Essays in Criticism and Critical Theory*. Ed. Michael Fischer. New York and London: Norton, 1989.

Adams, H. M. 'The Shakespeare Collection in the Library of Trinity College, Cambridge'. *Shakespeare Survey*, 5 (1952), 50–4.

Adams, Robert M. 'Empson and Bentley. *Scherzo*'. In his *Ikon: John Milton and the Modern Critics*. Ithaca: Cornell University Press, 1955, pp. 112–27.

Addison, Joseph, Richard Steele, *et al. The Spectator*. Ed. Donald F. Bond. 5 vols., Oxford: Oxford University Press, 1965.

Alexander, Peter. 'Restoring Shakespeare'. In Anne Ridler, ed., *Shakespeare Criticism 1935–1960*. London: Oxford University Press, 1963, pp. 117–31.

Anon. *Milton Restor'd, and Bentley Depos'd*. London, 1732.

Barney, Stephen A., ed. *Annotation and its Texts*. New York: Oxford University Press, 1991.

Barthes, Roland. *S/Z*. Trans. Richard Miller. London: Cape, 1975.

Image-Music-Text. Essays Selected and Translated by Stephen Heath. London: Fontana, 1984.

Bartine, David. *Early English Reading Theory: Origins of Current Debates*. Columbia: University of South Carolina Press, 1989.

Bate, Jonathan. *Shakespearean Constitutions: Politics, Theatre, Criticism 1730–1830*. Oxford: Oxford University Press, 1989.

Bateson, F. W. 'The application of thought to an eighteenth-century text: *The School for Scandal*'. In René Wellek and Alvaro Ribeiro, eds., *Evidence in Literary Scholarship*. Oxford: Oxford University Press, 1979, pp. 321–35.

Battestin, Martin. 'A rationale of literary annotation: the example of Fielding's novels'. In George L. Vogt and John Bush Jones, eds., *Literary and Historical Editing*. Lawrence: University of Kansas Libraries, 1981, pp. 57–79.

Baxter, Richard. *A Paraphrase on the New Testament, with Notes, Doctrinal and Practical. By Plainness and Brevity Fitted to the Use of Religious Families, in their Daily Reading of the Scriptures; and of the Younger and Poorer Sort of Scholars and Ministers*. London, 1685.

Bennett, Stuart. 'Jacob Tonson an early editor of *Paradise Lost*?' *Library*, 6th ser., 10 (1988), 247–52.

Bentley, G. E. *The Profession of Dramatist in Shakespeare's Time 1590–1642*. Princeton: Princeton University Press, 1971.

Bentley, Jerry H. *Humanists and Holy Writ: New Testament Scholarship in the Renaissance*. Princeton: Princeton University Press, 1983.

Bentley, Richard. *The Odes of Horace in Latin and English; with a Translation of Dr Bentley's Notes. To which are Added, Notes upon Notes; Done in the Bentleian Stile and Manner*. 2 vols., London: Lintot, 1712–13. (The satiric 'Notes upon notes' are probably by William Oldisworth.)

Remarks upon a Late Discourse of Free-Thinking. London, 1713.

Proposals for Printing a New Edition of the Greek Testament and St Hierom's Latin Version. London, 1721.

The Works of Richard Bentley. Ed. Alexander Dyce. 3 vols., London: Macpherson, 1836–8.

The Correspondence of Richard Bentley. Ed. Christopher Wordsworth. 2 vols., London: Murray, 1842.

Bentley, Richard, ed. *Q. Horatius Flaccus*. Cambridge, 1711.

Milton's Paradise Lost. London, 1732.

Berger, Harry. *Imaginary Audition: Shakespeare on Stage and Page*. Berkeley: University of California Press, 1989.

Blackwall, Anthony. *The Sacred Classics Defended and Illustrated: or, An Essay in Two Parts towards Proving the Purity, Propriety, and True Eloquence of the Writers of the New Testament*. 2 parts, London, 1725.

Bornstein, George, and Ralph G. Williams, eds. *Palimpsest: Editorial Theory in the Humanities*. Ann Arbor: University of Michigan Press, 1993.

Bossuet, Jacques Bénigne. *Exposition de la doctrine de l'église catholique sur les matières de controversie*. Paris, 1671.

Bourdette, Robert E., Jr. '"To *Milton* lending sense": Richard Bentley and *Paradise Lost*'. *Milton Quarterly*, 14 (1980), 37–49.

'A sense of the sacred: Richard Bentley's reading of *Paradise Lost* as "divine narrative"'. *Milton Studies*, 24 (1988), 73–106.

Bourdette, Robert E., Jr, and Michael M. Cohen. 'Richard Bentley's edition of *Paradise Lost* (1732): a bibliography'. *Milton Quarterly*, 14 (1980), 49–54.

Bowers, Fredson. 'Remarks on eclectic texts'. In his *Essays in Bibliography, Text, and Editing*. Charlottesville: University Press of Virginia, 1975, pp. 488–528.

Brown, A. D. J. 'The little fellow has done wonders'. *Cambridge Quarterly*, 21 (1992), 120–49.

'Pope's Shakespeare'. *Cambridge Quarterly*, 22 (1993), 184–6.

Bullough, Geoffrey. 'Theobald on Shakespeare's sources'. In J. C. Gray, ed., *Mirror up to Shakespeare: Essays in Honour of G. R. Hibbard*. Toronto: University of Toronto Press, 1984, pp. 15–33.

Burke, Seán. *The Death and Return of the Author: Criticism and Subjectivity in Barthes, Foucault and Derrida*. Edinburgh: Edinburgh University Press, 1992.

Authorship: From Plato to the Postmodern. A Reader. Edinburgh: Edinburgh University Press, 1995.

Burnet, Gilbert. *The History of the Reformation of the Church of England*. 3 parts, London, 1679, 1681, 1715.

Bury, Arthur. *The Naked Gospel*. London, 1690.

Callander, John. *Milton's Paradise Lost. Book 1*. Glasgow, 1750.

Capell, Edward. *Notes and Various Readings to Shakespeare: Part I*. 1774.

Catalogue of Mr Capell's Shakespeariana; Presented by Him to Trinity College Cambridge. 1779.

Notes and Various Readings to Shakespeare. 3 vols., 1779–83.

Capell, Edward, ed. *Prolusions; or, Select Pieces of Antient Poetry*. London, 1760.

Mr William Shakespeare his Comedies, Histories, and Tragedies, 10 vols., London, 1768.

Chambers, Ephraim. *Cyclopaedia*. 5th edition, 2 vols., 1741, 1743.

Chillingworth, William. *The Religion of Protestants a Safe Way to Salvation*. Oxford, 1638.

Churton Collins, John. 'The Porson of Shakspearian criticism'. *Quarterly Review*, 175 (1892), 102–31.

Clark, J. C. D. *Samuel Johnson: Literature, Religion and English Cultural Politics from the Restoration to Romanticism*. Cambridge: Cambridge University Press, 1994.

Clarke, Samuel. *The Scripture-Doctrine of the Trinity*. London, 1712.

Coleridge, S. T. *Biographia Literaria*. Ed. James Engell and W. Jackson Bate. 2 vols., London: Routledge, and Princeton: Princeton University Press, 1983. Vols. VII:i and VII:ii of *The Collected Works of Samuel Taylor Coleridge*. General Editor, Kathleen Coburn.

Collins, Anthony. *A Discourse of Free-Thinking*. London, 1713.

Corballis, Richard. 'Copy text for Theobald's "Shakespeare"'. *Library*, 6th ser., 8 (1986), 156–9.

Crane, R. S. 'The Yahoos, the Houhynhnms, and the history of ideas'. In his *The Idea of the Humanities and other Essays Critical and Historical* (2 vols., London and Chicago: University of Chicago Press, 1967), II. 261–82.

Crosse, Gordon. 'Charles Jennens as editor of Shakespeare'. *Library*, 4th ser., 16 (1935), 236–40.

Cuming, A. 'A copy of Shakespeare's Works which formerly belonged to Dr Johnson'. *Review of English Studies*, 3 (1927), 208–12.

Darbishire, Helen. 'The printing of the first edition of *Paradise Lost*'. *Review of English Studies*, 17 (1941), 415–27.

Milton's Paradise Lost. James Bryce Memorial Lecture. London: Oxford University Press, 1951.

De Grazia, Margreta. 'The essential Shakespeare and the material book'. *Textual Practice*, 2 (1988), 69–86.

Shakespeare Verbatim: the Reproduction of Authenticity and the 1790 Apparatus. Oxford: Oxford University Press, 1991.

'Shakespeare in quotation marks'. In Jean I. Marsden, ed., *The Appropriation of Shakespeare: Post-Renaissance Reconstructions of the Works and the Myth.* New York and London: Harvester Wheatsheaf, 1991, pp. 57–71.

De Grazia, Margreta, and Peter Stallybrass. 'The materiality of the Shakespearean text'. *Shakespeare Quarterly*, 44 (1993), 255–83.

De Maria, Robert, Jr. *The Life of Samuel Johnson: a Critical Biography*. Oxford: Blackwell, 1993.

Derrida, Jacques. 'Structure, sign and play in the discourse of the human sciences'. In David Lodge, ed., *Modern Criticism and Theory: a Reader.* London: Longman, 1988, pp. 107–23.

Dillon, Janette. 'Is there a performance in this text?' *Shakespeare Quarterly*, 45 (1994), 74–86.

Dixon, Peter. 'Edward Bysshe and Pope's "Shakespear"'. *Notes and Queries*, 209 (1964), 292–3.

'Pope's Shakespeare'. *Journal of English and Germanic Philology*, 63 (1964), 191–203.

Dobson, Michael. *The Making of the National Poet: Shakespeare, Adaptation and Authorship, 1660–1769.* Oxford: Oxford University Press, 1992.

Docherty, Thomas. *On Modern Authority: the Theory and Condition of Writing 1500 to the Present Day.* Brighton: Harvester, 1987.

Dowden, Edward. 'Milton in the eighteenth century (1701–1750)'. *Proceedings of the British Academy*, 3 (1907–8), 275–93.

Drury, John, ed. *Critics of the Bible, 1724–1873.* Cambridge: Cambridge University Press, 1989.

Eachard, John. *Some Observations upon the Answer to an Enquiry into the Grounds and Occasions of the Contempt of the Clergy.* 1671.

Eastman, Arthur M. 'Johnson's Shakespeare and the laity: a textual study'. *PMLA*, 65 (1950), 1112–21.

'The texts from which Johnson printed his Shakespeare'. *Journal of English and Germanic Philology*, 49 (1950), 182–91.

Eaton, Marcia Muelder. 'Good and correct interpretations of literature'. *Journal of Aesthetics and Art Criticism*, 29 (1970–1), 227–33.

Edwards, Thomas. *The Canons of Criticism, and Glossary, Being a Supplement to Mr Warburton's Edition of Shakespear*. 7th edition, London, 1765.

Empson, William. 'Milton and Bentley'. In his *Some Versions of Pastoral*. London: Chatto and Windus, 1935, pp. 149–91.

Erskine-Hill, Howard. 'On historical commentary: the example of Milton and Dryden'. In Howard Erskine-Hill and Richard A. McCabe, eds., *Presenting Poetry: Composition, Publication, Reception*. Cambridge: Cambridge University Press, 1995, pp. 52–74.

Evans, Arthur William. *Warburton and the Warburtonians: a Study in Some Eighteenth-Century Controversies*. London: Oxford University Press, 1932.

Evans, G. Blakemore. 'The text of Johnson's *Shakespeare* (1765)'. *Philological Quarterly*, 28 (1949), 425–8.

Felton, Henry. *A Dissertation on Reading the Classics, and Forming a Just Style. Written in the Year 1709*. 4th edition, London, 1730.

Fish, Stanley. *Surprised by Sin: the Reader in Paradise Lost*. New York and London: MacMillan and St Martin's, 1967.

Is there a Text in this Class? The Authority of Interpretive Communities. Cambridge, Mass., and London: Harvard University Press, 1980.

Fix, Stephen. 'Johnson and the "duty" of reading *Paradise Lost*'. *ELH*, 52 (1985), 649–71.

Ford, H. L. *Shakespeare 1700–1740: a Collation of the Editions and Separate Plays*. Oxford: Oxford University Press, 1935.

Fowler, Edward. *The Texts which Papists Cite out of the Bible, for the Proof of their Doctrine, Concerning the Obscurity of the Holy Scriptures, Examined*. London, 1688.

Fox, Adam. *John Mill and Richard Bentley: a Study of the Textual Criticism of the New Testament 1675–1729*. Oxford: Blackwell, 1954.

Friedman, Arthur. 'Principles of historical annotation in critical editions of modern texts'. *English Institute Annual* (1941), 115–28.

Gentleman of Christ-Church College, Oxon, A. *A Friendly Letter to Dr Bentley, Occasion'd by His New Edition of Paradise Lost*. London, 1732.

Goldberg, Jonathan. 'Textual properties'. *Shakespeare Quarterly*, 37 (1986), 213–17.

Gother, John. *A Papist Mis-represented and Represented*. London, 1685.

Reason and Authority: or the Motives of a Late Protestants Reconciliation to the Catholic Church. London, 1687.

The Catholic Representer. Or the Papist Misrepresented & Represented. Second part. London, 1687.

Graff, Gerald. *Professing Literature: an Institutional History*. Chicago: University of Chicago Press, 1987.

Grafton, Anthony. *Defenders of the Text: the Traditions of Scholarship in an Age of Science, 1450–1800*. Cambridge, Mass.: Harvard University Press, 1991.

Gray, Thomas, William Collins, and Oliver Goldsmith. *The Poems of Thomas Gray, William Collins, Oliver Goldsmith*. Ed. Roger Lonsdale. London: Longmans, 1969.

Green, George Smith. *The State of Innocence: and Fall of Man. Described in Milton's Paradise Lost. Render'd into Prose. With Historical, Philosophical and Explanatory Notes. From the French of the Learned Raymond* [or rather Nicolas François Dupré] *de St Maur. By a Gentleman of Oxford* [George Smith Green]. London: T. Osborne, and York: J. Hildyard, 1745.

Greetham, D. C. '[Textual] criticism and deconstruction'. *Studies in Bibliography*, 44 (1991), 1–30.

Greg, W. W. *Catalogue of the Books Presented by Edward Capell to the Library of Trinity College in Cambridge*. Cambridge: printed for Trinity College at the University Press, 1903.

'Principles of emendation in Shakespeare'. Annual Shakespeare Lecture of the British Academy (1928). *Proceedings of the British Academy*, 14 (1928), 147–216.

The Editorial Problem in Shakespeare: a Survey of the Foundations of the Text. Oxford: Oxford University Press, 1942.

'The rationale of copy-text'. In O. M. Brack and Warner Barnes, eds., *Bibliography and Textual Criticism: English and American Literature, 1700 to the Present*. Chicago and London: University of Chicago Press, 1969, pp. 41–58. First printed in *Studies in Bibliography*, 3 (1950), 19–36.

Grey, Zachary. *Critical, Historical, and Explanatory Notes on Shakespeare. With Emendations of the Text and Metre*. 2 vols., London, 1754.

Hale, John K. 'More on Bentley's Milton'. *Milton Quarterly*, 14 (1980), 131.

'Notes on Richard Bentley's edition of *Paradise Lost* (1732)'. *Milton Quarterly*, 18 (1984), 46–50.

'Paradise purified: Dr Bentley's marginalia for his 1732 edition of *Paradise Lost*'. *Transactions of the Cambridge Bibliographical Society*, 10 (1991), 58–74.

Hammond, Henry. *A Paraphrase and Annotations upon All the Books of the New Testament: Briefly Explaining all the Difficult Places thereof*. London, 1653.

Hancher, Michael. 'The science of interpretation, and the art of interpretation'. *Modern Language Notes*, 85 (1970), 791–802.

'Three kinds of intention'. *Modern Language Notes*, 87 (1972), 827–51.

Hanmer, Thomas, ed. *The Works of Shakespeare*, 6 vols., Oxford, 1744.

Harris, Wendell V. *Interpretive Acts: In Search of Meaning*. Oxford: Oxford University Press, 1988.

Hart, John A. 'Pope as scholar-editor'. *Studies in Bibliography*, 23 (1970), 45–59.

Harth, Philip. *Swift and Anglican Rationalism: the Religious Background of 'A Tale of a Tub'*. Chicago and London: University of Chicago Press, 1961.

Contexts of Dryden's Thought. Chicago: University of Chicago Press, 1968.

Hawkes, Terence. *That Shakespeherian Rag: Essays on a Critical Practice*. London, Methuen, 1986.

Meaning by Shakespeare. London and New York: Routledge, 1992.

Hay, Louis. 'Does "text" exist?' *Studies in Bibliography*, 41 (1988), 64–76.

Heath, Benjamin. *A Revisal of Shakespeare's Text, wherein the Alterations Introduced into it by the More Modern Editors and Critics are Particularly Considered*. London, 1765.

Hirsch, E. D., Jr. *Validity in Interpretation*. New Haven: Yale University Press, 1967.

The Aims of Interpretation. Chicago: University of Chicago Press, 1976.

Hobbes, Thomas. *Leviathan*. Ed. Richard Tuck. Revised edition, Cambridge: Cambridge University Press, 1996.

Hogan, Charles Beecher. *Shakespeare in the Theatre 1701–1800*. 2 vols., Oxford: Oxford University Press, 1952, 1957.

Honigmann, E. A. J. *The Stability of Shakespeare's Text*. London: Arnold, 1965.

Housman, A. E. 'The application of thought to textual criticism'. *Proceedings of the Classical Association*, 18 (1921), 67–84.

Howard-Hill, T. H. 'Playwrights' intentions and the editing of plays'. *TEXT*, 4 (1988), 269–78.
'Modern textual theories and the editing of plays'. *Library*, 6th ser., 11 (1989), 89–115.
Hume, Patrick. *Annotations on Milton's Paradise Lost*. London, 1695.
Ioppolo, Grace. '"Old" and "new" revisionists: Shakespeare's eighteenth-century editors'. *Huntington Library Quarterly*, 52 (1989), 347–61.
Revising Shakespeare. Cambridge, Mass.: Harvard University Press, 1991.
Jack, Ian. 'Novels and those "necessary evils": annotating the Brontës'. *Essays in Criticism*, 32 (1982), 321–37.
Jarvis, Simon. *Scholars and Gentlemen: Shakespearian Textual Criticism and Representations of Scholarly Labour, 1725–1765*. Oxford: Oxford University Press, 1995.
Jebb, R. C. *Bentley*. London: Macmillan, 1882.
Jennens, Charles, ed. *Lear . . . Collated with the Old and Modern Editions*. London, 1770.
Hamlet . . . Collated with the Old and Modern Editions. London, 1773.
Johnson, Samuel. *Miscellaneous Observations on the Tragedy of Macbeth: with Remarks on Sir T[homas] H[anmer]'s Edition of Shakespear; to which is affix'd, Proposals for a New Edition of Shakespear, with a Specimen*. London, 1745.
Proposals for Printing, by Subscription, the Dramatick Works of William Shakespeare. London, 1756.
Lives of the English Poets. Ed. G. Birkbeck Hill. 3 vols., Oxford: Oxford University Press, 1905.
Johnson on Shakespeare. Ed. Arthur Sherbo. New Haven: Yale University Press, 1968. Volumes VII and VIII of the Yale edition of the *Works* of Samuel Johnson.
Johnson, Samuel, ed. *The Plays of William Shakespeare, with the Corrections and Illustrations of Various Commentators*. 8 vols., London, 1765.
Johnson, Samuel, and George Steevens, eds. *The Plays of William Shakespeare*. 2nd edition, 10 vols., London, 1778.
Johnston, Joseph. *A Reply to the Defence of the Exposition of the Doctrin of the Church of England: Being a Further Vindication of the Bishop of Condom's Exposition of the Doctrin of the Catholic Church*. London, 1687.
Joliffe, Harold R. 'Bentley versus Horace'. *Philological Quarterly*, 16 (1937), 278–86.
The Critical Methods and Influence of Bentley's Horace. Chicago: University of Chicago Press, 1939.
Jones, Richard Foster. *Lewis Theobald: His Contribution to English Scholarship, with some Unpublished Letters*. New York: Columbia University Press, 1919.
Juhl, P. D. *Interpretation: an Essay in the Philosophy of Literary Criticism*. Princeton: Princeton University Press, 1980.
Kane, George. 'Conjectural emendation'. In D. A. Pearsall and R. A. Waldron, eds., *Medieval Literature and Civilisation: Studies in Memory of G. N. Garmonsway*. London: Athlone, 1969, pp. 155–69.
Keener, Frederick M. 'Parallelism and the poets' secret: eighteenth-century commentary on *Paradise Lost*'. *Essays in Criticism*, 37 (1987), 281–302.
Kenney, E. J. *The Classical Text: Aspects of Editing in the Age of the Printed Book*. Los Angeles and London: University of California Press, 1974.

Kümmel, Werner G. *The New Testament: the History of the Investigation of its Problems*. Trans. S. M. Gilmour and H. C. Kee. London: SCM, 1973.

Lamb, Jonathan. *Sterne's Fiction and the Double Principle*. Cambridge: Cambridge University Press, 1989.

Langhans, Edward A. *Eighteenth-Century British and Irish Promptbooks: a Descriptive Bibliography*. New York: Greenwood Press, 1987.

Lennox, Charlotte. *Shakespear Illustrated: or the Novels and Histories, on which the Plays of Shakespear are Founded, Collected and Translated from the Original Authors*. London, 1753.

Levine, Joseph M. *The Battle of the Books: History and Literature in the Augustan Age*. Ithaca and London: Cornell University Press, 1991.

Lim, C. S. 'Emendation of Shakespeare in the eighteenth century: the case of Johnson'. *Cahiers Elisabéthains*, 33 (1988), 23–30.

Lipking, Lawrence. *The Ordering of the Arts in Eighteenth-Century England*. Princeton: Princeton University Press, 1970.

Locke, John. *The Reasonableness of Christianity, as Delivered in the Scriptures*. London, 1695.

A Paraphrase and Notes on the Epistles of St Paul to the Galatians, Romans, I & II Corinthians, Ephesians. To which is Prefix'd, An Essay for the Understanding of St Paul's Epistles, by Consulting St Paul himself. London, 1707.

Lofft, Capel, ed. *Paradise Lost*. Bury St Edmunds, 1792. Book I only. The second edition of 1793 gives Books I and II.

Lounsbury, Thomas R. *The First Editors of Shakespeare: Pope and Theobald*. London: Nutt, 1906.

Lowth, Robert. *Lectures on the Sacred Poetry of the Hebrews*. Trans. G. Gregory. 2 vols., London, 1787. First published as *De sacra poesi Hebraeorum praelectiones*, London, 1753.

Lowth, William. *A Vindication of the Divine Authority and Inspiration of the Writings of the Old and New Testament*. Oxford, 1692.

Directions for the Profitable Reading of the Holy Scriptures. London, 1708.

Maas, Paul. *Textual Criticism*. Trans. Barbara Flowers. Oxford: Oxford University Press, 1958.

Mackail, J. W. 'Bentley's Milton'. Warton Lecture, 1924. *Proceedings of the British Academy*, 11 (1924–5), 55–73.

Mallet, David. *Of Verbal Criticism: an Epistle to Mr Pope, Occasioned by Theobald's Shakespear, and Bentley's Milton*. London, 1733.

Manilius, M. *Astronomicon*. Ed. A. E. Housman. Book I, London: Grant Richards, 1903.

Marsden, Jean I., ed. *The Appropriation of Shakespeare: Post-Renaissance Reconstructions of the Works and the Myth*. London: Harvester Wheatsheaf, 1991.

Martin, Peter. *Edmond Malone Shakespearean Scholar: a Literary Biography*. Cambridge: Cambridge University Press, 1995.

Mayali, Laurent. 'For a political economy of annotation'. In Barney, ed., *Annotation and its Texts*, pp. 185–91.

McDermott, Anne. 'The defining language: Johnson's *Dictionary* and *Macbeth*'. *Review of English Studies*, n.s. 44 (1993), 521–38.

McGann, Jerome J. *A Critique of Modern Textual Criticism*. Chicago: University of Chicago Press, 1983.

The Beauty of Inflections: Literary Investigations in Historical Method and Theory. Oxford: Oxford University Press, 1985.

'The monks and the giants: textual and bibliographical studies and the interpretation of literary works'. In McGann, ed., *Textual Criticism and Literary Interpretation*, pp. 180–99.

'Interpretation, meaning, and textual criticism: a homily', *TEXT*, 3 (1987), 55–62.

The Textual Condition. Princeton: Princeton University Press, 1991.

McGann, Jerome J., ed. *Textual Criticism and Literary Interpretation*. Chicago: University of Chicago Press, 1985.

McKenzie, Donald F. *Bibliography and the Sociology of Texts*. The Panizzi Lectures, 1985. London: British Library, 1986.

McKerrow, R. B. 'The treatment of Shakespeare's text by his earlier editors, 1709–1768'. *Proceedings of the British Academy*, 19 (1933), 89–122.

Prolegomena for the Oxford Shakespeare: a Study in Editorial Method. Oxford: Oxford University Press, 1939.

McLaverty, James. 'The concept of authorial intention in textual criticism'. *Library*, 6th ser., 6 (1984), 121–38.

'The mode of existence of literary works of art: the case of the *Dunciad Variorum*'. *Studies in Bibliography*, 37 (1984), 82–105.

McLeod, Randall. 'UNEditing Shak-speare'. *Sub-stance*, 33–4 (1982), 26–55.

'*Gon*. No more, the text is foolish'. In Gary Taylor and Michael J. Warren, eds., *The Division of the Kingdoms: Shakespeare's Two Versions of King Lear*. Oxford: Oxford University Press, 1983, pp. 153–93.

Metzger, Bruce M. *The Text of the New Testament: its Transmission, Corruption, and Restoration*. 3rd edition, enlarged, New York and Oxford: Oxford University Press, 1992.

Milton, John. *The Poetical Works of John Milton*. Ed. W. A. Wright. Cambridge: Cambridge University Press, 1903.

Poetical Works. Ed. Helen Darbishire. 2 vols., Oxford: Oxford University Press, 1952, 1955.

The Poems of John Milton. Ed. John Carey and Alastair Fowler. London: Longmans, 1968.

Minnis, A. J. *Medieval Theory of Authorship: Scholastic Literary Attitudes in the Later Middle Ages*. 2nd edition, Aldershot: Wildwood House, 1988.

Minnis, A. J., and A. B. Scott, eds., with David Wallace. *Medieval Literary Theory and Criticism c. 1100 – c. 1375: the Commentary Tradition*. Revised edition, Oxford: Oxford University Press, 1991.

Monk, James Henry. *The Life of Richard Bentley, D. D.* London, 1830.

Montagu, Elizabeth. *An Essay on the Writings and Genius of Shakespear*. London, 1769.

Mowat, Barbara. 'The form of *Hamlet*'s fortunes'. *Renaissance Drama*, 19 (1988), 97–126.

Moyles, R. G. 'Edward Capell (1713–1781) as editor of *Paradise Lost*'. *Transactions of the Cambridge Bibliographical Society*, 6 (1975), 252–61.

The Text of Paradise Lost: a Study in Editorial Procedure. Toronto: University of Toronto Press, 1985.

Mueller-Vollmer, Kurt, ed. *The Hermeneutics Reader: Texts of the German Tradition from the Enlightenment to the Present*. Oxford: Blackwell, 1986.

New, Melvyn. '"At the backside of the door of purgatory": a note on annotating *Tristram Shandy*'. In Valerie Grosvenor Myer, ed., *Laurence Sterne: Riddles and Mysteries*. London: Vision, and Totowa, N.J.: Barnes and Noble, 1984, pp. 15–23.

'Introduction'. In Laurence Sterne, *Tristram Shandy*, volume III: *The Notes*. Ed. Melvyn New, with Richard A. Davies and W. G. Day. Gainesville: University Presses of Florida, 1984, pp. 1–31.

Newton, Thomas, ed. *Paradise Lost: New Edition, With Notes of Various Authors*. 2 vols., London, 1749.

Paradise Regain'd. A Poem, in Four Books. To which is Added Samson Agonistes: and Poems upon Several Occasions. A New Edition with Notes of Various Authors. London, 1752. The third and culminating volume, following the two volumes of *Paradise Lost*, of Newton's *Poetical Works of John Milton*.

Newton-de Molina, David, ed. *On Literary Intention: Critical Essays*. Edinburgh: Edinburgh University Press, 1976.

Nichol Smith, David. *Eighteenth-Century Essays on Shakespeare*. 2nd edition, Oxford: Oxford University Press, 1963.

Nichols, John. *Illustrations of the Literary History of the Eighteenth Century*. 8 vols., London, 1817–58.

Norris, Christopher. 'Post-structuralist Shakespeare: text and ideology'. In *Alternative Shakespeares*. Ed. John Drakakis. London: Methuen, 1985, pp. 47–66.

Oras, Ants. *Milton's Editors and Commentators from Patrick Hume to Henry John Todd (1695–1801). A Study in Critical Views and Methods*. Tartu: University of Tartu, and London: Oxford University Press, 1931.

Orgel, Stephen. 'What is a text?' *Research Opportunities in Renaissance Drama*, 24 (1981), 3–6.

Osborn, J. M. 'Johnson on the sanctity of an author's text'. *PMLA*, 50 (1935), 928–9.

Parker, G. F. *Johnson's Shakespeare*. Oxford: Oxford University Press, 1989.

Parker, Hershel. *Flawed Texts and Verbal Icons: Literary Authority in American Fiction*. Evanston, Ill.: Northwestern University Press, 1984.

Paterson, James. *A Complete Commentary, with Etymological, Explanatory, Critical, and Classical Notes on Milton's Paradise Lost*. London, 1744.

Patrick, Simon. *Search the Scriptures. A Treatise Shewing that all Christians Ought to Read the Holy Books; with Directions to them therein*. 1685.

Pearce, Zachary. *A Review of the Text of Milton's Paradise Lost, in which the Chief of Dr Bentley's Emendations are Consider'd*. 3 parts, 1732, 1733.

Peck, Francis. *New Memoirs of the Life and Poetical Works of Mr John Milton: with an Examination of Milton's Stile: and, Explanatory & Critical Notes on Divers passages of Milton & Shakespeare*. 1740.

Peckham, Morse. 'Reflections on the foundations of modern textual editing'. *Proof*, 1 (1971), 122–55.

Pfeiffer, Rudolf. *History of Classical Scholarship, from 1300 to 1850*. Oxford: Oxford University Press, 1976.

Pollard, A. W. *Shakespeare's Fight with the Pirates and the Problems of the Transmission of his Text*. 2nd edition, revised, Cambridge: Cambridge University Press, 1920.

Pope, Alexander. *The Twickenham Edition of the Poems of Alexander Pope*. Ed. John Butt *et al.* 11 vols., London: Methuen, and New Haven: Yale University Press, 1938–68.

The Correspondence of Alexander Pope. Ed. George Sherburn. 5 vols., Oxford: Oxford University Press, 1956.

Pope, Alexander, ed. *The Works of Shakespear*. 6 vols., London, 1723–5.

The Works of Shakespear. 2nd edition, 8 vols., London, 1728.

Popper, Karl R. *Objective Knowledge: an Evolutionary Approach*. Revised edition, Oxford: Oxford University Press, 1983.

Preston, Thomas R. 'Biblical criticism, literature, and the eighteenth-century reader'. In Isabel Rivers, ed., *Books and their Readers in Eighteenth-Century England*. Leicester: Leicester University Press, 1982, pp. 97–126.

Real, Herman J., and Heinz J. Vienken. '"Interpretations the author never meant": problems of annotation in *A Tale of a Tub*'. *Notes and Queries*, 230 (1985), 201–3.

Reedy, Gerard. *The Bible and Reason: Anglicans and Scripture in Late Seventeenth-Century England*. Philadelphia: University of Pennsylvania Press, 1985.

Reinert, Thomas. 'Johnson and conjecture'. *Studies in English Literature, 1500–1900*, 28 (1988), 483–96.

Reynolds, L. D., and N. G. Wilson. *Scribes and Scholars: a Guide to the Transmission of Greek and Latin Literature*. 3rd edition, Oxford: Oxford University Press, 1991.

Richardson, J., father and son. *Explanatory Notes and Remarks on Milton's Paradise Lost*. London, 1734.

Ricks, Christopher. *Milton's Grand Style*. Oxford: Oxford University Press, 1963.

Rowe, Nicholas, ed. *The Works of Mr William Shakespear*. 6 vols., 1709.

Rushworth, William. *The Dialogues of William Richworth or the Iudgment of Common Sense in the Choise of Religions*. Paris, 1640. Facsimile edition, Ilkley and London: Scolar Press, 1975.

Sarpi (Servita Paolo). *Histoire du Concile de Trente, écrite en Italien par Fra-Paolo Sarpi*. Trans. (into French) Pierre François Le Courayer. 2 vols., London, 1736.

Seary, Peter. *Lewis Theobald and the Editing of Shakespeare*. Oxford: Oxford University Press, 1990.

Sergeant, John. *Sure-Footing in Christianity, or Rational Discourses on the Rule of Faith*. London, 1665.

Sewell, George, ed. *The Works of Mr William Shakespear. The Seventh Volume*. London, 1725.

Shakespeare, William. *Hamlet: a New Variorum Edition*. Ed. Horace Howard Furness. 2 vols., 1877. Reprinted New York: Dover, 1963.

The Arden Shakespeare: Hamlet. Ed. Harold Jenkins. London: Methuen, 1982.

The New Cambridge Shakespeare: Hamlet. Ed. Philip Edwards. Cambridge: Cambridge University Press, 1985.

The Oxford Shakespeare: Hamlet. Ed. G. R. Hibbard. Oxford: Oxford University Press, 1987.

The Complete Works. Ed. Stanley Wells, Gary Taylor, J. Jowett, and W. Montgomery. Oxford: Oxford University Press, 1988.

The Tragicall Historie of Hamlet Prince of Denmarke. Ed. Graham Holderness and Bryan Loughrey. Hemel Hempstead: Harvester Wheatsheaf, 1992.

Shawcross, John T. *Milton: the Critical Heritage*. London: Routledge and Kegan Paul, 1970. (Shawcross 1)

Milton, 1732–1801: the Critical Heritage. London: Routledge and Kegan Paul, 1972. (Shawcross II)

Sherbo, Arthur. 'Dr Johnson's *Dictionary* and Warburton's *Shakespear*'. *Philological Quarterly*, 33 (1954), 94–6.

Samuel Johnson, Editor of Shakespeare. Illinois Studies in Language and Literature, 42. Urbana: University of Illinois Press, 1956.

The Birth of Shakespeare Studies: Commentators from Rowe (1709) to Boswell-Malone (1821). East Lansing, Mich.: Colleagues Press, 1986.

Sherburn, George. *The Early Career of Alexander Pope.* Oxford: Oxford University Press, 1934.

Sherlock, William. *The Protestant Resolution of Faith.* London, 1683.

A Discourse Concerning a Judge of Controversies in Matters of Religion. London, 1686.

Sherwin, Oscar. 'Milton for the masses: John Wesley's edition of *Paradise Lost*'. *Modern Language Quarterly*, 12 (1951), 267–85.

Shillingsburg, Peter L. *Scholarly Editing in the Computer Age: Theory and Practice.* Athens, Georgia, and London: University of Georgia Press, 1986.

'Text as matter, concept, and action'. *Studies in Bibliography*, 44 (1991), 31–82.

Sidney, Philip. *An Apology for Poetry.* Ed. Geoffrey Shepherd. London: Nelson, 1965.

Simon, Irène. *Three Restoration Divines: Barrow, South, and Tillotson.* 2 vols. in 3, Paris: Société d'Edition 'Les Belles Lettres', 1967.

Simon, Richard. *A Critical History of the Old Testament. Written Originally in French, and translated into English by a Person of Quality* [i.e. Henry Dickinson]. London, 1682.

A Critical History of the Text of the New Testament. London, 1689.

Small, Ian. 'Annotating "hard" nineteenth-century novels'. *Essays in Criticism*, 36 (1986), 281–93.

'"Why edit anything at all?" Textual editing and postmodernism: a review essay'. *English Literature in Transition*, 38 (1995), 195–203.

Small, Ian, and Josephine Guy. *Politics and Value in English Studies: a Discipline in Crisis?* Cambridge: Cambridge University Press, 1993.

Spencer, Hazelton. *Shakespeare Improved: the Restoration Versions in Quarto and on the Stage.* Cambridge, Mass.: Harvard University Press, 1927.

Spinoza, Benedict. *A Theologico-Political Treatise.* Trans. R. H. M. Elwes. New York: Dover, 1951.

Steiner, George. 'On difficulty'. In his *On Difficulty and Other Essays.* Oxford: Oxford University Press, 1980, pp. 18–47.

Stone, George Winchester, Jr. 'Garrick's long lost alteration of *Hamlet*'. *PMLA*, 49 (1934), 890–921.

'Garrick's presentation of *Antony and Cleopatra*'. *Review of English Studies*, 13 (1937), 20–38.

Strugnell, John. 'A plea for conjectural emendation in the New Testament, with a coda on 1 Cor 4:6'. *Catholic Biblical Quarterly*, 36 (1974), 543–58.

Sutherland, James R. 'The dull duty of an editor'. *Review of English Studies*, 21 (1945), 202–15.

Swift, Jonathan. *Mr C[olli]ns's Discourse of Free-Thinking, Put into English, by Way of Abstract, for Use of the Poor. A Proposal for Correcting the English Tongue, Polite Conversation, Etc.* Ed. Herbert Davis and Louis Landa. Oxford: Blackwell, 1957.

A Tale of a Tub. Ed. A. C. Guthkelch and D. Nichol Smith. 2nd edition, corrected, Oxford: Oxford University Press, 1973.

Tanselle, G. Thomas. 'Textual study and literary judgment'. In his *Textual Criticism and Scholarly Editing*, pp. 325–37. First published in *Papers of the Bibliographical Society of America*, 65 (1971), 109–22.

'The editorial problem of final authorial intention'. *Studies in Bibliography*, 29 (1976), 167–211.

'The editing of historical documents'. *Studies in Bibliography*, 31 (1978), 1–56.

'Literary editing'. In *Literary and Historical Editing*. Ed. George L. Vogt and John Bush Jones. Kansas: University of Kansas Libraries, 1981, pp. 35–56.

'Recent editorial discussion and the central questions of editing'. *Studies in Bibliography*, 34 (1981), 23–65.

'Classical, Biblical, and medieval textual criticism and modern editing'. *Studies in Bibliography*, 36 (1983), 21–68.

'Historicism and critical editing'. *Studies in Bibliography*, 39 (1986), 1–46.

A Rationale of Textual Criticism. Philadelphia: University of Pennsylvania Press, 1989.

'Textual criticism and deconstruction'. *Studies in Bibliography*, 43 (1990), 1–33.

Textual Criticism and Scholarly Editing. Charlottesville and London: University Press of Virginia, 1990.

'Textual criticism and literary sociology'. *Studies in Bibliography*, 44 (1991), 83–143.

Taylor, Gary. 'Inventing Shakespeare'. *Deutsche Shakespeare-Gesellschaft West Jahrbuch 1986*, pp. 26–44.

Re-inventing Shakespeare: a Cultural History from the Restoration to the Present. New York: Vintage, 1991.

Taylor, Gary, and Michael Warren, eds. *The Division of the Kingdoms: Shakespeare's Two Versions of King Lear*. Oxford: Oxford University Press, 1983.

Theobald, Lewis. *Shakespeare Restored: or, A Specimen of the Many Errors, as well Committed, as Unamended, by Mr Pope in his Late Edition of this Poet*. London, 1726.

Theobald, Lewis, ed. *The Works of Shakespeare*. 7 vols., London, 1733.

Tillotson, John. *The Works of the Most Reverend Dr John Tillotson*. 3rd edition, London, 1701.

Toland, John. *Christianity Not Mysterious*. London, 1696.

Tyrwhitt, Thomas. *Observations and Conjectures upon some Passages of Shakespeare*. Oxford, 1766.

Upton, John. *Critical Observations on Shakespeare*. 2nd edition, London, 1748.

Urkowitz, Steven. 'The base shall to th'legitimate: the growth of an editorial tradition'. In Taylor and Warren, eds., *The Division of the Kingdoms*, pp. 23–43.

Vickers, Brian. *Appropriating Shakespeare: Contemporary Critical Quarrels*. New Haven and London: Yale University Press, 1993.

Vickers, Brian, ed. *Shakespeare. The Critical Heritage*. 6 vols., London: Routledge and Kegan Paul, 1974–81.

Wake, William. *A Defence of the Exposition of the Doctrine of the Church of England, against the Exceptions of Monsieur de Meaux, late Bishop of Condom*. London, 1686.

Walker, Alice. 'Principles of annotation: some suggestions for editors of Shakespeare'. *Studies in Bibliography*, 9 (1957), 95–105.

'Edward Capell and his edition of *Shakespeare*'. *Proceedings of the British Academy*, 46 (1960), 131–45.

Walsh, Marcus. 'Editing poetry: theory and practice'. In *Talking about Text: Studies Presented to David Brazil*. Ed. Malcolm Coulthard. Birmingham: English Language Research, 1986, pp. 75–87.

'Literary annotation and Biblical commentary: the case of Patrick Hume's *Annotations* on *Paradise Lost*'. *Milton Quarterly*, 22 (1988), 109–14.

'Text, "text", and Swift's *Tale of a Tub*'. *Modern Language Review*, 85 (1990), 290–303.

'Bentley our contemporary: or, editors, ancient and modern'. In Ian Small and Marcus Walsh, eds., *The Theory and Practice of Text-Editing*. Cambridge: Cambridge University Press, 1991, pp. 157–85.

'The fluid text and the orientations of editing'. In Warren Chernaik, Caroline Davis, and Marilyn Deegan, eds., *The Politics of the Electronic Text*. Oxford: Office for Humanities Communication, 1993, pp. 31–9.

'Profession and authority: the interpretation of the Bible in the seventeenth and eighteenth centuries'. *Literature and Theology*, 9 (1995), 383–97.

Walton, Brian. *Biblia Sacra Polyglotta*. 6 vols., London, 1655–7.

Warburton, William. 'Remarks on Milton's *Paradise Lost*'. *The History of the Works of the Learned* (1740), Article xviii, 273–80.

Warburton, William, ed. *The Works of Shakespear*. 8 vols., London, 1747.

Warner, Richard. *A Letter to David Garrick, Esq. Concerning a Glossary to the Plays of Shakespeare, on a More Extensive Plan than has Hitherto been Attempted*. London, 1768.

Warton, Thomas, the younger, ed. *John Milton. Poems upon Several Occasions*. London, 1785.

Watts, Isaac. *The Improvement of the Mind*. Supplement to his *Art of Logick*. London, 1741.

Weinbrot, Howard D. *Britannia's Issue: the Rise of British Literature from Dryden to Ossian*. Cambridge: Cambridge University Press, 1993.

Wellek, René. *The Rise of English Literary History*. New York: University of North Carolina Press, 1941.

Wells, Stanley, and Gary Taylor, with J. Jowett and W. Montgomery. *William Shakespeare: a Textual Companion*. Oxford: Oxford University Press, 1987.

Wesley, John. *An Extract from Milton's Paradise Lost. With Notes*. 1763.

Milton for the Methodists. Emphasized Extracts from Paradise Lost Selected, Edited, and Annotated by John Wesley. With an Introduction by Frank Baker. London: Epworth Press, 1988.

West, Martin L. *Textual Criticism and Editorial Technique Applicable to Greek and Latin Texts*. Stuttgart: B. G. Teubner, 1973.

White, R. J. *Dr Bentley: a Study in Academic Scarlet*. London: Eyre and Spottiswoode, 1965.

Wilson, F. P. *Shakespeare and the New Bibliography*. Rev. and ed. Helen Gardner. Oxford: Oxford University Press, 1970.

Wilson, John. *The Scriptures Genuine Interpreter Asserted: or, a Discourse Concerning the Right Interpretation of Scripture*. London, 1678.

Wilson, Penelope. 'Classical poetry and the eighteenth-century reader'. In Isabel

Rivers, ed., *Books and their Readers in Eighteenth-Century England*. Leicester: Leicester University Press, 1982.

Wimsatt, W. K. *The Verbal Icon: Studies in the Meaning of Poetry*. New York: Noonday, 1966.

Wolf, F. A. *Prolegomena to Homer (1795)*. Trans. and ed. Anthony Grafton, Glenn W. Most, and James E. G. Zetzel. Princeton: Princeton University Press, 1985.

Zuntz, Günther. '"The critic correcting the author"'. *Philologus*, 99 (1955), 295–303.

Index

CAMBRIDGE STUDIES IN EIGHTEENTH-CENTURY ENGLISH LITERATURE AND THOUGHT

General Editors
Professor HOWARD ERSKINE-HILL LITT.D., FBA, *Pembroke College, Cambridge*
Professor JOHN RICHETTI, *University of Pennsylvania*

1 *The Transformation of* The Decline and Fall of the Roman Empire
by David Womersley

2 *Women's Place in Pope's World*
by Valerie Rumbold

3 *Sterne's Fiction and the Double Principle*
by Jonathan Lamb

4 *Warrior Women and Popular Balladry, 1650–1850*
by Dianne Dugaw

5 *The Body in Swift and Defoe*
by Carol Flynn

6 *The Rhetoric of Berkeley's Philosophy*
by Peter Walmsley

7 *Space and the Eighteenth-Century English Novel*
by Simon Varey

8 *Reason, Grace, and Sentiment*
A Study of the Language of Religion and Ethics in England, 1660–1780
by Isabel Rivers

9 *Defoe's Politics: Parliament, Power, Kingship and* Robinson Crusoe
by Manuel Schonhorn

10 *Sentimental Comedy: Theory & Practice*
by Frank Ellis

11 *Arguments of Augustan Wit*
by John Sitter

12 *Robert South (1634–1716): an Introduction to his Life and Sermons*
by Gerard Reedy, SJ

13 *Richardson's* Clarissa *and the Eighteenth-Century Reader*
by Tom Keymer

14 *Eighteenth-Century Sensibility and the Novel*
The Senses in Social Context
by Ann Jessie Van Sant

15 *Family and the Law in Eighteenth-Century Fiction*
The Public Conscience in the Private Sphere
by John P. Zomchick

16 *Crime and Defoe: A New Kind of Writing*
by Lincoln B. Faller

17 *Literary Transmission and Authority: Dryden and Other Writers*
edited by Earl Miner and Jennifer Brady

18 *Plots and Counterplots*
Sexual Politics and the Body Politic in English Literature, 1660–1730
by Richard Braverman

19 *The Eighteenth-Century Hymn in England*
by Donald Davie

20 *Swift's Politics: A Study in Disaffection*
by Ian Higgins

21 *Writing and the Rise of Finance*
Capital Satires of the Early Eighteenth Century
by Colin Nicholson

22 *Locke, Literary Criticism, and Philosophy*
by William Walker

23 *Poetry and Jacobite Politics in Eighteenth-Century Britain and Ireland*
by Murray G. H. Pittock

24 *The Story of the Voyage: Sea-Narratives in Eighteenth-Century England*
by Philip Edwards

25 *Edmond Malone: a Literary Biography*
by Peter Martin

26 *Swift's Parody*
by Robert Phiddian

27 *Rural Life in Eighteenth-Century English Poetry*
by John Goodridge

28 *The English Fable: Aesop and Literary Culture, 1651–1740*
by Jayne Elizabeth Lewis

29 *Mania and Literary Style*
The Rhetoric of Enthusiasm from the Ranters to Christopher Smart
by Clement Hawes

30 *Landscape, Liberty and Authority*
Poetry, Criticism and Politics from Thomson to Wordsworth
by Tim Fulford

31 *Philosophical Dialogue in the British Enlightenment*
Theology, Aesthetics, and the Novel
by Michael Prince

32 *Defoe and the New Sciences*
by Ilse Vickers

33 *History and the Early English Novel*
Matters of Fact from Bacon to Defoe
by Robert Mayer

34 *Narratives of Enlightenment*
Cosmopolitan History from Voltaire to Gibbon
by Karen O'Brien

35 *Shakespeare, Milton and Eighteenth-Century Literary Editing*
The Beginnings of Interpretative Scholarship
by Marcus Walsh